The Subtle Revolution

WOMEN AT WORK

RALPH E. SMITH
EDITOR

THE URBAN INSTITUTE • WASHINGTON, D.C.

THE URBAN INSTITUTE is a nonprofit research organization established in 1968 to study problems of the nation's urban communities. Independent and nonpartisan, the Institute responds to current needs for disinterested analyses and basic information and attempts to facilitate the application of this knowledge. As part of this effort, it cooperates with federal agencies, states, cities, associations of public officials, and other organizations committed to the public interest.

The Institute's research findings and a broad range of interpretive viewpoints are published as an educational service. The interpretations or conclusions are those of the authors and should not be attributed to The Urban Institute, its trustees, or to other organizations that support its research.

CONTENTS

PREFACE

We are undergoing a revolution—at times obvious, at times only dimly perceived—in the traditional relationship of women to work, money, marriage, and family. One indicator of this revolutionary change is that in less than a generation the size of the female labor force has more than doubled and now includes the majority of working-age women. It is estimated, moreover, that between now and 1990 an additional one million women will enter the labor force each year. But while the ranks of wage-earning women are highly visible, this phenomenon is not easily grasped as a whole—not in its origins, nor in the predictability of its course, nor in its consequences. This is a subtle revolution.

In 1975, The Urban Institute launched a concentrated program of policy research on the changing social and economic status of women and families. The first focus of this research was on the phenomenon of families headed by women, a family type that was growing ten times faster than the traditional husband and wife family. Published under the title *Time of Transition: The Growth of Families Headed by Women,* this study explores the evidence that when women had an economic alternative, such as the social and economic leverage they could obtain through paid jobs, they divorced from unsatisfactory marriages. Over time, though, it became clear that their choices were not directed against marriage itself, since most of them remarried within a few years. The research also showed, however, that while government policies can assist families, they can also intrude upon them: for example, single and divorced mothers on welfare, who lose money if they marry or remarry, tend to remain unmarried in higher proportions than do women like them who are not on welfare.

In subsequent studies, the research program on Women and Family Policy has explored the impact of various government policies, programs, and institutions which now manage responsibilities that were

ix

once considered exclusively the family's—the provision of education and income, and support in sickness, unemployment, old age, and, more recently, childbearing and child care. The United States today accepts responsibility for individual survival to a degree undreamed of in earlier times. But while government programs and policies have freed the family from many extreme burdens, they have also at times exacerbated the conflict between the old tradition of caring for one's own and the host of opportunities to commit one's time and energy to other goals.

What is particularly striking about the recent growth of the female labor force is that the majority of working women are now married and that one-third of all employed women have children under eighteen years of age. Apart from the tension between their roles as homemakers and employees, these women are subject to provisions of the federal income tax and the social security system which penalize their wage-earning. They also face occupational overcrowding in "women's jobs"—those that are clerical and deal with health care, education, domestic work, or food service. Once in the labor force, they suffer more unemployment than men and lower wages than men in the same occupations. Moreover, for working wives, an average week includes not only the hours of paid work but also another twenty-seven hours of housework at home.

When we ask why women go to work, we are forced to reexamine our assumptions. The traditional family of past generations has undergone many changes. Families are much smaller now than in the past. Homemakers have more time and fewer functions in an age of new technologies for housekeeping, compulsory child education, and abundant consumer goods. In going to work, a woman obtains a higher market value for her time, thanks to the significant increases in real wages over the past decades. She and her family can raise their standard of living. In addition, the workplace a woman enters today is not the environment from which women—as well as their husbands and their children—needed to be rescued at the turn of the century. Workers' safety and health are protected by law; many employers support attractive environments as investments in productivity; medical care and life insurance are commonly provided as part of the work benefit package.

It is easy to overlook one of the biggest changes in environment, however—the changing character of the neighborhood, the community. In the early 1970s, our culture became more suburban than urban, separating, for many of us, where we work from where we live. This polarization of place, and the isolation of functions between work and family, men and women, and women and children have never been so extreme as in suburbia. Working wives and mothers may be signaling the failure of human environments segregated by age, income, race, and sex during the work day of a traditional family. Citizens across the country express needs for more participation in, and more control over, government policies which affect them.

One of the aims of this study is to help citizens and policy makers improve their decisions by identifying needs and directions of change in our society. Recognizing that no change takes place in isolation, and that some changes are more significant than others, the research covered in this volume traces the growth and increasing diversity of the female labor force since the turn of the century, examines the prospects for women in the labor market itself (including the possibility of more rigid sexual stereotyping in the labor market), and highlights their problems and needs. The authors demonstrate that, contrary to belief, the expansion of the female labor force is not likely to mean the end of the American family but will lead to important changes, with working women marrying at a later age and with an increasing number of families in which both husband and wife work for pay. These developments will affect consumption patterns, living standards, and the market for home services and will generate pressures for change in private and public institutions that are still largely predicated on the notion of a society dominated by one-earner families. Here, appropriately, the authors also examine the problems that arise when institutions fail to adjust to women's changing role and present alternatives for amending the provisions of the federal income tax and social security laws.

In consolidating what is known, projecting trends, and analyzing malfunctions of our social and economic systems, *The Subtle Revolution: Women at Work* helps us to know what we can do now to ease the tensions of change and allow those changes to be the basis for a rewarding future.

September, 1979

William Gorham
President
The Urban Institute

ACKNOWLEDGMENTS

This book was made possible by the generosity and foresight of the Ford Foundation, which helped establish the Program of Research on Women and Family Policy within The Urban Institute in 1975 and provided institutional funds that enabled the Program to integrate the results of its research in this volume. The financial support provided to the Program by the following organizations is also gratefully acknowledged: American Telephone and Telegraph Company, Atlantic Richfield Foundation, Columbia Broadcasting System, EXXON Corporation, General Motors Corporation, and IBM Corporation.

In addition to the foregoing institutional support, the research on which two of the chapters is based was funded by federal agencies: a grant from the U.S. Department of Labor, Employment and Training Administration, supported much of the research underlying Chapter 1 and the Congressional Budget Office provided funding for the research reported in Chapter 8.

I am indebted to Nancy Barrett and Isabel Sawhill for the major roles they played in the development of this book. I am grateful for the assistance provided by Sheila Keeny and Priscilla Taylor in preparing the manuscript for publication. Responsibility for the views expressed and for any errors rests solely on the chapter authors and myself as editor.

R.S.

ABOUT THE AUTHORS

Ralph E. Smith, the editor of this volume, is an economist with the National Commission for Employment Policy in Washington, D.C. From 1969 to 1978, Dr. Smith was on the staff of The Urban Institute, first associated with a research project on unemployment, inflation, and labor markets, and then with the Program of Research on Women and Family Policy. The results of his analyses of labor market processes, problems, and policies have been presented before many professional gatherings and in testimony before Congress, as well as published in professional and government reports.

Nancy S. Barrett, Deputy Assistant Secretary for Economic Policy and Research, U.S. Department of Labor, and a Professor of Economics at American University, was director of The Urban Institute's Program of Research on Women and Family Policy from 1977 to 1979. She received her Ph.D. in economics from Harvard University. The author of several books and numerous articles on economic policy, labor markets, and the economic situation of women, Dr. Barrett has served on the staff of the Congressional Budget Office and the President's Council of Economic Advisers.

Nancy M. Gordon, now Executive Director of President Carter's Interdepartmental Task Force on Women, was a senior research associate at The Urban Institute from 1976 through 1978. While at the Institute and previously when she was on the Stanford University and Carnegie-Mellon University faculties, Dr. Gordon conducted research concerning salary differentials related to sex and race, determinants of alimony and child support payments by absent fathers, and the treatment of women under both the Social Security system and the federal income tax system.

Sandra L. Hofferth, a sociologist, has been a research associate with The Urban Institute's Women and Family Policy Program since 1977.

xv

During this period she has worked with Kristin Moore on the consequences of early childbearing. Dr. Hofferth is now researching factors affecting the early career paths of the post-World War II baby boom cohorts and the consequences of these groups' low fertility.

KRISTIN A. MOORE, acting director of The Urban Institute's Program of Research on Women and Family Policy, is a social psychologist whose areas of specialization include fertility, survey methodology, and sex roles. During her four years with The Urban Institute's Program of Research on Women and Family Policy, Dr. Moore has completed several studies on the determinants and consequences of teenage and out-of-wedlock childbearing.

CLAIR VICKERY is a labor economist in the Department of Economics, University of California, Berkeley. Her areas of specialty include unemployment, income support programs, and labor supply. Dr. Vickery has conducted research projects on welfare (Aid to Families with Dependent Children), unemployment insurance, and the labor supply decisions of married women. Currently she is writing a book on how the changes in women's work in twentieth-century America have affected the labor market and the way people live.

Chapter 1

THE MOVEMENT OF WOMEN INTO THE LABOR FORCE

RALPH E. SMITH

A revolution in American society has been taking place, one that affects virtually all of our social and economic arrangements. Increasingly women are either working or looking for work outside the home. The work place is no longer a man's world. The family with a working husband supporting a wife who stays home to rear the children still exists, but certainly is no longer typical.

At the turn of the century, only 5 million of the 28 million Americans in the labor force were female. One-quarter of these women were teenagers and only a few were married. As recently as 1947, fewer than 17 million of the 59 million labor force participants were women. But over the past thirty years, six out of ten additions to the work place have been female. During this short period in our history, it has become widely acceptable—even fashionable—for married women to seek work outside the home. Half are now doing so, including more than one-third of mothers of young children.

The movement of women into the paid labor market is a revolution in the sense that it is bringing about a fundamental change in social and economic conditions. The division of labor between the sexes in which men work outside the home for pay while women engage in unpaid housework is breaking down. And, as more women work outside the home, the fight for equal treatment in the job market and equal responsibilities for unpaid domestic work has intensified. Indeed, female-male relationships in every aspect of society are being questioned and are changing. The movement of women into the labor force is part of this larger social revolution, both as a cause and as an effect. The economic power provided by paid employment enhances the bargaining power of an individual in the marketplace, the political arena, and the home.

But the revolution associated with women's movement into the paid labor force is, in many ways, a subtle revolution. It is subtle in that it has been gradual, not traceable to any abrupt change. Decade after decade the percentage of the female population in the labor force (that is, women's participation rate) has been increasing. Since 1947, when statistics began to be collected on a regular basis, the participation rate of women has increased in all but four years, but never by more than 1.5 percentage points in any one year.

The revolution is subtle in that its origins are difficult to understand. Many economists point to the increasing attractiveness of the paid labor market to women, as real wages have risen and work opportunities (particularly in white-collar jobs) have expanded. Many sociologists point to changes in sex-role attitudes, rising divorce rates, and falling birthrates. Other explanations offered at one time or another include the invention of labor-saving devices for the home, rising education levels, inflation, unemployment, and movement away from rural areas. Probably all have been important in various periods.

It is subtle in that its course has been difficult to predict. Time after time, projections of the size of the female labor force have seriously underestimated future growth. Official government forecasts repeatedly have predicted a tapering off of past growth rates, and repeatedly they have been wrong.

This book is about some of the consequences of women's changing roles. Although much has been written about the origins of these changes, surprisingly little has been said about their impacts. How are men and women interacting in the work force? What occurs in households when the full-time homemaker is no longer available to take care of domestic responsibilities? What are the effects of public policies which have presupposed that most families consist of a single earner and dependents?

This chapter presents the context within which the changes are occurring. The growth of the female labor force since the turn of the century is reviewed. Next, a picture of today's female workers—who they are and what they are doing—is presented. Forecasts of the growth of women in the labor force through 1990 are offered. These projections are then used as a frame of reference by the other authors. The final sections of this chapter discuss several of the issues arising from women's movement into the labor force and provide a summary of the remainder of the volume.

GROWTH OF THE FEMALE LABOR FORCE*

Although stereotypes are often based on fact, they are seldom revised as quickly as the facts change. Stereotypes about the roles of men and women and the structure of families provide excellent examples of this phenomenon. In 1890, the first year for which usable labor force information is available, few women worked outside the home. That year's census revealed that 3.7 million women were in the labor force. They accounted for only 17 percent of all workers and 18 percent of the female population age fourteen and over. All but a million of these working women were single. Only 4.5 percent of married women were in the labor force at that time.

Expansion of the female labor force since that era has resulted from both population growth and from the dramatic increase in the proportion of women who have chosen (or been required) to seek paid work. Meanwhile, the male labor force has grown much less rapidly. Although the male population has expanded at about the same rate as the female population, the proportion of the male population in the labor force has actually fallen. Between 1890 and 1978 the female labor force participation rate grew from 18 percent to 50 percent while that of males declined from 84 percent to 78 percent.

While the decrease for men is largely attributable to longer education, earlier retirement, and longer life spans, most of the increase for women is associated with a profound change in the activities of married women. By 1978 nearly half of all married women were in the labor force. The increases in participation rates among single women or women who were in other marital categories (separated,

---

* The discussion of the determinants of past labor force growth and the projection of future growth are based on research conducted under Grant No. 21–11–77–09 from the Employment and Training Administration, U.S. Department of Labor. The complete analysis is presented in Ralph E. Smith, *Women in the Labor Force in 1990* (Washington: The Urban Institute, 1979).

divorced, and widowed) were much less pronounced, because a substantial percentage of them have always worked. In 1890, 37 percent of single women were in the labor force, compared with 60 percent in 1978; the rate for women no longer married increased from 29 percent to 42 percent.

The sharpest sustained increases in the participation rates of women, including married women, have occurred in the past few decades. Between 1947 and 1978, the participation rate of women increased by eighteen percentage points. To appreciate the magnitude of this change, consider how many women are in the labor force now who would not be there if no change had occurred. In 1978, 42 million women were in the labor force, 50 percent of the female population age sixteen and over. If, instead, the percentage of working women had remained the same as in 1947 (32 percent), only 27 million women would now be in the labor force.

The post-World War II participation rate increase is primarily a result of increased participation by married women. Between 1947 and 1978, married women's rate increased from 20 percent to 48 percent. Nearly all of the 15 million added to the labor force as a result of participation rate increases were married. The question, then, is: Why are so many married women working?

Economists and sociologists have made many attempts to answer this question. From their studies, it is possible to identify the factors likely to have been significant, but difficult to estimate the sizes of their contributions. The theory of decision making developed by economists provides one conceptual framework. An individual decides whether to participate in the labor force based on the perceived rewards to seeking paid employment relative to the rewards of spending this time outside the labor force. The latter may include going to school full time, homemaking, volunteer work, and leisure. As we have seen, an increasing proportion of women have opted to participate. This fact suggests that the perceived benefits of being in the labor force have been increasing, the benefits of not participating have been decreasing, or both. What has changed?

Most economists who have investigated this subject rely heavily on economic explanations. As the economy has expanded throughout most of this century, real wages (adjusted for inflation) have increased manyfold, but there has been no corresponding increase in the rewards of working within the home. Therefore, more women have shifted part of their work activity into the marketplace. The "opportunity cost" of staying at home all day has become too great for an increasing proportion of women.

The economic model on which this conclusion is based takes into account two opposing forces set in motion by rising wages. The first is the positive relationship between participation in the labor force and the wage rate discussed above. As wages rise, paid labor is substituted for unpaid activities outside the labor market. The opposing force is an "income effect," through which the rising income within a family associated with higher wages is translated into less economic pressure to work and greater financial means to enjoy leisure pursuits, go to school, and so forth.

For married women with husbands present the former effect has outweighed the latter effect. Even though the increases in husbands' earnings throughout most of the century have permitted improvement in living standards without wives' entering the labor force, many wives have chosen to do so. The economic explanation is that these women were facing a three-way choice, rather than a simple labor versus leisure choice. For them, the third option was unpaid work within the home. An increase in family income permits reduction in unpaid work through the purchase of labor-saving devices, restaurant meals, domestic service, and the like. Thus, increases in real wages over time may stimulate more participation in the labor force for married women, as has been the case throughout this century.[1]

Additional economic explanations for the long-term increase include the tremendous growth in the kinds of jobs which are thought to be most appealing to married women or for which employers are most willing to hire women: service jobs, office employment, and jobs that permit part-time schedules. Also, the importance of physical strength in many industrial sector jobs has diminished. In addition, women are acquiring increasing amounts of education, which enables them to qualify for jobs that are both better paying and more interesting.

These explanations are closely related to the wage explanation in that they help to account for the continual rise in women's wages, even as so many women enter the market. Had demand for female workers not increased, it is likely that women's wages, relative to men's, would have fallen. In fact, the ratio of median female to male wage rates has been remarkably stable, remaining near six-tenths of the male wage throughout this century. Nonetheless, some independent effects of the shifts in the mix of job opportunities and in

---

1. Jacob Mincer, "Labor Force Participation of Married Women: A Study of Labor Supply," in *Aspects of Labor Economics* (Princeton: Princeton University Press, 1962); Glen Cain, *Married Women in the Labor Force: An Economic Analysis* (Chicago: University of Chicago Press, 1966).

educational advancement should be expected because both affect the nonmonetary benefits of paid employment as well.

Other economic factors that may affect the decision of an individual married woman to participate include her likelihood of finding a job, her husband's employment status, and inflation. Changes in these variables cause temporary changes either in the expected rewards to being in the labor market or in income levels. Each may account for the pace of labor force growth in particular periods of unemployment fluctuations or inflation, but not for the long-term growth.

Sociologists have focused on other influences, involving demographic and attitudinal changes, that have reinforced these economic factors. Later marriages, rising divorce rates, declining birthrates, and other demographic trends certainly have been responsible for some of the participation rate growth, especially in recent years. Women who have never married are much more likely to participate in the labor force than are married women of the same age. Women who are divorced or separated are more likely to participate than are women who are living with their husbands. The increase in the proportion of women whose marriages have dissolved means an increase in women in the labor force-prone categories. The explanation is actually somewhat more complicated than this, inasmuch as causation goes in both directions; that is, increasing labor force participation of women may have helped to bring about later marriage and more marital disruption.

Similarly, among women in otherwise comparable situations, those with no children are most likely to be in the labor force; those with school-age children are next most likely; and those with very young children are least likely. Hence, the decline in the birthrate since the mid-1960s has contributed to recent labor force growth. The same qualification about causation applies; women who are otherwise committed to the labor force may want fewer children.

Finally, increasing acceptance of nontraditional, and especially nonfamilial, roles for women has been credited with contributing to the rapid rise in the female participation rate in recent years. In 1964, for example, 54 percent of women surveyed agreed that a mother who worked could still establish a close relationship with her children.[2] Within only six years, the percentage of women with this

---

2. Karen Oppenheim Mason, John L. Czajka, and Sara Arber, "Changes In U.S. Women's Sex-Role Attitudes, 1964–1974," *American Sociological Review* 4 (August 1976): 573–96.

view increased to 73 percent. These proportions are a far cry from the attitudes prevailing in the 1930s, when only 18 percent of women in a national opinion survey answered with an unconditional yes to the question, "Do you believe that married women should have a full-time job outside the home?" and 41 percent said no.[3] Sociologists have assembled convincing evidence that an increasing proportion of women believe that work outside the home is compatible with their other roles and that this increasing conviction is related to the growth in their labor force.[4] Once again, causation is difficult to disentangle. For example, attitudes may have changed largely in response to the economic factors cited. Nonetheless, it seems likely that, whatever the original reason, the result will be either to increase the perceived benefit of being in the labor force or to decrease the perceived benefit of staying at home.

In sum, during most of the period since World War II, all the factors discussed here—improvement in job opportunities, demographic change, and liberalization in attitudes—have contributed to the expansion of the female labor force. The next section provides a picture of what this work force looks like. Then, the changes in the size and composition of the female labor force that should be anticipated and the consequences of these changes are examined.

THE FEMALE LABOR FORCE TODAY

Who are the women in the job market today? Why are they there? What are they doing? These kinds of questions are often answered with reference to the "typical" or average woman in the labor force. She is married, living with her husband, and working in a clerical job to raise or maintain her family's standard of living. This kind of a word picture provides the illusion of contributing to one's understanding of the female labor force. In fact, it contributes to the widespread misunderstanding of women's present role in the labor market.

With more than 40 million women in the labor force—half of all women age sixteen and over—it is nearly as misleading to attempt to describe them with a few averages as it would be to do so for men

---

3. Valerie Kincade Oppenheimer, *The Female Labor Force in the United States: Demographic and Economic Factors Governing Its Growth and Changing Composition* (Berkeley: University of California, 1970).

4. Linda J. Waite, "Projecting Female Labor Force Participation From Sex-Role Attitudes," *Social Science Research*, forthcoming.

in the labor force. The distinguishing feature of the female work force is its diversity. Some indication of this can be seen by examining frequency distributions of their characteristics, rather than averages. A few will serve to demonstrate that the phenomenon of women working outside the home is not restricted to any particular group.

The review of the factors that have been responsible for the rapid growth of the female labor force does suggest certain characteristics or conditions that tend to increase the chances that a woman will be working or looking for work. Women who are in particular *need* of money—those with no husbands or with husbands who are not working or have low earnings—are more likely to be in the labor force than are women in high-income families. Women with *few competing responsibilities* outside the labor market are more likely to seek work. For example, women who are child-free or whose youngest child is already in school are more likely to participate. Finally, women with especially *good job prospects*—as indicated by educational attainment, for example—are attracted to the labor market. Nonetheless, millions of women who are married to husbands with above-average earnings or who have preschool age children or who are not able to find particularly good jobs are also in the labor force.

Statistics on the marital and family characteristics of the women in the labor force illustrate the extent to which the composition of the female labor force is affected by some of these factors.[5] In March 1978, the most recent month for which detailed tabulations are available, 41 million women were in the labor force, of whom all but 5.6 million were under age fifty-five. Among the 35 million female labor force participants under age fifty-five, 56 percent were married and living with their husbands; 16 percent were divorced, separated, or widowed; and the remaining 28 percent had not married (see Figure 1).

The labor force participation rates reveal that marriage and child rearing do inhibit participation. Figure 1 shows that about 55 percent of married women were in the labor force, compared with 63 percent of women who had never married and 72 percent of formerly married women. Figure 2 shows that within each marital group, women with no children under age eighteen are more likely to work than

---

5. U.S. Department of Labor, Bureau of Labor Statistics, unpublished tabulations from the March 1978 Current Population Survey.

FIGURE 1

**LABOR FORCE STATUS OF ALL U.S. WOMEN
AGES 16-54   MARCH 1978**

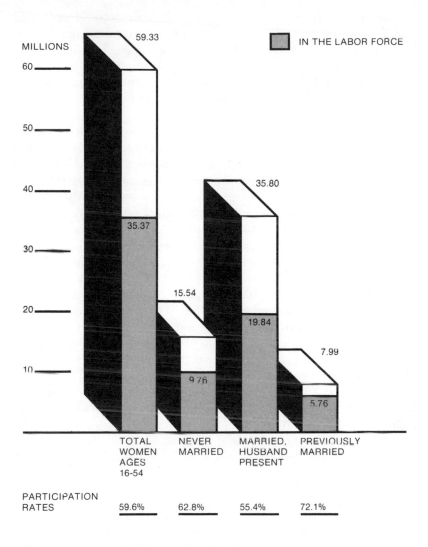

SOURCE: U.S. Department of Labor, Bureau of Labor Statistics,
          unpublished tabulations from the March 1978
          Current Population Survey.

are those with children between the ages of six and seventeen, while these women are more likely to participate than are those with children under age six. Analysis of more detailed data revealed similar patterns for most age groups.

What are all these women doing in the labor force? Here again, there is considerable diversity. Three-quarters are working at least thirty-five hours per week (that is, full time) or are looking for full-time work, and the rest have or seek part-time jobs.[6] The latter group includes a disproportionate number of teenagers and of women over age fifty-four. Female workers can be found in all kinds of jobs and under all kinds of conditions.

Despite the heterogeneity of the female work force, however, women are concentrated in a narrow range of activities. In fact, occupational and industrial concentration of female workers in a few "women's" jobs is the biggest problem facing women in the labor market today. One-third work in clerical occupations. Another quarter work in the fields of health care (not including physicians), education (not including higher education), domestic service, and food service.[7] The extreme form of occupational segregation in which women remained at home may have ended years ago, but the majority are still doing "women's work."

Chiefly because of the limited range of jobs held by women, women's earnings tend to be very low. The predominantly female occupations have below-average pay and offer limited opportunities for advancement. In addition, women often earn less than men within the same occupation. Thus the median annual earnings of women working full time, year round, are only 60 percent of those of men.

Women in the labor force come from all points in the income distribution. Within husband-wife families, a woman is slightly more likely to be in the labor force if her husband's income is below average. This income effect would be much stronger were it not for the tendency of the potential wages of wives to be correlated with

---

6. U.S. Department of Labor, Bureau of Labor Statistics, *Employment and Earnings* 26 (January 1979): 163. In 1978 there were 31.8 million women working full-time schedules (35 hours per week), working part time for economic reasons, or looking for full-time work. There were 10.0 million women voluntarily employed part time or looking for part-time work.

7. Computed from Current Population Survey estimates of employment by sex and detailed occupation in 1978 reported in U.S. Department of Labor, Bureau of Labor Statistics, *Employment and Earnings* 26 (January 1979): 172–73. Among the 38.9 million women employed in 1978, 13.5 million were clerical workers; 3.3 million were nurses, health technicians, and health service workers; 2.1 million were teachers; 1.1 million were service workers in private households; and 3.0 million were food service workers.

FIGURE 2

**LABOR FORCE STATUS OF EVER-MARRIED
U.S. WOMEN AGES 16-54 MARCH 1978**

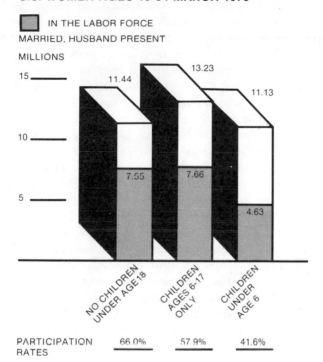

■ IN THE LABOR FORCE

MARRIED, HUSBAND PRESENT

MILLIONS

| PARTICIPATION RATES | 66.0% | 57.9% | 41.6% |

PREVIOUSLY MARRIED

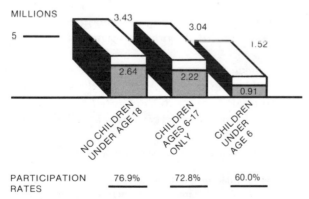

MILLIONS

| PARTICIPATION RATES | 76.9% | 72.8% | 60.0% |

SOURCE: U.S. Department of Labor, Bureau of Labor Statistics, unpublished tabulations from the March 1978 Current Population Survey.

the earnings of their husbands and for women with high potential earnings to be in the labor force.

The earnings of working wives, on average, contribute about 26 percent of total family income. Among families in which the wife worked full time, year round, the median contribution is 38 percent. The additional money income provided by the working wife is sufficient to put their families ahead of families in which the wife has no earnings. Thus, casual examination can lead to the correct, but misleading, conclusion that wives who work are in higher-income families than are wives who do not. Their families are in higher-income brackets precisely *because* they work.

In 1977, the median income of husbands under age fifty-five whose wives were in the labor force was approximately $2,000 below that of husbands whose wives were not in the labor force. Ten percent of the husbands of working wives had incomes above $25,000, compared with 17 percent of the husbands of nonparticipants.[8] When a wife's earnings are added to family income, the relative position of families in which both spouses work is reversed. In 1976 (the most recent year for which these data are available), the median income of husband-wife families in which the husband was under age fifty-five and the wife was in the labor force was about $3,000 above that of families in which the wife was not in the labor force. Twenty-five percent of the families with working wives had incomes above $25,000, compared with only 18 percent of the families with non-participating wives.[9]

In addition, the difference in money incomes between families in which the wife works and families in which the wife does not work overstates the difference in their standards of living. The family in which the wife works outside the home has given up something in return. As a result of her job, the wife (and sometimes other members of the family) has less time to do other things and has additional expenses.

The earnings of women are especially important in households in which there is no adult male present. Although these families constitute only one-seventh of all families in the United States, they include one-half of all families living in poverty. Virtually all the increase in

---

8. Calculated from unpublished data, from the March 1978 Current Population Survey.

9. Calculated from data provided in U.S. Department of Commerce, Bureau of the Census, "Money Income in 1976 of Families and Persons in the United States" *Current Population Reports*, series P-60, no. 114, (Washington, D.C.: U.S. Government Printing Office, 1978), pp. 79 and 82.

the number of families living in poverty over the past decade was among these families. In 1977, there were more than 8 million of these families, of which one-third had incomes below the poverty line. The likelihood that these families were living in poverty was closely linked to the employment status of the woman. In those in which the woman did not work at all during the year, 51 percent were in poverty; 19 percent of the ones in which the woman worked (including ones in which she worked part time or part year) were poor; and only 7 percent of the families in which the woman worked full time, year round, were poor. The kind of job held was also important. For example, 33 percent of the families in which the woman's main job was as a service worker (including domestic service) were poor, compared with only 6.6 percent of the ones in which the woman was employed as a professional or managerial worker.[10]

In sum, the female labor force in the United States consists of more than 40 million women from diverse backgrounds, family situations, and income levels. The work they are doing, however, is more uniform; it consists largely of employment that is separate from jobs held by men, and less remunerative.

FUTURE GROWTH OF THE FEMALE LABOR FORCE

We have seen that the female labor force has grown rapidly during this century, particularly since World War II. Women from backgrounds as varied as the female population itself are now participating We have also seen that the work they are doing is still largely confined to occupations that have come to be known as "women's work." What about the future? Will the size of the female labor force continue to grow? How rapidly? With what consequences?

Each of the authors of the chapters that follow proceeds on the assumption that the labor force participation rate of the female population will continue to increase at a fairly rapid pace at least throughout the next decade. The effects of this increase, especially its implications for current policies, are then examined in several critical areas. This section presents the labor force projections on which the analyses are based (see Table 1).

By 1990 about 55 percent of the female population ages sixteen and over are expected to be in the labor force, an increase of more

---

10. U.S. Department of Commerce, Bureau of the Census, "Money Income and Poverty Status of Families and Persons in the United States: 1977" (advance report) *Current Population Reports*, series P-60, no. 116, (Washington, D.C.: U.S. Government Printing Office, 1978), p. 27.

Table 1

PROJECTIONS OF THE FEMALE LABOR FORCE IN 1990

	Population			Labor Force			Participation Rate		
	Actual 1978 (March)	Projected 1990	Projected Change	Actual 1978 (March)	Projected 1990	Projected Change	Actual 1978 (March)	Projected 1990	Projected Change
	(thousands)			(thousands)			(percent)		
Total, ages 16 and over	83,374	94,690	11,316	40,971	51,890	10,919	49.1	54.8	5.7
Ages 16–24	18,277	15,535	−2,742	10,580	10,420	−160	57.9	67.1	9.2
Ages 25–54	41,059	52,023	10,964	24,790	35,706	10,916	60.4	68.6	8.2
Ages 55 and over	24,038	27,132	3,094	5,601	5,764	163	23.3	21.2	−2.1
Total, ages 16–54	59,336	67,558	8,222	35,370	46,126	10,756	59.6	68.3	8.7
Never-married	15,544	13,757	−1,787	9,763	9,464	−299	62.8	68.8	6.0
Married, husband present	35,802	44,390	8,588	19,842	29,600	9,758	55.4	66.7	11.3
No children under age 18	11,439	12,942	1,503	7,549	9,561	2,012	66.0	73.9	7.9
Children ages 6–17 only	13,231	17,859	4,628	7,661	12,520	4,859	57.9	70.1	12.2
Children under age 6	11,132	13,589	2,457	4,633	7,519	2,886	41.6	55.3	13.7

Other ever-married	7,989	9,410	1,421	5,764	7,062	1,298	72.1	75.0	2.9
No children under age 18	3,433	3,740	307	2,639	3,063	424	76.9	81.9	5.0
Children ages 6–17 only	3,042	3,882	840	2,216	2,865	649	72.8	73.8	1.0
Children under age 6	1,515	1,788	273	908	1,134	226	60.0	63.4	3.4

Source: Smith, *Women in the Labor Force in 1990.*

than fifteen percentage points from the figure in 1978. This participation trend, combined with the anticipated population growth, leads to a projection of 52 million women working or looking for work in 1990—11 million more than in 1978. Most of the net additions to the labor force will be women between the ages of twenty-five and fifty-four, most will be married, and many will have young children.

These projections are based on an extensive analysis of the determinants of future labor force growth, described elsewhere.[11] Estimating the future size of the labor force involves projecting the size of the female population and projecting the percentage of this population that will be in the labor force. The size of the 1990 female adult population is known with a high degree of accuracy, for all women who will be at least sixteen that year have already been born. The Census Bureau provides projections by sex and detailed age categories. But projecting the percentage of women within each age group who will be in the labor force is much more difficult. The record of past projections of women's labor force participation rates is not good.

To estimate the future size of the female labor force we first projected the demographic composition of the female population and then projected the participation rates for thirty-five separate age-marital-family status groups.

In the past the overall percentage of women in the labor force has grown both because the participation rates within many of the specific age-marital-family status groups have increased and because the demographic composition of the female population has shifted toward groups more likely to be in the labor force, specifically women without husbands or young children.

We first assumed that, within each age group, the marital and family composition of the female population would remain approximately as it was in 1977. The resulting marital and family composition is similar to the central projection made by the Census Bureau, but is still subject to error. The labor force projections are not sensitive to a wide range of alternative assumptions regarding marital status, but are sensitive to the fertility assumptions. In particular, if there should be a baby boom before the year 1990, the overall labor force projection would be too high, but the projection of the number of working mothers would probably be too low (assuming no other errors). This uncertainty is further discussed later.

---

11. Smith, *Women in the Labor Force in 1990*.

The next step—projecting participation rates within each group—is by far the most difficult. The rates of most female groups under age fifty-five have risen sharply in recent years. Will these increases continue? The answer depends on what happens to the many factors that influence the decision to participate. Will role attitudes continue to change? Will job opportunities and wages continue to grow? Will women's relative position in the labor market improve? To what extent will these and other factors continue to affect labor force decisions?

We concluded that most of the economic, social, and demographic factors that have contributed to the rapid growth in the female labor force in recent years will continue to propel women into the labor market and encourage them to remain there. As long as married women continue to be attracted to the labor force by improved labor market opportunities, anticipated growth in the economy over the next decade should be an important positive factor. Will women continue to share in the job opportunities that are created by economic growth? There are several reasons to expect that they will. First, the job outlook in the white-collar and service sector occupations (except for teachers) looks particularly good. Second, continued enforcement of equal opportunity laws should open opportunities in other fields, such as the skilled trades, that have long been male preserves. Third, the educational level of the adult female population is expected to continue to increase in various fields including law and medicine, which offer particularly large rewards. Fourth, women are developing increased work experience which, by itself, may pay off in higher wages, promotion opportunities, and seniority rights.

In addition to the economic reasons, the role of attitudes should not be ignored. The women who will be between the ages of twenty and sixty-four in the year 1990 are now between the ages of nine and fifty-three. There is considerable evidence that younger women's attitudes toward the role of women in the labor market are more liberal than are those of older women. Even if no individual woman's attitude changed any further, just the replacement of the less liberal older women with the younger ones over time will itself result in a working-age population more oriented toward the labor market.

Another factor that may be decisive for many women is the momentum built up as more and more women participate in the labor force. As women who do not work outside the home become a minority, keeping up with the Joneses will increasingly require Ms. Smith to enter the labor force. A family's place in the income distribution used to depend almost exclusively on the earnings of the husband. Now, even if the husband has above-average wages, the family could have below-average income if the wife stays home. Moreover, the full-time homemaker is finding that her occupation is becoming atypical.

The labor force projections reported here are based on the simple assumption that the increase in each age-marital-family group's participation rate over the next thirteen years will be similar to its trend from the preceding thirteen-year period. The resulting participation rates are slightly lower than those that would result from fitting trends directly to the age groups; the latter would reflect the past decline in birthrates that caused fewer women to be in low-participation family categories.[12]

These projections do not suggest a sharp break with recent history. Nonetheless, when added to the changes in labor force patterns that have occurred during the past few decades, they depict a dramatic departure from the prevailing picture of what American women are doing. If these projections are accurate, by the end of the next decade, two-thirds of all married women under the age of fifty-five will be in the labor force, including more than half of the mothers with young children. Even though the number of married women in this age group is expected to increase from 35.8 million in 1978 to 44.4 million in 1990, the number staying home with children under age eighteen is not expected to grow. The stereotype of a wife who stays home to look after her children will therefore fit only one-quarter of the 44.4 million women under age fifty-five who are expected to be married in 1990.

Several patterns deserve discussion. First, virtually all of the projected labor force increase is in the age group twenty-five through fifty-four. This pattern is due mainly to the aging of the post-World War II babies who, by 1990, will be in their prime working years. Fifty-five percent of the female population age sixteen and over will be in the twenty-five to fifty-four age group, compared with 49 percent in 1978. The absolute number of women ages sixteen to twenty-four will fall; even with a projected nine percentage-point increase in their participation rate, the number of young women in the labor force in 1990 will be virtually the same as in 1978.

---

12. For example, between 1964 and 1977 the proportion of women between ages twenty and twenty-four with children under age six declined from 48 percent to 29 percent. This demographic shift, which is unlikely to continue (at least at that rate), accounted for a considerable share of the growth in the participation rate of women in this age group. The complete report contains several alternative projections, based on different estimation periods and behavioral assumptions.

Second, married women are expected to account for a larger proportion of the female population and a larger proportion of the female labor force in 1990 than they did in 1978. The change in the age distribution will account for the first development, while the same reason plus the projected continued growth in women's labor force participation rate will account for the latter.

Finally—and most important—a very large jump is forecast in the number of working mothers with children under age six. By 1990, an increase of 3.1 million is expected in the number of working mothers with young children, a 56 percent increase over the 1978 level. An additional increase of 5.5 million working mothers with children between the ages of six and seventeen (and none under age six) is projected, also a 56 percent rise over the 1978 level. Increases of this magnitude, especially for the mothers of younger children, could have tremendous consequences for child care policy, work schedules, and other issues that affect an individual's ability to juggle the demands of a job with the demands of a child.

How likely is a substantial increase in working mothers with young children? Although the specific number is sensitive to the assumptions built into the projections, there seems little room for doubt that there will be a large increase and, with it, a large rise in the number of young children with working mothers. Three factors contribute to the expected increase: First, the number of women in their central childbearing years will continue to expand until the middle of the next decade. Second, most demographers anticipate a leveling-off of the recently declining fertility rates or an increase; there is no basis for expecting a further decline. The fertility rate projection used here may be conservative. Third, the labor force participation rates of women with young children have risen more rapidly than has the rate of any other group, in part because of the increasing acceptability of combining motherhood and work outside the home. Most of the women who will be bearing children in the 1980s will have been in their teens and early twenties in the 1970s and therefore are likely to hold the newer views; also, they will have had more role models who combined child rearing with labor market activities. Thus, the participation rate increases that have occurred in recent years are likely to continue.

CONSEQUENCES

The remainder of this volume is concerned with the implications of the continued movement of women into the labor force during the next decade. This subtle revolution has already significantly changed the lives of women who have come into the labor force and the lives of those with whom they interact. Unless the projections presented here are greatly misconceived, we should plan for the consequences of further changes in the same direction: more women working or looking for work; more wives splitting their time between unpaid work in the home and paid work outside the home; and more women trying to be both good mothers and good employees.

Some people view the prospect of a growing female labor force with enthusiasm. Others view it with apprehension and nostalgia for the days when women's role was more clearly delineated. But, for better or worse, many more women will be joining and remaining in the labor force, and planners—private and public—must anticipate the consequences.

Failure of individuals to plan in accordance with these projections will result in needless frustration. Marriages entered into with the unstated assumption that the wife will follow her husband as his job moves around the country or world and that she will leave her own job to rear their children will be shaken when these demands conflict with her own career. Women who, as students, choose their courses with the unstated assumption that their principal or exclusive life's work will be as wives and mothers will, when they enter the job market, come to regret that they did not prepare themselves for paid employment as well.

Failure of public policy makers to anticipate continuing growth of the female labor force will result in poorly planned government activities that affect us all. For example, total employment will need to increase by a larger amount to achieve a given unemployment reduction. Future Social Security tax receipts and payments will depend on the number of women who will be working.

The subjects of the chapters that follow are grouped according to the main sphere of activity within which the topics occur, although the overlap should be apparent: (a) the problems and opportunities that arise within the job market as a consequence of the rapidly growing female labor force (Chapters 2 and 3); (b) the impact of this movement on home and family life (Chapters 4 through 6); and (c) the responsiveness of public institutions to the changing needs of a society in transition (Chapters 7 and 8). In each area, the authors discuss the anticipated changes, the issues prompted by these changes, and some ways of resolving these issues. Some highlights of their studies follow.

Women in the Job Market

The most obvious change to anticipate is that there will be more women looking for jobs. Will they find them? What kinds of jobs will they be? In particular, will women's position in the labor force, relative to that of men, noticeably improve over the next decade? What can be done to increase the odds that women working in the year 1990 will fare better than women in the labor market today? These questions are the subject of Chapters 2 and 3, by Nancy Barrett.

Although an ever-increasing proportion of women are participating in the labor force and for longer periods, working women still have a long way to go to achieve parity with working men. Despite much attention to individual success stories and more than a decade of equal opportunity legislation, the statistics on women's position in the labor market do not show great progress. Women today still earn much less than men, have higher unemployment rates, and are more likely to be involuntarily working on a part-time schedule. Barrett examines some of the reasons for this lack of progress, emphasizing the principal barriers that must be overcome as women's commitment to the labor market increases and as attitudes change.

The critical problem that women in the labor force face today and will continue to face is occupational segregation. As mentioned earlier, the majority of women in the labor force today are engaged in activities that could be characterized as "women's work." Most are clerical workers, nurses, elementary school teachers, sales clerks, and waitresses—not managers, physicians, college and university professors, or skilled crafts workers. Nobody is under the illusion that this pattern of segregation will have ended by the year 1990. Its causes are complex and varied, relating in part to employer discrimination, but also to the attitudes and preparation of the female workers themselves. The key issue is how to absorb more women into the labor market in such a way that integration will occur.

Barrett points out that if women continue to enter occupations that already employ chiefly women, conditions in these jobs could deteriorate further. Women's jobs already pay less than men's jobs and often have lower status. Unless the demand for workers in these fields happens to keep pace with the growing female labor supply, wages in these occupations could fall further behind and/or higher female unemployment could result.

Many people still believe that women's participation in paid labor market activities is incidental to their major life's work as wives and mothers. This view has already been made obsolete by the decisions many women have made to participate in the labor force in circumstances that a generation ago would have kept them out; in particular, the presence of young children is not nearly so great a barrier. This view will represent an accurate description of an even smaller proportion of the female population in the years to come.

When people persist in holding this preconception, it can seriously affect their evaluation of women as workers or potential workers. Young women who do not expect to be in the labor force for long are unlikely to acquire the education and training that will prepare them for good jobs. Similarly, their parents, teachers, and counselors are unlikely to provide good vocational guidance if they do not expect the young women to work for long. Employers hesitate to hire women for jobs that require considerable training if they do not expect the trained employees to stay on the job.

As long as women who work outside the home earn much less than men earn, they will continue to be viewed as "secondary" workers. This second-class designation not only affects women's position within the job market, but also influences women's decisions about whether it is worthwhile for them to enter or remain in the labor force. This secondary-worker designation also affects how women are viewed by society in general and by their families in particular. In our society, a person's status is often defined in terms of the work the person does. If the wife's job pays less than her husband's and offers less opportunity for advancement, it is clear which job will take precedence when a child needs to be taken to the doctor or when the husband has an opportunity for promotion by moving to another city. Women's acquiescence in treatment as secondary workers in turn perpetuates the view that women's home responsibilities make them less valuable workers outside the home.

Barrett is optimistic that, with government support, women, through their increasing commitment to the labor force, can improve their position there. Yet, she notes, traditional views about "women's place" may simply be translated into more rigid stereotypes in the labor market. To speed up integration, she suggests vigorous enforcement of equal employment opportunity legislation already on the books, especially to open up opportunities in occupations such as the skilled crafts, in which men continue to predominate. In addition, women—especially young women—need counseling on career planning and on the opportunities for them in predominantly male occupations. To meet the needs and desires of tomorrow's work force, Barrett also calls for changes in employer practices. These include measures that would help women to maintain job continuity, such as maternity leave, improved child care facilities, and arrangements for flexible work schedules. More basic changes in the way work is organized may also be called for in order to encourage men to compete for jobs in the predominantly female occupations and vice versa. At a minimum, many firms will find it in their self-interest to accommodate the needs of couples in which both spouses work. For example, firms with rigid nepotism rules and with career ladders that require employees to move around the country to advance will find it increasingly difficult to attract and retain the best workers.

Home and Family Life

What changes in home and family life should we expect as more women, especially wives and mothers, move into the labor force? What issues will need to be resolved and what are the options for their resolution? Chapters 4, 5, and 6 deal with these questions.

The fundamental changes that will occur will stem directly from the increase in the number of women who spend some time in the labor force. A family will have a higher money income after the wife enters the labor force, but there will be less time for other activities. The time drain is, in turn, the source of many real and imagined problems for working women and their families. To the extent that other productive or enjoyable activities are sacrificed in order for a wife to work, the increase in the standard of living is less than that indicated by the increase in money income.

Sociologists Sandra Hofferth and Kristin Moore examine the state of knowledge concerning the impact of women's increasing participation in the labor force on marriage and child rearing (Chapters 4 and 5). They find that marriage as an institution does not seem to be dying but evolving. Young people seem to be postponing marriage but not forgoing it. Although the number of unmarried people living together has increased, such an arrangement seems to be a transient one for most couples rather than a substitute for formal marriage. In addition, despite a slight increase in the proportion of couples who plan to be childless, the vast majority still intend to have children. Family sizes, however, are likely to remain small; this trend already has contributed to a decline in the proportion of adult life devoted to child rearing. Although most people who divorce do remarry, the frequency of divorce has risen dramatically, an indication of a significant change in the meaning or at least the permanence of marriage.

To the extent that employment provides a woman with a reason and the means to postpone marriage, with meaningful roles other than motherhood, and with the ability to support herself after a divorce, women's employment has contributed to these changes in marriage formation and dissolution. It is not clear, however, whether employment is the cause or effect of these changes. It seems most likely that the increased employment of women is only one of many interrelated factors that have altered the American family. Nevertheless, those families in which the wife works are different from other families in important ways.

One of the clearest differences is in the way decisions are made; employed wives enjoy greater influence and responsibility in household decision making. The evidence on marital satisfaction is more complicated. As long as employment is elective, and particularly in households in which the woman works part time and/or has no small children, marital satisfaction is high. There is, however, a tendency for husbands whose wives work to be less satisfied with their marriages than are those men whose wives stay home, while working wives seem to be more satisfied than nonworking wives are with their marriages. The studies on which these findings are based reflect research done at a time when employment outside the home was less socially acceptable for women. In the future, the advantages of having a second income may compensate for the disruptions and tensions that more frequently receive attention.

The number of preschool children with working mothers is expected to grow rapidly over the next decade, both because the total number of women in the childbearing ages is increasing and because a higher proportion of mothers will be employed. This situation raises an important concern, because the supply of individual providers, such as the neighborhood woman who cares for several small children in her home or the in-home "baby-sitter," appears to be shrinking at the same time that the need for such care increases. Most evidence points to increased parental dependence on group care, not only for their three- to five-year-olds, but also for infants and toddlers. Because of the increased number of children in group care, it is important to examine the effects of such care on the children of working mothers.

One common fear seems to have been resolved. Working mothers and their infants do appear to establish normal attachment relationships. The quality of the relationship when parents and children are together as well as the quality and continuity of substitute care seem to be more important factors than maternal employment per se.

Overall, the evidence does not suggest that day care harms children. Effects depend on a number of factors, including particularly the mother's reasons for working. Because of the variation in types and quality of day care and family life itself, conclusions about broader effects are hard to reach. For example, the research done thus far has failed to take into account critical variables, such as the husband's attitude, characteristics of the caretaker, family income, sex of child, and hours the mother worked. Even if evidence were found that two-parent employment harms children, however, one could not conclude that the only solution is for women to quit their jobs.

Hofferth and Moore call for policy changes to help two-earner families, particularly those families with children, cope with their heavy workloads. Opportunities for meaningful part-time employment, flexible hours, high-quality and affordable day care, and parental leave after childbirth could expand the options of parents, while equal pay and job opportunities for women could remove the stigma of secondary employment from women's jobs and increase women's chances of becoming equal partners in both home and working environments. Work and family life may be inimical only because employers and policy makers have not taken into consideration the family involvements of both men and women.

Economist Clair Vickery, in a related study (Chapter 6), focuses on the impact of a wife's participation in the labor force on resource allocation within families, with resources defined to include both money and time. Although she approaches this subject from a very different perspective from that of Hofferth and Moore, there is a fair amount of agreement in identifying the main problems that arise within the home when the wife works and in identifying the kinds of changes needed to resolve them.

Vickery's analysis focuses on what the increased money income associated with a wife's job buys and what she and her family give up as a result of the absence of a full-time homemaker. Clearly, a wife's earnings contribute to the material well-being of her family, but the increase in total well-being is less than that indicated by the added money income. Vickery demonstrates this by examining how one-earner and two-earner couples spend their money and by discussing the concept of "full income," which includes both money and time resources. She finds, for example, that two families with the same money income—one obtained from the earnings of both husband and wife and the other from the husband alone—have significantly different full incomes. In particular, the two-earner couple has much higher work-related expenses, such as transportation, Social Security taxes, and clothing, and has less time for other activities, be they homemaking or leisure.

Vickery also questions the common assumption that two-earner couples are necessarily more financially secure than are one-earner couples. Of course the two-earner couple has more money income than would be the case if one spouse stayed home, and presumably the risk of both spouses' losing their jobs at the same time is small. But once expenditure patterns are adjusted to the expectation of two pay-checks, the pair becomes more dependent on the marketplace. In the past, when wives were much less likely to work outside the home, a husband's job loss was sometimes the occasion for his wife to seek temporary employment to offset some of the income loss. This "income cushion" role of the full-time homemaker is not available to two-earner couples. In the meantime, as families become accustomed to purchasing most of their goods and services in the marketplace, rather than producing them in the home, they become less self-sufficient.

What, then, does the wife's paycheck buy? Vickery finds that, after work-related expenses are deducted, the additional income brought home by the wife is spent on items similar to those that would be purchased if the income came from the husband's job. For the woman, personally, the job also is likely to buy greater economic independence; this independence is especially important in the event of divorce, separation, or the death of her husband. Based on the available data on how husbands and wives divide homemaking responsibilities, Vickery finds that the working wife continues to do the bulk of the housework. Thus, her total work week is much longer than that of the full-time homemaker.

Two issues Vickery raises are examined in other chapters as well. First, as two-earner couples become even more common, the average amount of paid work performed by married couples will increase unless the length of the standard work week falls or jobs with part-time schedules become more common. It is certainly reasonable for both husbands and wives to want to take some of their additional income from the wife's job in the form of more leisure. But unless more satisfactory part-time jobs become available, the danger exists that part-time work will remain systematically inferior to full-time work and be considered mainly for wives.

Second, families in which the wife remains a full-time homemaker will fall further behind in the income distribution. A comparison of money incomes will overstate this difference, however, because families in which the wife stays home have fewer work-related expenses and more time for nonmarket activities. Policy makers should not overlook this important distinction because it is relevant to how these families are treated. Perhaps the most important concern with respect to federal policy is that the income tax system does not now recognize the difference, as Chapter 7 points out.

Institutional Responses

The movement of women into the work force has been cited as a vital impetus to change in our rapidly evolving society. In the preceding summary of Chapters 2 through 6, the focus has been on some of the issues that have arisen within the labor market and within the home, in part because familiar ways of doing things are being questioned and are being modified. At various points government actions to ease the transition have been proposed. In addition, government institutions themselves should be reviewed to determine whether they have kept up with the needs of a society in transition. The final chapters (Chapters 7 and 8), by Nancy Gordon, examine problems that have arisen in the federal personal income tax system and the Social Security system. In both cases it is argued that the government has failed to adjust to the fact that the picture of a traditional family in which the husband works outside the home and the wife is a full-time homemaker is descriptive of a dwindling percentage of the American population.

The key issue Chapter 7 addresses is what to do about the so-called "marriage penalty" that now exists in the federal personal income tax system. Simply put, this penalty is the added tax that many couples pay if two individuals who work choose to marry. The amount can be quite large, even in the middle income brackets. For example, if a woman with a $10,000 salary marries a man with a $15,000 salary (and they have typical deductions) their combined federal income tax liability is more than $400 above what it would be if they were to live together without marrying and file tax returns as single individuals. The exact size of the penalty depends on the family's income and the proportion of the income earned by each spouse. The higher and more evenly divided the earnings, the larger the penalty. Two professional workers each of whom earns $20,000 pay $1,200 more tax if they marry. Gordon estimates that, in 1976, 23 percent of all tax-paying couples and 46 percent of all tax-paying couples in which both spouses worked paid more tax because they were married. It is anticipated that by 1990, 37 percent of all tax-paying couples, including 65 percent of the two-earner couples, would pay a penalty if the system is not changed.

In arguing for reform, Gordon considers a number of alternatives. She is particularly concerned that families with full-time homemakers should not have the rules of the game abruptly changed and sharp tax increases imposed on them. Among the alternatives that have been proposed, Gordon finds most promising one that would permit, but not require, married couples to file as single persons. This practice would be preferable to the present system because two-earner couples would no longer be penalized for marrying. It would be preferable to abolishing the joint tax return because it would not unduly penalize one-earner families for labor force decisions that were made under the present system. In this transition period, providing couples with a choice has much to recommend it.

The final chapter, also by Nancy Gordon, addresses problems within the Social Security system that have become more serious as women's participation in the labor force has increased and as divorce has become more common. The Social Security system was established in the 1930s, at a time when the stereotype of the American family was closer to reality than it is today or will be in 1990. An important feature of the retirement part of the system is that the monthly benefit levels are related to the indexed earnings histories that individual workers developed and on which workers and their employers paid payroll taxes. Dependents' benefits are included in the system: aged spouses of recipients are entitled to the higher of the benefits they earned as workers in their own right or 50 percent of their spouses' benefits.

In cases in which the wife never worked in employment covered by the Social Security system, the result is to provide "free" benefits. In cases in which the wife did work, but because of low or intermittent earnings has benefits in her own right that are less than those she could claim as a dependent, her Social Security contributions have no impact on her retirement income. Even when her own benefits as a worker exceed her benefits as a dependent, the net return from her contributions (over what she would receive anyway as a dependent) is small.

One result of this system is to favor families in which only one spouse contributes to the Social Security system, at the expense of families in which both spouses contribute and at the expense of individuals who never marry. One-earner families are favored in the sense that their benefits relative to Social Security taxes paid are much higher than are those of two-earner families and single persons. Another problem arises if a divorce occurs. Until recently a dependent wife's claim was not vested unless the marriage had lasted at least twenty years. Beginning in 1979, vesting will occur when the marriage has lasted ten years. Yet benefits for divorced homemakers remain low; they amount to half of the ex-husband's benefits while he is alive and equal his full benefits only after his death. Both these problems with the current system have created pressure to change it. As the proportion of husband-wife families in which both spouses participate in the labor force increases, and as high divorce rates continue, pressure to change the system will increase.

A number of proposals have been made in recent years to resolve existing problems. After analyzing the likely benefits and costs of the main alternatives, Gordon concludes that "earnings sharing" would best serve the needs of our heterogeneous society. Under this plan, Social Security earnings records would be shared equally between spouses each year the couple is married and spouses would receive retirement benefits on the basis of their own shared records. Protection for divorced homemakers would be improved because each spouse would have accrued identical claims during the years they were married. Gordon estimates that this proposal could be implemented with little increase in the total cost of the Social Security program. She proposes that the new system be implemented gradually, however, perhaps over a twenty- or thirty-year period, in order not to disrupt the financial plans of people whose expectations are based on the present system.

The recommendations for changes in government institutions that Gordon makes—optional individual filing within the personal income tax system and phased-in earnings sharing within the Social Security system—would move the federal government toward a neutral policy regarding the labor force participation decisions made by married women. The changes would reduce the penalties now being imposed on the increasing number of married women who opt to work outside the home, but would not establish compelling incentives for women to enter the labor force. The rights of women who choose to be full-time homemakers would be preserved.

Many important consequences of women's movement into the labor force are not considered in this book, or are given scant attention. For example, what will happen to the many community services that are now performed primarily by homemakers as volunteers? Much more research remains to be done. Nonetheless, I believe that the authors have made an important contribution to our understanding of the challenges that lie ahead.

Chapter 2

WOMEN IN THE JOB MARKET: OCCUPATIONS, EARNINGS, AND CAREER OPPORTUNITIES

NANCY S. BARRETT

The rapid growth and changing character of the female labor force together with new attitudes and conceptions about women's role in society pose new opportunities and challenges for the American labor market in the years ahead. Indeed, the past decade has witnessed many changes in the stereotypical views of women's work and in the career expectations of young women. The growing propensity of women to remain continuously in the labor force while their children are young and the recognition that women are quite likely to depend on their jobs for financial support and status have already had an effect on people's attitudes about women workers.

Despite the widespread view that a revolution in societal sex roles is taking place, most economists agree that women's progress in the job market—as measured by their earnings and employment opportunities—has not matched the pace of expectations. Although the increased emphasis on paid employment and careers for women and a lessening of sex-role stereotypes point in the direction of an upgrading of women's labor market status, women workers have made relatively little progress toward equality, at least according to the official statistics. In 1977, for instance, the median income of female college graduates (including those with advanced degrees) who worked full time, year round, was below the median income of male high school dropouts.[1] And there has been remarkably little increase in women's relative earnings over the past decade, despite the upsurge in female labor force participation, an increase in the average number of years spent in the labor force, and the enactment of legislation outlawing sex discrimination in pay and employment.

Although it would be naive to expect that historical and institutional practices that have relegated women to second-class status in the past will miraculously disappear as women exhibit a strengthened commitment to the labor force, it is clear that new responses by employers, government policy makers, and women themselves are needed if society is to take full advantage of the opportunities presented by the growing female labor force. This chapter analyzes recent employment and income patterns of women workers with a view to identifying the barriers to progress to date, and assessing the likelihood that changing aspirations and attitudes will erode the inequalities that currently exist between women and men in the labor market.

THE MALE-FEMALE EARNINGS GAP

Although women have increased their labor force participation, demonstrated a growing stability in their commitment to paid employment, and sought more responsible job opportunities, their average earnings have remained far below those of men. In 1977, less than 20 percent of men working full time, year round, earned less than $10,000, compared with more than half the full-time, year-round women workers (Figure 3). The ratio of median earnings of full-time, year-round women workers to male workers actually dropped from about 63 percent in the mid-1950s to below 60 percent in the mid-1960s and 1970s. (See Table 2.)

Regardless of the criterion chosen—age, education, or prior work experience—women in each category earn far less than men with the same characteristics, even when they work the same number of hours.

---

1. U.S. Department of Commerce, Bureau of the Census, *Current Population Reports*, series P-69, no. 116, 1978.

FIGURE 3

**EARNINGS DISTRIBUTIONS
OF MEN AND WOMEN, 1977**

WOMEN

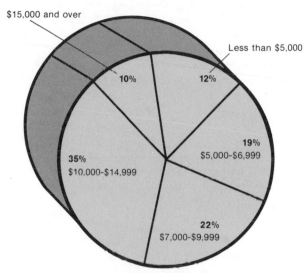

$15,000 and over

Less than $5,000

10%

12%

19%
$5,000-$6,999

35%
$10,000-$14,999

22%
$7,000-$9,999

MEN

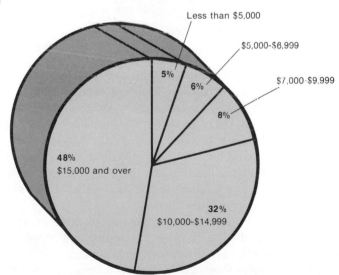

Less than $5,000

$5,000-$6,999

5%

6%

$7,000-$9,999

8%

48%
$15,000 and over

32%
$10,000-$14,999

NOTE: Median earnings of full-time, year-round workers 14 years
of age and older. Numbers have been rounded, so percentages
do not total 100 exactly.

SOURCE: U.S. Department of Commerce, Bureau of the Census.

Table 2

WOMEN'S RELATIVE EARNINGS BY OCCUPATION, 1956–75

*(Median Earnings of Full-Time, Year-Round Women Workers as a
Percentage of Men's Median Earnings)*

Occupational Group	1956	1960	1965	1970	1975
All Workers	63.3	60.7	59.9	59.4	58.8
Professional and technical workers	62.4	61.3	65.2	64.1	65.9
Teachers, primary and secondary	NA	75.6	79.9	79.5	83.0
Managers and administrators	59.1	52.9	53.2	54.6	56.7
Clerical workers	71.7	67.6	67.2	64.0	62.2
Sales workers	41.8	40.9	40.5	42.7	38.9
Operatives	62.1	59.4	56.6	58.4	56.1
Service workers (nondomestic)	55.4	57.2	55.4	55.6	57.1

Source: U.S. Department of Commerce, Bureau of the Census, *Current Population Reports*, series P-60, various issues.

As Table 2 shows, women's earnings are far below men's earnings within all the major occupational groups. And for many occupations, women's relative position has deteriorated over the past decade. What accounts for the stubborn persistence of the pay gap between men and women?

Historical Antecedents

The existence of a sizable gap between the earnings of women and men is as old as recorded history. There is even a biblical reference to sex-segregated pay scales. Leviticus (27:1–4) describes a conversation between the Lord and Moses in which adult males are valued at fifty shekels of silver and adult females at thirty shekels—a ratio strikingly like that encountered today. Possibly the different pay rates for men and women in primitive society were linked to their relative ability to perform hard manual labor—a rationale that today's advanced technology has made obsolete.

During the Industrial Revolution in nineteenth-century England, workers had practically no bargaining power and employers based wages on the perceived subsistence requirements of the workers. Contemporary records show that women's wages were set at around 60 percent of men's, purportedly because of women's lower subsistence requirements. Because single women workers' subsistence needs were presumed to be less than the needs of men with families to support, and married women were assumed to be merely supplementing husbands' income, employers felt justified in paying women less. Moreover, equal pay would have been inconsistent with the established order of male dominance.[2] As labor market rewards increasingly determined an individual's status, lower pay scales for women were at once a cause and effect of women's inferior social position.[3]

Although these events are now history, the fact remains that the average wage for full-time, year-round women workers still stands today at around 60 percent of the male wage. Although many changes in women's social and political status have occurred since the Industrial Revolution, the relative economic position of women workers has not advanced greatly in modern times.

Equal Pay But Different Work

Equal pay for equal work became the law with the passage of the Equal Pay Act of 1963. (The details of this and subsequent legislation affecting women's earnings will be discussed later in this chapter.) Yet the statistics show that women's earnings have remained far below those of men since equal pay was mandated.

How is the equal pay principle consistent with the persistent gap between men's and women's earnings? Quite simply, the law does not mandate equal pay for individuals doing different work. And much of the discrepancy between women's and men's earnings is accounted for by differences in their job assignments.[4]

Sex differences in job assignments can take the form of allotting men and women different qualitative tasks. In business concerns, for instance, personnel officers may routinely seek women for secretarial positions and men as management trainees. Some professions, such as nursing or teaching young children, are socially stereotyped as "women's work," while other jobs like airline pilot and police officer are considered "men's work." In most cases, jobs that are perceived as

---

2. For a revealing account of the employment and pay practices and attitudes toward women workers during this period see Ivy Pinchbeck, *Women Workers and the Industrial Revolution* (London: G. Routledge, 1930).

3. The tendency of the industrial wage structure to reproduce preindustrial status hierarchies rather than reflect the relative skill or productivity of classes of workers was noted by John Stuart Mill in 1848. See J. S. Mill, *Principles of Political Economy*, vol. 2.

4. Occupational segregation that is done with the clear intent of paying women less than men for work of equal value is illegal. But it is difficult to demonstrate intent and to determine what constitutes work of equal value.

"women's work" pay less than do "men's" jobs requiring comparable levels of skill and effort.

A related mechanism that perpetuates a wage gap between men and women is the assignment of men to jobs needing specialized skills and training that can only be learned on the job, or to supervisory positions with extra responsibility. In practice, differences in upward mobility for men and women interact with the practice of giving men and women qualitatively different job assignments. Career-ladder jobs are often restricted to male turf, while women's jobs afford fewer opportunities for advancement. The male management trainee, for instance, will receive specialized training and will be assigned to positions of ever-increasing responsibility with, of course, higher pay. The secretary, meanwhile, often finds herself in a dead-end job, with much smaller increases in pay than those the male executive receives, even if she spends years in the company.

LIFE-CYCLE EARNINGS OF MEN AND WOMEN

Examination of the pattern of earnings over the life cycles of men and women reveals a marked contrast between the sexes. The earnings profile for males rises sharply from the postschool years through their twenties and thirties, peaks in their mid-forties, and declines somewhat thereafter (see Figure 4). In marked contrast, women's earnings rise hardly at all, and, on average, they peak at about age thirty.

Table 3 shows the same pattern. The youngest women who worked full time, year round, in 1975 earned 75 percent as much as men of the same age, in contrast to women aged forty-five to fifty-four, whose earnings averaged 52 percent of earnings for men in their age group.

Adjusting for such factors as education and occupation does not affect the general picture portrayed by these statistics. Alan Blinder, in a study that corrected age-earnings data for women and men by education and occupation, concluded that "the failure of women *in the same education-occupation category* [as men] to rise in the economic ladder over their working lives is seen to be the single largest cause of the male-female difference [in earnings] among whites."[5]

One factor frequently alleged to depress older women's wages is their relative lack of work experience. Certainly, women who drop out of the labor force to raise families cannot expect to earn as much when they return as persons with uninterrupted careers are earning. If

---

5. Alan S. Blinder, "Wage Discrimination: Reduced Form and Structural Estimates," *Journal of Human Resources* 8 (Fall 1973): 448.

FIGURE 4

**LIFE-CYCLE EARNINGS PROFILES
OF MEN AND WOMEN, 1975**

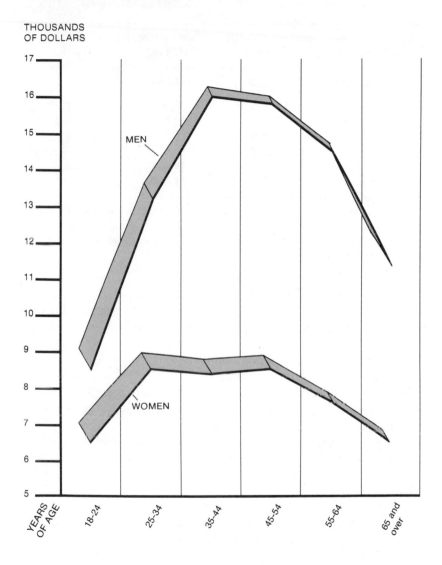

NOTE: Mean earnings of full-time, year-round workers.

SOURCE: U.S. Department of Commerce,
Bureau of the Census.

Table 3

THE SEX DIFFERENTIAL IN EARNINGS, BY AGE, 1975

(Mean[1] Earnings of Full-Time, Year-Round Workers)

Age Group	Female Earnings (Mean)	Male Earnings (Mean)	Ratio
All Ages	$7,940	$14,047	56.5
18–24	6,345	8,360	75.9
25–34	8,462	13,071	64.7
35–44	8,320	16,030	51.9
45–54	8,358	15,919	52.5
55–64	7,916	14,405	55.0
65+	6,309	11,286	55.9

1. The Census Bureau does not tabulate median earnings broken down by sex and age.

Source: U.S. Department of Commerce, Bureau of the Census, *Current Population Reports*, series P-60, no. 105, 1977.

women work only intermittently, they cannot expect much upward mobility over their life cycle. Yet Isabel Sawhill has found that single (never-married) women had age-earnings profiles that were almost identical to those of married women despite the fact that single women's average job tenure was about the same as tenure for men in the same age bracket. Her study found that continuous work experience raised the earnings ratio of females by only one percentage point.[6] Even after adjusting for differences in age, education, hours worked, and other factors, she found that, compared with married women who earned, on average, 56 percent of the average earnings of men, women who never married averaged 57 percent of men's earnings.

Dead-End Jobs

If the failure of women's earnings to rise over the life cycle cannot be accounted for by a lack of stability in their attachment to the labor market, how can we account for the flat age-earnings profiles for women that we observe in the official statistics? One possibility is that women find it more difficult than men to move up the ladder to high-status jobs.

6. Isabel V. Sawhill, "The Economics of Discrimination Against Women: Some New Findings," *Journal of Human Resources* 8 (Fall 1973): 383–96.

A case in point is the distribution of women among the classification grades of the Federal Government Civil Service system. Although the government professes to be an equal opportunity employer, it is clear from Table 4 that women are disproportionately employed at the bottom end of the scale. More than three-fourths of the jobs in classifications 1 through 3 (paying $6,561 to $8,366) are held by women. In contrast, women hold only around 4 percent of jobs in classifications 14 through 18 (paying more than $32,000).[7]

Similar patterns are characteristic of the distribution of women in the job hierarchies of large private corporations. Barbara Bergmann notes the case of an insurance company that achieved notoriety as a result of a sex-discrimination lawsuit brought by some of its employees under Title VII of the Civil Rights Act of 1964.[8] Between 1965 and 1970, the company recruited 2,000 individuals from outside the company for professional positions designated "claims adjuster" and "claims representative." For each category, the only formal requirement was a college degree. Yet, only men were designated claims adjusters, while claims representatives were almost exclusively women. New claims adjusters were paid $2,500 more than claims representatives, but what is more important, only adjusters could obtain promotions beyond a low supervisory level. While the men who stayed with the firm advanced into higher-paying jobs as they gained experience and were given increased responsibility, women were stuck in jobs paying little more than their starting salary. Thus, although the designation of women as claims representatives resulted in a starting wage $2,500 lower than the wage for male claims adjusters, this gap was small compared with the later discrepancy associated with the fact that claims adjusters were promoted to higher-paying jobs while claims representatives were not.[9]

---

7. For a more detailed breakdown, see U.S. Civil Service Commission, *Equal Employment Opportunity Statistics* (Washington, D.C.: U.S. Government Printing Office, 1978).

8. Barbara R. Bergmann, "Reducing the Pervasiveness of Discrimination," in Eli Ginzberg, ed., *Jobs for Americans*, by the American Assembly (Englewood Cliffs, N.J.: Prentice-Hall, Inc., 1976).

9. A growing body of academic literature has addressed itself to this phenomenon. One approach conceptualizes two distinct labor markets. One set of jobs, generally the low-paying, dead-end positions, is filled by recruits of new workers from outside the firm. The other set of higher-paying jobs is filled internally, through the promotion and upgrading of currently employed workers. For a complete discussion, see Peter B. Doeringer and Michael J. Piore, *Internal Labor Markets and Manpower Analysis* (Lexington, Mass.: D. C. Heath and Company, 1971).

Table 4

EARNINGS OF WOMEN AND MEN IN THE
FEDERAL GOVERNMENT CIVIL SERVICE SYSTEM

*(Full-Time, White-Collar Employees of Federal Government Agencies as of
November 30, 1977)*

General Schedule (GS) Grade	Salary	Number of Women Employed	Women as a Percentage of Total Employed
Total GS Employees	—	615,342	43.1
1	$ 6,561	1,277	65.7
2	7,422	15,818	74.1
3	8,366	73,187	77.5
4	9,391	134,602	77.5
5	10,507	126,060	68.1
6	11,712	60,560	69.6
7	13,014	64,631	49.4
8	14,414	16,374	50.3
9	15,920	54,455	35.1
10	17,532	8,547	32.4
11	19,263	30,621	19.4
12	23,087	16,997	11.1
13	27,453	7,670	6.8
14	32,442	2,878	4.9
15	38,160	1,435	4.5
16	44,756	159	3.4
17	47,500	55	3.2
18	47,500	16	3.7

Note: The salary rate shown is basic pay for employees in step 1 of the grade as of October 1978.

Source: U.S. Civil Service Commission, *Equal Employment Opportunity Statistics* (Washington, D.C.: U.S. Government Printing Office, 1978), p. 2.

Are Women Committed Workers?

The perception that women are temporary participants in the work force is often cited as a rationale for paying women low wages and offering them limited opportunities for advancement. How committed are women to work outside the home, and what effect does their commitment or lack of it have on their working lives?

Labor force participation and continuity of experience obviously help shape the life-cycle earnings profiles of women. One explanation for why men's age-earnings profiles rise while women's are relatively flat is that men are more likely to invest early in education and training that pay off later in higher earnings. Because men view their careers in long-term perspective, they are allegedly willing to forgo short-term earnings opportunities and to undertake costly education and training with a view toward a later payoff. Women, conversely, are said to invest less in education and training because they expect to have fewer years of labor force activity in which to benefit from education and training.[10]

Another explanation for the differences in men's and women's age-earnings profiles is that employers provide superior training opportunities for men in the expectation that men will stay with the firm longer than will most women. Training decisions are usually made early in a worker's career, before he or she has had the opportunity to establish a work history. To the extent that employers hold traditional attitudes regarding the intermittency or unreliability of women employees, even women who never leave the firm will have received fewer training opportunities than will similarly qualified men. Hence, on average, women have flatter life-cycle earnings profiles.[11]

There seems to be some truth in each of these explanations. Both women and employers underestimate how long the average woman will remain in the labor force. A national survey that followed the labor market experiences of two groups of women for five years revealed that younger women (ages fourteen to twenty-four in 1968) grossly underestimated their future labor market participation when their predictions were compared with the actual work experience of older women.[12] Young white women predicted a participation rate of 29 percent at age thirty-five, compared with an actual rate of 48 percent for the older women at age thirty-five. Black women predicted a rate of 51 percent compared with an actual rate of 67 percent. And the gap between the responses of the younger women and the actual

---

10. See, for instance, Gary S. Becker, *Human Capital: A Theoretical and Empirical Analysis* (New York: Columbia University Press, 1964); Jacob Mincer, "Investment in Human Capital," *Journal of Political Economy* 66 (August 1958); and Jacob Mincer and Solomon W. Polachek, "Family Investments in Human Capital: Earnings of Women," *Journal of Political Economy* 82 (March/April 1974): S76–S108.

11. See Barbara R. Bergmann, "Sex Discrimination in Wages: Comment," in Orley Ashenfelter and Albert Rees, eds., *Discrimination in Labor Markets* (Princeton: Princeton University Press, 1973), pp. 152–54.

12. Reported in U.S. Department of Labor, Employment and Training Administration, *Women and Work*, Manpower Research Monograph No. 46 (Washington, D.C.: U.S. Government Printing Office, 1977), p. 15.

participation rate they will experience at age thirty-five is likely to be
even greater than these numbers show, given the national trend to
higher female labor force participation.

When women underestimate their future labor market participation,
they will invest in less education and training than their prospects
warrant. Moreover, they may be less concerned about the quality of
their education and may be careless about career planning. Women in
college still tend to specialize in the arts and humanities, while men
predominate in science and business. Part of this difference is, no
doubt, the result of an educational system that encourages boys to
excel in science and competitive sports and girls to pursue artistic and
literary studies. Further, our society does not emphasize career planning for girls. Marriage has been seen as the primary mechanism
through which a woman achieves status; hence many women's efforts
have been concentrated on securing desirable husbands, rather than
on achieving through their own merits. In the past, a woman's college
education has sometimes been viewed more as a way to improve social
acceptability than as a vehicle for acquiring the skills requisite to a
career.

But myopia about future work experience is only one factor in
explaining women's relatively flat life-cycle earnings profiles. Studies
indicate that women get less payoff from education and training than
men do in terms of earnings.[13] Figure 5 shows the life-cycle income
profiles of men and women by years of education. For men in their
mid-forties, the income of the average college graduate is about $9,000
a year more than for high school graduates. For women, the difference
between high school and college graduates' earnings is only about
$4,000. Furthermore, women who have finished college have lower
incomes than do male high school graduates of all ages; in fact, as
already noted, their median incomes are about on a par with those of
male high school dropouts.

Not all the differential between male and female college graduates
can be explained by differences in their choice of major or in the
quality of the institution attended. One study paired female college
graduates with male counterparts with the same academic degree from
the same institution. The outcome showed a substantial wage gap
between the sexes, even when quality of output and work experience
were taken into account.[14]

13. See, for instance, Gary D. Brown, "How Type of Employment Affects Earnings
Differences by Sex," *Monthly Labor Review* 99 (July 1976): 25–30.

14. Nancy M. Gordon and Thomas E. Morton, "The Staff Salary Structure of
A Large University," *Journal of Human Resources* 11 (Summer 1976): 374–82.

FIGURE 5

THE EFFECTS OF EDUCATION ON THE LIFE-CYCLE INCOMES OF MEN AND WOMEN, 1975

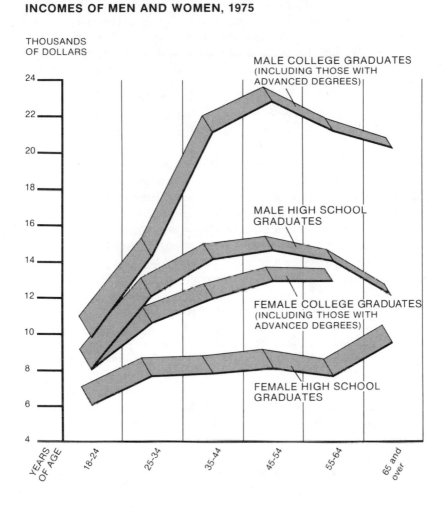

NOTE: Median incomes of full-time, year-round workers, 1975.

SOURCE: U.S. Department of Commerce, Bureau of the Census.

It appears, then, that a combination of factors adversely affects the upward mobility of women. To the extent that women discount their probable future labor market participation, they will invest in less education and training, but because of externally imposed barriers to their upward mobility, women also get less payoff for education and training than do men. Thus there is a vicious circle in which women have less incentive to undertake costly education and training than men do, not only because they expect to spend less time in the labor market, but also because education and training do not pay off in higher earnings for women to the same degree that they do for men.

Women's Labor Force Commitment and Upward Mobility

Although years of experience in the job market enhance earnings, women's progress in the labor market may ultimately depend on whether they strengthen their job attachment. In low-income families, for instance, a large percentage of the women work, but they work intermittently and change jobs often. These practices mean loss of seniority, a principal avenue of advancement. In more affluent families, women often drop out of the labor force during their childbearing years, just when their male counterparts are aggressively moving up the career ladder. When women return to work, they have to compete for jobs with younger men who are preferred because presumably they have more working years ahead during which the firm can benefit from its investment in them.

Of course childbearing and child rearing are not the only reasons women leave their jobs. If women's employment is viewed as secondary within the family, the wife may be expected to relocate as her husband's career may require. Studies show that among couples who migrate, the husband's wage generally increases while the wife's wage declines.[15] This fact suggests that the average couple moves because of a better opportunity for the husband, at the cost of a drop in earnings for the wife. The longer-range consequences of the move may be even more adverse, if the woman forgoes a job that would have provided upward mobility in later years.

Employers may expect that if they invest in training a man and he receives a better offer, they can retain him by paying a higher wage. By the same token, they may feel they have less prospect of retaining a woman's services if a family's moves are determined by the husband's needs.

As in the case of education and training investments, many factors contribute to women's relatively weak job commitment. High rates

---

15. See Solomon W. Polachek and Francis W. Horvath, "A Life Cycle Approach to Migration: Analysis of the Perspicacious Peregrinator," in Ronald G. Ehrenberg, ed., *Research in Labor Economics*, vol. 1 (Greenwich, Conn.: Jai Press, 1977).

of job turnover are common among low-paid workers of both sexes who correctly perceive little advantage to job continuity. From the employer's perspective, job continuity rather than labor force commitment is the principal concern; yet it is often assumed that the two are synonymous. Actually, the concentration of women in low-paying, dead-end jobs weakens their *job* attachment, regardless of whether their *labor market* commitment is continuous. This reduced job attachment results in another vicious circle in which women are perceived to be less stable workers than men, and hence are not given responsible positions. But studies document that when account is taken of job status, men and women show very little difference in job attachment.[16] Further, although workers in the lowest-ranked jobs have relatively high absentee rates, absenteeism in equivalent job categories is no higher for women than for men.[17]

Women have begun to realize that dropping out of the labor force in the early years can adversely affect their job prospects should they eventually want to return to work. One reason the overall female labor force participation rate has risen so fast is that women who enter the labor force are remaining longer than before. The Bureau of Labor Statistics reports that although the average number of years men spend in the labor force has been declining since 1950, the average number of years women work has been sharply rising, especially among married women with children. After 1950, work-life expectancy among women rose at a faster rate than did overall life expectancy, and the time women spent out of the labor force began to decline.[18]

Many young women are postponing childbearing until they have established careers and demonstrated a commitment to continuous

16. See, for instance, John B. Parrish, "Employment of Women Chemists in Industrial Laboratories," *Science*, April 30, 1965; and U.S. Department of Labor, Women's Bureau, *Facts About Women's Absenteeism and Labor Turnover* (Washington, D.C.: U.S. Government Printing Office, 1969).

17. Ibid. According to the Women's Bureau report, among federal government workers in 1961, sick leave averaged 9.6 days for women and 7.9 days for men. However, among those earning $9,000 to $10,000 per year, sick leave averaged 6.9 days for women versus 6.3 days for men. Further, a Public Health Service study showed an average of 5.6 days lost by women as compared with 5.3 by men in all employment in 1967. "Current Estimates from the Health Interview Survey," *Vital and Health Statistics* (Washington, D.C.: U.S. Government Printing Office, 1967).

18. Howard N. Fullerton, Jr., and James J. Byrne, *Length of Working Life for Men and Women, 1970*, U.S. Department of Labor, Bureau of Labor Statistics, Special Labor Force Report No. 187 (Washington, D.C.: U.S. Government Printing Office, 1977).

participation in the labor force. Provided they drop out for only a
short period, it is often possible for them to return to similar positions.
The prospect of good, well-paying jobs is likely to entice them to
return to the labor force more quickly than would be the case if less
desirable options are available. Hence working women who have
delayed childbearing until they have established careers or seniority
are expected to have higher labor force participation rates when they
have children than do those women who dropped out earlier and have
less attractive reentry prospects.

OCCUPATIONAL SEGREGATION BY SEX

An important factor that keeps the equal pay principle from closing
the male-female earnings gap is so-called *occupational segregation*.
Traditional conceptions of women's work, derived from societal sex
roles and sex-based division of labor at home, characterize the jobs
women do in the paid labor force. As Figure 6 shows, more than two-
thirds of employed women hold jobs in stereotypically female occupations as nurses, librarians, teachers, social workers, clerical workers, and
service workers.

Several traits characterize jobs typically held by women. First, women
are rarely put in positions of authority. The assignment of male
supervisors to a predominantly female work force limits women's upward mobility even in female-dominated occupations. In elementary
and secondary schools, for example, two-thirds of the teachers are
women, but only a third of the principals and other school adminis-
trators are women.[19]

Both white-collar and blue-collar jobs that women hold are
stereotyped according to certain attributes commonly perceived as
feminine. Jobs that require caring for others and nurturing small
children are viewed as appropriately feminine, since these are tasks
to which females are exposed from childhood.

Another characteristic of women's work assignments is that women
are allowed only vicarious rather than direct achievements. The
secretary who prepares her boss for business dealings, the nurse who
assists the doctor in the operating room, and even the school teacher
whose success lies in the achievements of her students exemplify
indirect achievers. Society has long encouraged women to accept
vicarious satisfactions. Girls have been taught to enjoy competitive

19. U.S. Department of Labor, Bureau of Labor Statistics, *Employment and
Earnings* 25 (January 1978): 153.

FIGURE 6

OCCUPATIONAL PROFILE OF THE FEMALE LABOR FORCE, 1977

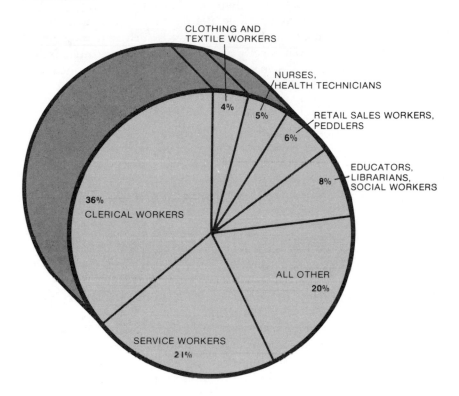

PERCENTAGE OF THESE GROUPS THAT ARE FEMALE			
CLERICAL WORKERS	79%	SALES CLERKS, ETC.	67%
SERVICE WORKERS	62%	NURSES, ETC.	83%
EDUCATORS, ETC.	64%	TEXTILE WORKERS, ETC.	76%

SOURCE: U.S. Department of Labor, Bureau of Labor Statistics, 1977.

sports as spectators or cheerleaders. Women have learned home economics with a view to pleasing husbands and raising healthy children.

Among blue-collar workers, too, sex-role attitudes affect job assignments. Women allegedly are better than men at tedious, repetitive tasks and at jobs requiring manual dexterity. Further, women are supposed to be more sensitive than men to loud noises and dirty places, and are presumed less able than men to work with heavy equipment (even though modern technology is such that most heavy equipment operates mechanically and physical strength often is not particularly important). As in the white-collar world, traditional sex roles dictate that blue-collar women should be supervised by men.

Social and Psychological Pressures

Although occupational segregation of women may be a rather obvious way for employers to circumvent the Equal Pay Act, the mechanisms that perpetuate segregation are extremely powerful. When women attempt to move out of vicarious roles, they are often seen as unfeminine and in many cases they are ridiculed. Women who try to achieve directly are said to "threaten" men and may be subjected to ostracism by fellow workers. The psychological impact of male disapproval can be devastating for many women, particularly because society has taught them the importance of pleasing men as a way to obtain status.

Overt sex harassment is common when blue-collar women try to do traditionally masculine work. Pornographic material is sometimes displayed to embarrass women and show them "their place." Work areas are sometimes arranged so as to make it difficult for anyone of short stature to have access to the equipment used. In many cases, rearrangement of the work place would not inhibit production, but male workers resist changes and ridicule women who try to work under the adverse conditions.[20]

The male buddy system also operates. In many factory environments, teamwork is essential for effective completion of jobs, and men often refuse to cooperate with a woman who dares to invade male territory, particularly if she refuses to exchange sexual favors.[21]

Among blue-collar workers a genuine conflict exists between union solidarity and the question of women's rights. The problem becomes acute when equal employment opportunity for women comes into conflict with union seniority systems.

---

20. For a discussion of some of these factors in the construction trade, see Sandra Hofferth, Katharine Fisher, and Donna Heins, "Occupational Segregation in Construction: A Case Study in Washington, D.C.," (mimeographed), The Urban Institute, Washington, D.C., 1977.

21. Ibid.

Many of the work rules that make it difficult for women to perform traditionally male jobs are set by the male-dominated trade unions. Union meetings are often held in bars and male lodge halls where working-class women do not go. Women workers report that their husbands will not allow them to go to union meetings, even if they could find the time when the housework is completed.

As long as sex roles within the family presuppose male dominance and female submission, occupational segregation in the marketplace will be hard to overcome. Women and men have trouble adjusting to different sex-role patterns at home and in the office. A man who is accustomed to a submissive wife has trouble taking orders from a woman at work, while a female executive with a position of authority in the office may find it hard to accept a dominant husband at home.

Wages in Female-Dominated Occupations

Female occupations are noted for their low wages; hence occupational segregation of women has contributed to the persistence of the male-female wage gap. If women are disproportionately concentrated in the low-wage sectors of the economy, a redistribution more in line with male employment patterns would result in an increase in relative earnings for women.

One study of men's and women's wages in more than 400 detailed occupations concluded that about 28 percent of the male-female wage rate differential among whites and about 22 percent among blacks is attributable to sex differences in the occupational distribution of employment.[22] (The rest of the wage gap is accounted for by sex differences in earnings *within* occupational categories.) The study revealed that the relative contribution of occupational segregation in explaining wage differentials varied considerably by age, marital status, and education. Occupational segregation had the largest effect on married, white college graduates; among them, it accounted for nearly 70 percent of the differential.[23]

Estimates of this kind understate the losses to women from occupational segregation to the extent that segregation itself causes lower

22. The amount of the wage gap attributable to occupational segregation depends on how detailed the occupational definition is. The greater the detail, the more the wage gap appears to be affected by occupational differences. For instance, in the extreme case in which each job is treated as a separate occupation, all wage differences would be attributed to occupational differences.

23. Barry Chiswick, J. Fackler, June O'Neill, and Solomon Polachek, "The Effect of Occupation on Race and Sex Differences in Hourly Earnings," *Proceedings of the American Statistical Association*, 1974, pp. 219–28.

wages in predominantly female occupations. Unless the number of jobs in the female job sector keeps pace with the number of women seeking employment, or unless job segregation by sex is alleviated, the rapid growth of the female labor force will drive down wages in female-oriented occupations.

Occupational Crowding

Many observers attributed the rapid growth of the female labor force during the 1960s to the increase in job opportunities in the traditionally female sector—particularly in clerical work, teaching, and health services. More recently, however, the growth in job opportunities in the female sector does not appear to have kept pace with the large number of female job seekers.

Trends in the clerical field have particular significance for the female work force as a whole because one in three women workers is employed in clerical work and 80 percent of all clerical workers are women. Between 1968 and 1977, female jobholders increased by 8.9 million, and 3.3 million of these were in clerical occupations. As Table 5 shows, clerical employment as a percentage of total female employment has risen from less than 32 percent in the mid-1960s to about 35 percent in the mid-1970s.

Although clerical employment has been increasing at a faster rate than the overall labor force has grown, clerical wages have not kept pace with the earnings of other female workers. Median earnings of female full-time, year-round clerical workers rose only 4.9 percent in real terms between 1965 and 1975 (less than 0.5 percent a year), compared with a 25.4 percent increase in real median earnings for all other female full-time workers over the same period.[24] At the same time, unemployment among clerical workers increased substantially. In 1965, clerical workers represented 11 percent of all unemployed workers, compared with nearly 15 percent in 1977 (see Chapter 3).

These figures suggest that the demand for clerical workers since 1968 simply has not kept up with the supply of women seeking clerical work. Occupational crowding in this field makes it a poor career choice, yet

---

24. In 1975, median earnings for male clerical workers were $12,152, compared with $7,562 for women clericals working full time, year round. This suggests considerable segmentation on the basis of sex within the clerical category. Most male clerical workers are post office mail carriers, shipping and receiving clerks, and stock clerks and storekeepers, all categories with a minority of women. Secretaries, typists, telephone operators, bank tellers, and bookkeepers are almost exclusively female.

Table 5

EMPLOYMENT OF WOMEN IN CLERICAL
AND SERVICE OCCUPATIONS, 1960–77

Year	Total Female Labor Force (thousands)	Clerical Number (thousands)	Clerical Percent-age of Total	Nondomestic Service Number (thousands)	Nondomestic Service Percent-age of Total
1960	21,374	6,617	30.3	3,236	14.8
1965	24,748	7,862	31.8	3,826	15.5
1970	29,667	10,233	34.5	4,909	16.5
1971	29,875	10,132	33.9	5,192	17.4
1972	31,072	10,777	34.7	5,435	17.5
1973	32,446	11,140	34.3	5,678	17.5
1974	33,417	11,676	34.9	5,955	17.8
1975	33,553	11,773	35.1	6,116	18.2
1976	35,095	12,248	34.9	6,282	17.9
1977	36,685	12,730	34.7	6,567	17.9

Source: U.S. Department of Labor, Employment and Training Administration, *Employment and Training Report of the President, 1978*, p. 205.

the number of people in clerical jobs continues to increase at a rapid pace. Similar trends are evident among service workers and in some female dominated occupations within the professional and technical categories.

Trends Among Younger Workers

Why are women continuing to enter the clerical field when job opportunities there seem less attractive than in the past? One factor in the growth of clerical employment is the change in the age composition of the female labor force—a much higher proportion of younger women now participate—that has accompanied its rapid growth. In 1977, 45 percent of the members of the adult female labor force were twenty to thirty-four years old, up from 35 percent in 1968. (The comparable figures for men are 40 percent versus 33 percent.)

Younger women are much more likely to be in clerical occupations than are older women. According to the Bureau of Labor Statistics, more than 42 percent of women age twenty to twenty-four were in clerical jobs in 1977, compared with 29 percent of women over fifty-four. But in 1968 more than 48 percent of younger women compared with about 24 percent of older women were in clerical jobs. For many women, clerical employment seems to have become a way station to other jobs. A higher proportion of older women are employed in the professional, technical, and managerial categories than are younger women.

That the rise in clerical employment is associated with the greater representation of younger workers in the female labor force is apparent from Table 6. Between 1968 and 1977, the occupational distribution of younger women age twenty to thirty-four shifted slightly away from clerical work toward the professional, technical, and managerial occupations. Because of the higher proportion of younger women in the work force, who are still more likely than older women to be employed as clerical workers, however, the absolute proportion of clerical workers among all employed women has risen. But if the trend among younger workers away from clerical jobs continues, the proportion of women in clerical employment should decline in the future, thereby easing the crowding. The simultaneous trend toward the professional and

Table 6

OCCUPATIONAL DISTRIBUTION OF YOUNG WOMEN
WORKERS (AGES 20–34) in 1977 COMPARED WITH 1968

Occupation	Distribution (percent)	
	1977	*1968*
Professional, technical, and managerial	24.5	20.0
(of which, teachers[1])	(7.1)	(7.1)
Clerical	38.0	41.7
Services	17.4	16.7
(of which, private household)	(1.4)	(3.0)
Operatives	10.4	14.5
Craftsmen	1.8	0.6
Sales	5.6	4.4
Other	2.3	2.1

1. Excludes college and university teachers.

Source: Unpublished tabulations provided by the U.S. Department of Labor, Bureau of Labor Statistics.

managerial categories is encouraging. It suggests that the male-female wage gap might be expected to narrow somewhat in the future.

Other occupational trends among young women workers are less significant, but suggest a generally positive outlook. For example, although the proportion of young female workers in the service category has increased, fewer are in private household employment. The decline in blue-collar employment reflects a general shift in the economy toward service-producing industries; hence some of the increase in service employment is directly associated with a decline in manufacturing employment. But it is notable that the younger women have increased their representation among craft workers, although they are still grossly underrepresented in the skilled blue-collar trades.

Although these trends among younger workers are important and encouraging as indicators of potential improvement, occupational segregation of women remains widespread and most women coming into the labor force are taking jobs in traditionally female occupations. A recent survey of 5,000 young women aged twenty-one to thirty-one revealed that of those who expected to be working outside the home by age thirty-five, the overwhelming majority aspired to traditionally female occupations. Of the noncollege females, 81 percent of the whites and 87 percent of the blacks said they would prefer to be in a typically female job by age thirty-five; among college females, the numbers aspiring to traditional careers were 75 percent for whites and 78 percent for blacks.[25]

Thus, although there are a few encouraging signs in the occupational statistics, there is also evidence that attitudes about job options for women are changing very slowly. Even though barriers to women in previously male sectors are eroding as a result of affirmative action plans and enforcement of equal opportunity guidelines, these changes have not occurred rapidly enough to keep pace with the growth of the female labor force. And although the struggle for equal rights and the egalitarian ideology accompanying it have produced a philosophical environment that encourages women to seek new opportunities, many still opt for traditionally female labor market activities even as they reject the role of full-time homemaker.

Sex-based division of labor has taken many forms as our society has evolved. In primitive times, men were the hunters, women the gatherers. During industrialization, men worked primarily outside the

---

25. Patricia K. Brito and Carol L. Jusenius, "Occupational Expectations for Age 35," in U.S. Department of Labor, *Years for Decision*, vol. 4, R&D Monograph No. 24, 1978.

home; women in domestic activities and cottage industry. The rapid growth of the female labor force over the past decade has signaled the emergence of a new era in which the major distinction between men's work and women's work will no longer be associated with market versus nonmarket labor. This development could portend greater economic and social equality between the sexes. But another possibility is that traditional views about "women's place" will simply be translated into more rigid sexual stereotypes in the labor market, and crowding in traditionally female jobs will continue to depress women's wages relative to those of male workers.

Sex Discrimination

If so much of the male-female earnings gap is to be explained by differences in opportunities for advancement and occupational segregation, is the root of the problem then not pure discrimination?

The most blatant forms of discrimination—separate pay schedules for men and women and rules prohibiting women from taking certain jobs—are illegal. But occupational segregation of the sexes makes it fairly easy to circumvent the Equal Pay Act in many cases and the pervasive gap in male-female earnings suggests that much remains to be accomplished.[26] The female administrative assistant may do the same work as a male executive, but usually she does it for far less pay. The female operative may aspire to learn a skill that would increase her earnings, but often is unable to pass the test without the cooperation of male coworkers, who routinely provide assistance to male trainees. To the extent that such behavior derives from traditional attitudes about women's place rather than deliberate attempts to shut women out of better-paying jobs, it may be difficult to agree on whether it constitutes discrimination in a legal sense. But the effect is the same.

LAWS AND REGULATIONS GOVERNING WOMEN'S EMPLOYMENT

While outdated stereotypes regarding women's long-range commitment to work and traditional views about "women's place" in the job market are changing rather slowly, legislation governing women's employment has changed radically since the early 1960s. Over the years prior to that time, the so-called protective labor laws (which limited

---

26. For an excellent discussion and specific documentation of the practice of reclassifying jobs solely to sanction separate pay scales for women and men, see Winn Newman, "Combatting Occupational Segregation: Policy Issues," in Martha Blaxall and Barbara Reagan, eds., *Women and the Workplace* (Chicago: University of Chicago Press, 1976), pp. 265–72.

women's total hours of work and prohibited women from lifting heavy objects, working during pregnancy, and working at night) had become mechanisms through which firms could legally refuse to hire women for certain jobs. In many cases, appeals to these laws were the basis on which women were denied equal employment opportunity.[27] But beginning with the Equal Pay Act of 1963, which amended the 1938 Fair Labor Standards Act, a new policy evolved. With it came a set of laws and regulations that not only overturned the protective labor laws of individual states, but also provided a legislative and psychological climate in which overt discrimination on the basis of sex is more difficult to achieve.

The Equal Pay Act outlaws separate pay scales for men and women for work requiring similar skills and performed under the same working conditions. Inasmuch as it did not require nondiscrimination in hiring, promotion, or work assignments, however, the Equal Pay Act did not mandate equal employment opportunity. Some say the motivation of the Equal Pay Act was actually to increase employment security for men who feared competition from women who would do their jobs for lower wages.[28] Nonetheless, this piece of legislation represented a watershed, a turning away from a legal system that facilitated and sanctioned discrimination against women to a legal environment that prohibits sex discrimination in employment.

The Civil Rights Act was passed in 1964 on a wave of public concern over the injustices of racial discrimination. Legislative historians note that inclusion of the word "sex" in Title VII of the bill that sought to prohibit discrimination in employment was an attempt by the bill's opponents to engineer its defeat.[29] Yet, with the strong support of Congresswoman Martha Griffiths, the bill became law, closing the major loophole of the Equal Pay Act. Title VII prohibits all forms of discrimination in employment, including hiring, firing, promotion, training, and fringe benefits.

Title VII also established an enforcement agency, the Equal Employment Opportunity Commission (EEOC). Although initially the EEOC concentrated its efforts on prohibiting racial discrimination,

---

27. Two excellent discussions of the adverse effects on women of the protective labor law are Jo Freeman, "The Legal Basis of the Sexual Caste System," *Valparaiso Law Review* 5 (1971): 213–30; and Mary Eastwood, "Legal Protection Against Sex Discrimination," in Ann H. Stromberg and Shirley Harkess, eds., *Women Working* (Palo Alto, Calif.: Mayfield Publishing Company, 1978), pp. 111–13.

28. Freeman, "The Legal Basis of the Sexual Caste System," pp. 226–27.

29. Jo Freeman, *The Politics of Women's Liberation* (New York: Longman, 1975), pp. 53–54.

more recently it has increased its efforts to monitor discrimination on the basis of sex.[30] The EEOC still lacks effective enforcement powers and is overburdened with a heavy caseload, but its guidelines have clarified important legal issues. For instance, the guidelines have made it illegal for firms to attribute characteristics to individuals based on the attributes of a group. Further, since 1972, EEOC has been empowered to bring civil action suits against private firms engaged in discriminatory practices.

In 1967 Executive Order 11375 extended an earlier prohibition against racial discrimination in employment under federal contracts and subcontracts to sex discrimination. This action was followed in 1969 by Executive Order 11478 prohibiting sex discrimination by the federal government as an employer. In 1978 President Carter announced a reorganization plan to consolidate federal equal employment activities. He also took action to strengthen EEOC as an enforcement agency.[31]

Because the Equal Pay Act does not cover professional employees, and because Title VII of the Civil Rights Act excludes educational institutions, additional legislation was needed to satisfy the grievances of women teachers who were denied promotional opportunities. The Educational Amendments Act of 1972 and the Women's Educational Equity Act of 1974 enabled women teachers to seek legal redress. At the same time, these pieces of legislation nullified school board practices requiring pregnant teachers to take leave without pay, and opened the door to elimination of sex biases in school curricula and academic programs.[32]

The legislative and judicial record of the post-1963 period has clearly established the principle of equal employment opportunity for women. Various class-action suits charging sex discrimination have won sizable back pay settlements, including an out-of-court agreement in 1973 under which the American Telephone and Telegraph Company agreed to pay $38 million to women employees in back pay and salary adjustments.[33]

---

30. See Phyllis A. Wallace, "Employment Discrimination: Some Policy Implications," in Orley Ashenfelter and Albert Rees, eds., *Discrimination in Labor Markets* (Princeton: Princeton University Press, 1973), pp. 163–64.

31. Office of the White House Press Secretary, February 23, 1978.

32. Terry Tinson Saario, "Title IX: Now What?" in Allan C. Ornstein and Steven I. Miller, *Policy Issues in Education* (Lexington, Mass.: Lexington Books, D. C. Heath and Company, 1976).

33. Freeman, *The Politics of Women's Liberation*, p. 190. Also see Phyllis A. Wallace, ed., *Equal Employment Opportunity and the AT&T Case* (Cambridge, Mass.: The MIT Press, 1976).

By the beginning of the 1970s, policy gradually shifted, without congressional action, away from simple prohibition of discrimination to affirmative action to remedy the effects of past discrimination and to eliminate more subtle institutional barriers to equal employment opportunities. This policy shift meant that firms were required to seek out women for jobs in which they were underrepresented, and to give preference to qualified women (and minorities) even if male candidates appeared to have better credentials.

Various rulings have prohibited the denial of employment to mothers of preschool children and have upheld the rights of husbands of women employees to receive the same dependents' benefits as dependents of male employees.[34] In a reversal of these trends, however, the Supreme Court in 1976 upheld the constitutionality of disability insurance systems that deny benefits to women unable to work because of pregnancy or childbirth.[35]

The rapid evolution of the law from sanctioning sex discrimination in the guise of protecting the weaker sex, to establishing the principle of equal employment opportunity, and finally to mandating the eradication of discrimination through affirmative action is one of the most significant legislative developments of the post-World War II era. However, affirmative action as policy is extremely difficult to enforce. In an attempt to facilitate the enforcement effort, the federal courts have, since around 1971, shifted the burden of proof to employers. Where women workers as a group are paid less than men, employers must demonstrate that the discrepancy is not the result of discrimination. Further, employers must show that the lower earnings of women result from less education, less prior experience, or other relevant factors. In addition, where women are underrepresented in high-paying jobs and in management, employers must establish an acceptable affirmative action plan and demonstrate a "good faith" attempt to recruit and hire more women (and minorities) for these posts.[36]

The effectiveness of these laws and judicial rulings for improving the labor market prospects of women will depend to a large extent on whether women and employers take advantage of the opportunities they offer. Women must seek wider horizons, move out of traditional occupations, and plan for long-term careers. Equal employment legislation may open new doors for women, but women themselves must be prepared to walk through them.

---

34. Mary Eastwood, "Legal Protection Against Sex Discrimination," pp. 117–21.
35. Ibid., p. 118.
36. Freeman, *The Politics of Women's Liberation*, pp. 191–93.

Then too, employers must recognize that it will be unproductive, in the long run, to relegate women to traditionally female roles. Employment opportunities in female occupations are limited and the growing female labor force needs to enter other areas where there is a scarcity of workers. Of course, moving women into "men's turf" means a breaching of the age-old practice of paying women less than men, and will be met with considerable opposition from male workers who will view integration of the work place as a threat to their jobs and self-esteem.

Equal employment for women will not be an easy road, as prejudices against women are strongest in traditionally male strongholds. But the law that mandates affirmative action to increase the representation of women in these fields will be a powerful ally.

Legislative support for equal employment opportunity for women has never been stronger, and the requirement that firms take affirmative action to promote women and move them into formerly male occupations is a major achievement in the struggle for women's rights in the labor market. But it must be emphasized that the effective application of these laws is facilitated by a strong and growing economy. In a prosperous economy, mobility barriers and prejudicial attitudes about women workers will erode much faster than under the slack economic conditions that have typified the recent past.

CONCLUSIONS AND RECOMMENDATIONS

Today the average married woman with children will spend about twenty-five years in the labor force.[37] Some women will never marry, others will be divorced or widowed, and will—at some point in their lives—be dependent on their own earnings for financial support and status.

This chapter has examined some of the factors behind the persistent gap in men's and women's earnings, a gap that has not narrowed appreciably as women have increased their labor force participation and long-term career commitment. Segregating the labor market by sex has been a mechanism that has perpetuated the practice of paying women less than men. Moreover, the belief that women are intermittent workers affects both their job content and opportunities for advancement. Women continue to underestimate their future work life,

---

37. U.S. Department of Labor, Bureau of Labor Statistics, *Length of Working Life for Men and Women, 1970*, Special Labor Force Report No. 187 (Washington, D.C.: U.S. Government Printing Office, 1977).

and hence fail to consider careers that will lead to higher earnings over the life cycle. Employers continue to view women as less stable workers than men and hence resist placing women in training or management positions that will lead to higher pay.

Assignment to low-status jobs, in turn, has reinforced the view of women within their own families as secondary earners. This subordinate status has meant that women are expected to do a disproportionate share of the housework, and to relocate or perform unpaid services (like entertaining) to further their husbands' careers. These demands, in turn, make it more difficult for women to compete on an equal basis with men in the most challenging and demanding jobs.

Many factors contribute to the vicious circle that prevents women's earnings from achieving parity with men's. But this diversity means that there are also many potential points of intervention to break the self-reinforcing process. From a policy perspective, intervention at several points simultaneously is likely to pay off most effectively. Affirmative action laws must be accompanied by more realistic career counseling of young women to encourage them to plan for a lifetime of labor market activity and to consider nontraditional career options. Employers, too, need up-to-date information about the probable job tenure of women workers. And married couples need to become more sensitive to the likelihood that the wife's long-term job prospects must be taken into account when planning the division of household responsibilities and deciding where to live.

Maintaining job continuity is important if women are to expect equal access to training and career-ladder spots. Unfortunately, the time for women and men to begin building a career coincides with the peak of domestic responsibilities associated with child rearing. Marital strains arise when the peak effort associated with moving up the career ladder occurs simultaneously for both partners. Working women and the firms that train them need to consider ways to relieve some of the tensions of two-earner couples so as to make the individuals more effective employees. Many young couples have postponed childbearing until both careers are solidly grounded. Some couples alternate moves in response to the job requirements of each; others move only when better opportunities can be found for both. In a few cases, couples live apart when job requirements so dictate.

Employers can help by providing parental furloughs to men and women with guaranteed restoration of seniority within certain limitations. A worker is more likely to return to a firm in which he or she had acquired job-specific skills and a responsible position than to go to a new firm and begin at the bottom.

Provision of improved child care facilities and arrangements for more flexible work schedules are some other steps companies can take to reduce the strains on two-earner families in the crucial years when young children are present. All these programs increase the probability that women will remain on the job after children are born, enhancing the payoff to their training. Just as life-cycle wage increases are the most logical way to ensure retention of male workers, good wages will shorten periods of labor force inactivity for women and attract them to their old jobs.

Job restructuring is needed not only in traditionally female-dominated occupations but also in male strongholds. Historically, as occupations have become "feminized" they have been adapted to the needs of an intermittent work force. But as female commitment to work continues to strengthen, more on-the-job training and increased responsibility are likely to pay off.

Some job restructuring may be needed for male employees, too. Married men with working wives—about half the population of married men—need more flexibility than they did in the past to relocate, to work shorter hours, and in some cases to interrupt market work to participate in housework and child care. The trend for couples to locate only where both can find suitable jobs greatly reduces the flexibility of employers to transfer male employees and increases the financial risks associated with training them. Outdated nepotism rules must surely go by the board when two valuable executives marry, or when the firm cannot secure an attractive prospective employee unless a job can be found for the spouse.

Restructuring jobs in male-dominated occupations to allow more flexibility, and increasing possibilities for career advancement in female-dominated occupations, should reduce some of the built-in incentives for men and women to pursue traditional careers. Men who seek flexible and less demanding work arrangements will begin to find attractive career options in formerly "female" areas, while women will be able to take advantage of the more attractive career opportunities and new flexibility to be found in the "male" labor market.

As women gain economic independence they will be less susceptible to psychological pressures to pursue feminine careers. The threat of ostracism by men is less important to a woman with an independent source of income and status. Also, as women move into responsible jobs with good pay, their economic power will be reflected in increased leverage in the home. And they will learn ways of taking an active role in many areas of life in which women's activity traditionally has been vicarious.

Affirmative action plans must stress the importance of increasing female representation in male-dominated fields, regardless of the inevitable resistance from employers, coworkers, and sometimes women themselves. The reasons that this approach is essential have been outlined above. First, there simply is not room in traditionally female occupations for the growing female labor force; the crowding phenomenon is depressing women's wages. Second, sex segregation of jobs permits employers to circumvent both the Equal Pay Act and Title VII of the Civil Rights Act, allowing firms to pay women less than men for comparable work and denying women equal access to training and promotional opportunities. Finally, unless women increase their representation in jobs formerly dominated by men, a status differential based on sex will be perpetuated in the labor market, with women workers clearly second-class citizens. Until they achieve status parity with male workers, women cannot expect to exercise their rights on an equal basis with men in the broader range of economic, social, and political activities.

Chapter 3

WOMEN IN THE JOB MARKET: UNEMPLOYMENT AND WORK SCHEDULES

NANCY S. BARRETT

The previous chapter explored some of the reasons why women's wages have not risen so fast as those of men during the past decade. Some women who enter the labor force, however, are unable to find jobs even at relatively low wages, while others are forced to accept part-time work even though they want full-time jobs. On the other hand, some women, especially married women with young children, prefer part-time to full-time employment.

In 1976, only 39.5 percent of all women who worked or looked for work actually had full-time jobs for the entire year, compared with 63 percent of the men. The rest were unemployed, or for some part of the year were out of the labor force or working part time. This chapter analyzes some of the factors behind female joblessness and the relatively high propensity of women to work part time.

UNEMPLOYMENT OF WOMEN

Unemployment has become a major policy issue in the 1970s. The unemployment rate for all groups has far exceeded the average of the 1950s and 1960s. Prior to the heavy influx of women into the work force in the 1960s, the female unemployment rate was generally no more than one percentage point higher than the male rate. But in the mid-1960s the female unemployment rate increased relative to the rate for men, and the gap has widened to nearly two percentage points during the 1970s (see Figure 7).

Unemployment has important adverse consequences. It represents an underutilization of resources and hence a rate of economic activity that is below the economy's potential. Economists and policy makers regard the unemployment rate as a principal indicator of economic performance. Reducing unemployment is widely viewed as a major test of the government's ability to improve the economic climate, and the growth of the female labor force has raised problems in this area.

Higher rates of female unemployment, combined with the rapid increase in the female labor force, have contributed to higher unemployment rates for the nation as a whole compared with those experienced before the mid-1960s. In 1977, for instance, the overall unemployment rate was 7 percent—6.2 percent for men and 8.2 percent for women.

The labor force was composed of proportionately more women in 1977 than it was in 1960—more than 40 percent as compared with one-third—and the gap between the unemployment rates of women and of men has widened from one-half percentage point in 1960 to two points in 1977. If these changes had not occurred, the overall unemployment rate in 1977 would have been only 6.4 percent. This figure would still have reflected considerable slack in the economy, suggesting the need for further economic expansion. As the economy continues to grow, however, policy makers are questioning whether the 4 percent unemployment rate that had been the policy target in the 1960s is attainable without incurring substantial inflation.[1]

The answer to this question depends in part on why the female unemployment rate rose more than the rate for males did over the past decade, and on whether policies can be adopted to bring the female unemployment rate down to previous levels. In other words, has the recent increase in the female labor force brought with it special prob-

1. See Council of Economic Advisers, *Economic Report of the President* (Washington, D.C.: U.S. Government Printing Office, 1978), pp. 168–72; and Clair Vickery, Barbara R. Bergmann, and Katherine Swartz, "Unemployment Rate Targets and Anti-Inflation Policy as More Women Enter the Workforce," *American Economic Review* 68 (May 1978): 90–98.

FIGURE 7

**THE GAP BETWEEN MEN'S AND WOMEN'S
UNEMPLOYMENT RATES FROM 1950 TO 1977 . . .**

UNEMPLOYMENT RATE

...AND THE RISING PERCENTAGE OF WOMEN
PARTICIPATING IN THE LABOR FORCE

FEMALE
LABOR
FORCE

SOURCE: U.S. Department of Labor, Bureau of Labor Statistics,
Employment and Earnings, Vol. 25 (January 1978), p. 137.

lems that have rendered female unemployment particularly resistant to traditional economic remedies?

A related issue concerns the social burden of women's unemployment. Although there is general agreement that unemployment of women represents a loss of potential output, there is disagreement about the hardship associated with female joblessness. It has even been proposed that one comprehensive measure of national economic hardship, one that would include not only jobless individuals but also the working poor, exclude unemployed married women altogether.[2] The notion that female unemployment is not a serious social problem has contributed to a somewhat ambivalent attitude toward high unemployment in general. Because people do not consider unemployment of married women a serious social problem, there is less opposition to government policies that result in unemployment than there used to be when most of the unemployed were thought to be men. Indeed, the growth of the female labor force and the rise in the number of female job seekers has weakened the national consensus that full employment should be a prime goal for national economic policy.

Alternative Measures of Female Joblessness

Official unemployment statistics are not the only source of information about joblessness. Other indicators confirm the fact that as the female labor force has grown, women workers have experienced difficulty finding work. Many people who are unable to find full-time work take part-time jobs rather than not work at all. As Figure 8 shows, this involuntary part-time employment is highly cyclical, with far more people working part time because they cannot find full-time jobs in years of relatively high unemployment. Prior to the mid-1960s, more men than women worked part time because they could not find full-time work, but since then the number of women in involuntary part-time schedules has exceeded the number of men, and the gap is widening. As percentages of the female and male labor forces, the gap is even more pronounced. In 1977, 4.8 percent of all employed adult women were on involuntary part-time schedules, compared with 2.7 percent of adult men.

The official unemployment count includes only persons who are actively seeking work. Many people who become discouraged after weeks of futile job searching are no longer counted as unemployed,

---

2. Sar A. Levitan and Robert Taggart III, *Employment and Earnings Adequacy: A New Social Indicator* (Baltimore: Johns Hopkins University Press, 1974).

FIGURE 8

THOSE WHO WORK PART TIME BECAUSE THEY CANNOT FIND FULL-TIME WORK: MEN VS. WOMEN, 1957-1977

NOTE: Excludes agricultural workers.

SOURCE: U.S. Department of Labor, Employment and Training Administration, 1978 Employment and Training Report of the President, p. 227.

even though they are out of a job and want work. Because there is less social and psychological pressure for women to remain in the labor force, and because opportunities for productive household work outside the labor market are more likely to be taken up by women than by men, women are more apt than men are to give up fruitless job seeking. The Labor Department estimates that the number of discouraged jobless women in 1977 (694,000) was more than double the number of such men (317,000).

Because women are more inclined than men are to drop out of the labor force when they cannot find work, or to work on involuntary part-time schedules, the disparity between men and women with respect to joblessness is actually more pronounced than the official unemployment statistics indicate. Furthermore, the gap has been widening in recent years, despite the recovery from the 1974–75 recession and a decline in the official unemployment rate. Table 7 shows a relatively comprehensive measure of joblessness that includes discouraged workers and the underemployed who want full-time work but can find only part-time employment. This measure takes account of the

Table 7

JOBLESSNESS AMONG MEN AND WOMEN

| Year | *Joblessness* (percent) | |
	Women	*Men*
1970	9.3	5.9
1971	10.8	6.9
1972	10.4	6.4
1973	9.3	5.5
1974	10.2	6.4
1975	14.0	10.1
1976	12.8	9.0
1977	12.4	8.1

Note: The measure of joblessness illustrated above is (1) total full-time job seekers, plus one-half of the part-time job seekers, plus one-half of total workers on part-time for lack of full-time work, plus discouraged workers, all as a percentage of (2) the civilian labor force, plus discouraged workers, less one-half of the part-time labor force. The Bureau of Labor Statistics publishes this statistic each month along with the official unemployment statistics, but it is not broken down by sex.

Source: Compiled from data in U.S. Department of Labor, Bureau of Labor Statistics, *Employment and Earnings, 1970–77,* and from unpublished data provided by the Bureau of Labor Statistics.

fact that more women than men are looking only for part-time work, and hence the loss in potential work hours due to their unemployment is less than that for full-time job seekers. In 1977, the comprehensive female jobless rate was 12.4 percent, compared with 8.1 percent for men.

Why Women Work

The common view that most women can depend on men for financial support gives rise to the attitude that women's unemployment is not a major social problem. This misconception distorts the truth about the contemporary female labor force. In fact, of the nearly 37 million women in the labor force in 1975, 8.5 million were single (never married); 6.9 million were widowed, divorced, or separated; and 9.5 million were married to husbands who earned less than $10,000 per year.[3] These figures total 24.9 million women—68 percent of the female labor force—who are clearly working because of necessity.[4] Many of the remaining 32 percent make important contributions to their households' incomes; these earnings often provide the margin that enables a family to purchase a home, provide education for children, and the like.

Unfortunately, the burden of unemployment falls most heavily on the least skilled and most needy workers. According to the Bureau of Labor Statistics, for instance, unemployment among women who head families was 9.3 percent in 1977, compared with 3.6 percent for married men in families with children. In March 1977, the unemployment rate for women who had not completed high school was 13.5 percent, compared with a rate of 7.1 percent for those who had completed high school or had higher education.

Apart from the question of need, unemployment can be a demoralizing experience and, for women in particular, may produce hostility to the world of work that prompts them to drop out of the labor force for a time. As Chapter 2 emphasized, intermittent workers have much lower earnings than do persons with continuous work experience.[5]

---

3. The Bureau of Labor Statistics estimates that it took $9,838 for a family of four to maintain a low standard of living in 1975.

4. Some of the single women workers are teenagers who are living with their parents or are in school and who should not necessarily be included in this hardship category. This group comprises at most about 2 million persons.

5. Jacob Mincer and Solomon Polachek, "Family Investments in Human Capital: Earnings of Women," *Journal of Political Economy* 82 (March/April 1974): S76–S108. For a critique of Mincer and Polachek's work and disputation of their findings,

In view of the high rate of marital dissolution, many women who are now married will find themselves on their own at some point, perhaps with children to support and with little of the valuable work experience necessary to get a decent job. Many such women—even some who were formerly married to men with high incomes—end up on welfare or in greatly reduced economic circumstances.[6] In 1976, one of every three female-headed families was below the official poverty line, and 52 percent of children under age eighteen in families headed by women were living below the poverty level.[7]

Causes of Female Unemployment

Women's unemployment is often described as a phenomenon different from men's unemployment. For one thing, most adult men are continuously in the labor force and become unemployed because they have quit or lost their jobs. Women move more frequently in and out of the labor force and may experience some unemployment as they look for new jobs.

It must be kept in mind, however, that the greater propensity of women to drop out of the labor force during recessions may serve to reduce unemployment, too. Persons out of the labor force are not counted as unemployed, even if they have lost their previous jobs and would like to work if employment were available. In fact, in 1977, 25.4 percent of adult women between the ages of twenty-five and fifty-nine who had stopped work in the previous year and left the labor force did so because they could not find work; this was true of only 17.7 percent of men.[8] This statistic belies the popular perception

see Steven H. Sandell and David Shapiro, "The Theory of Human Capital and the Earnings of Women: A Re-examination of the Evidence," *Journal of Human Resources* 13 (Winter 1978): 103–117, followed by Mincer and Polachek's rebuttal, pp. 118–34.

6. An Urban Institute study showed that a high proportion of single, divorced, and separated women who have custody of their children never receive any financial assistance from the children's fathers, and that the payments that are made are small and irregular. In the 1976 study, fathers earning more than $7,000 paid an average of 12 percent of their gross incomes to support their former families. Unless the wife had access to other resources, her income and standard of living (together with that of the children) would fall much more than the former spouse's. See Carol Adaire Jones, Nancy M. Gordon, and Isabel V. Sawhill, "Child Support Payments in the United States," The Urban Institute Working Paper 992–03, Washington, D.C., October 1976.

7. Beverly L. Johnson, "Women Who Head Families, 1970–77: Their Numbers Rose, Income Lagged," *Monthly Labor Review* 101 (February 1978): 32–37.

8. U.S. Department of Labor, Bureau of Labor Statistics, *Employment and Earnings* 25 (January 1978): 169.

that women more readily leave the labor force for noneconomic reasons than men do.

Unemployment may occur as a result of losing one's job, quitting a job, or entering the labor force to look for a job. It is sometimes hard to distinguish among these causes. For instance, because women are more likely than men to drop out of the labor force when they lose their jobs and reenter when economic conditions improve, an unemployed female who is classified as a "reentrant" may be very similar in other respects to an unemployed male who is classified as a "job loser" but who continues to look for work.

Consider the case of two workers, one female and one male, both of whom lose their jobs on the same day and obtain new jobs six months later on the same day. Further, suppose the woman drops out of the labor force for three months in the interim, while the man continues his search. According to the official statistics, he is unemployed twice as long as she even though she has a higher rate of labor force mobility, that is, movement into and out of the labor force. Thus, movement into and out of the labor force does not necessarily add to unemployment. In this case, the intermittent female labor force participant actually experiences less unemployment than the "permanently attached" male does.

But two aspects of women's movement into and out of the labor force do add to unemployment. First, there are many more women than men who lack recent work experience and who therefore encounter special difficulties in finding jobs. In 1977, for instance, more than 1 million unemployed adult women were classified as entrants or reentrants to the work force compared with about 626,000 men.[9]

The difference between the male and female entry and reentry rates is not so large as commonly supposed, however, and does not account for the large differences in the growth rates of the male and female labor force. The high growth rate in female participation in the labor force reflects the recent trend for women to remain in the labor force rather than dropping out when they marry and have children; reentry has had little influence on this growth rate. Table 8 shows the trend in labor force entry and exit probabilities for women. Since 1968, entry probabilities for both full-time and part-time female workers have increased only slightly, while exit probabilities have declined dramatically for both groups. To the extent that the growth in the female labor force results from increased commitment to work,

9. Ibid., p. 147.

Table 8

PROBABILITY OF LABOR FORCE ENTRY AND EXIT FOR FEMALES AGES 16+,
1968–77 ANNUAL AVERAGES

Probability of—	1968	1969	1970	1971	1972	1973	1974	1975	1976	1977
Entry into full-time labor force[1]	2.3	2.4	2.5	2.6	2.6	2.6	2.7	2.8	2.9	2.9
Exit from full-time labor force	4.2	4.1	3.6	3.4	3.6	3.7	3.5	3.0	3.2	3.0
Exit from seeking full-time work	30.5	32.1	33.4	31.4	26.7	25.4	28.9	33.1	22.0	23.0
Entry into part-time labor force[2]	2.7	2.8	2.9	2.9	2.9	3.0	3.0	2.9	3.0	3.0
Exit from part-time labor force	17.9	16.4	14.8	13.6	13.8	13.7	12.7	11.9	12.1	11.5
Exit from seeking part-time work	58.0	61.1	63.8	60.4	46.5	50.1	51.0	54.0	42.1	44.1

1. Full-time labor force includes persons working full time, persons working part time involuntarily (part time for economic reasons), and persons seeking full-time work.

2. Part-time labor force includes persons working part time voluntarily and unemployed persons looking for part-time work.

Note: Probability of entry into or exit from the labor force is equal to the number of persons who entered (or left) the labor force in period t (where t is an average month in the year under study) divided by the number of persons in the labor force in period t − 1.

Source: Carol Len and Robert W. Bednarzik, "A Profile of Women on Part-Time Schedules," *Monthly Labor Review* 101 (October 1978): 10.

the average woman should be gaining work experience, and women's related unemployment rate should decline.

Table 9 shows a breakdown of unemployment by reason for adult men and women since 1968. Most of the unemployed are either job losers or leavers rather than labor force entrants or reentrants. In 1977, 57.2 percent of unemployed adult women and 77.1 percent of unemployed adult men fell into these two categories. Among those who have lost or left their jobs, women have a slightly higher quit rate than men, while men are more likely to be job losers. In many cases the distinction between job losers and leavers is somewhat arbitrary. Many people quit in anticipation of being fired, and because women lack seniority and job-specific skills, they are more apt than men are to be threatened with involuntary terminations.

But, statistical problems aside, low-paid workers of both sexes tend to be the most frequent job leavers, as they perceive no opportunities for upward mobility in their jobs and hence have little incentive to remain in them. Because women are disproportionately represented in the lowest-paid jobs, it is not surprising that the overall female quit rate is somewhat higher than the male quit rate.

Thus, despite the conventional view of unemployed women as inexperienced or casual job seekers, the major cause of unemployment among women is that they are laid off or fired. In 1977, 40.7 percent of unemployed adult women had lost their jobs and were unable to find work.

The table shows that the proportion of unemployed women who are just entering or reentering the job market has declined somewhat in recent years, but a greater proportion of unemployed females than of unemployed males continue to be labor force entrants or reentrants It is worth noting, moreover, that even if all entrants and reentrants are excluded, the female unemployment rate is still at least as high as the male rate.

It is tempting to dismiss as unimportant—or at least as not susceptible to traditional policy remedies—the unemployment of persons who have recently entered the labor force. To a large extent, women's proportionately high "reentry" rate reflects the greater prevalence of women among reentering discouraged workers, but even women who are entering the labor force after a long period of inactivity should not be ignored. Many are recently separated or divorced; often they are the sole support of young children. According to the Bureau of Labor Statistics, the unemployment rate for separated (not divorced) women with preschool children was 27 percent in March 1975. The comparable rate for divorced mothers of preschool children also was

Table 9

NUMBER OF UNEMPLOYED PERSONS BY REASON FOR
UNEMPLOYMENT AND UNEMPLOYMENT RATE

Year and Reason for Unemployment	Unemployed	Distribution			Unemployment Rate		
		Teenagers	Adult Men	Adult Women	Teenagers	Adult Men	Adult Women
							(percent)
1968							
Total: Number (thousands)	4,304	839	993	985	12.7	2.2	3.8
Job loser	1,070	15.5%	60.4%	34.7%	1.9	1.3	1.3
Job leaver	431	11.6	16.8	17.0	1.5	.4	.6
Reentrant	909	33.5	20.7	42.9	4.2	.4	1.6
New entrant	407	39.4	2.2	5.6	5.0	*	.2
1970							
Total: Number (thousands)	4,088	1,105	1,636	1,347	15.3	3.5	4.8
Job loser	1,809	18.1%	65.1%	40.4%	2.8	2.2	1.9
Job leaver	549	11.4	12.8	15.9	1.7	.4	.8
Reentrant	1,227	34.3	19.4	39.4	5.2	.7	1.9
New entrant	503	36.2	2.7	4.3	5.5	.1	.2

1973							
Job loser	1,666	1,225	1,594	1,485	14.5	3,2	4.8
Job leaver	674	17.2%	59.1%	34.6%	2.4	1.9	1.6
Reentrant	1,323	11.8	15.9	18.6	1.7	.5	.9
New entrant	642	29.5	21.6	41.5	4.3	.7	2.0
Total: Number (thousands)	7,830	41.5	3.4	5.3	6.0	.1	.3
1975							
Job loser	4,341	1,752	3,428	2,649	19.9	6.7	8.0
Job leaver	812	25.6%	75.0%	50.0%	5.0	5.1	4.0
Reentrant	1,865	8.7	8.5	13.9	1.7	.6	1.1
New entrant	812	29.9	14.5	31.9	6.0	1.0	2.6
Total: Number (thousands)	5,855	35.8	2.1	4.2	7.1	.1	.3
1977							
Job loser	3,103	1,642	2,727	2,486	17.7	5.2	7.0
Job leaver	889	19.2%	65.2%	40.7%	3.4	3.4	2.8
Reentrant	1,926	9.4	11.9	16.5	1.7	.6	1.2
New entrant	938	28.7	19.3	37.3	5.1	1.0	2.6
Total: Number (thousands)	2,817	42.8	3.6	5.5	7.6	.2	.4

* Less than 0.05 percent.

Note: Numbers may not add to the totals shown because of rounding.

Source: U.S. Department of Labor, Employment and Training Administration, *Employment and Training Report of the President, 1978,* p. 218.

high, 11 percent.[10] The difference between these rates undoubtedly reflects the effect of more recent family breakup for separated women, and hence a higher probability that a jobless woman is a new entrant or reentrant without recent work experience.

These women generally have special problems in gaining access to labor market information and acquiring the skills necessary to find a job and keep one. Largely through ignorance, desperation, and inadequate counseling, many of them end up in low-paying, traditionally female clerical or service jobs, even when they have the potential to move into higher-paying jobs. Many have problems arranging for child care and accommodating work schedules to household responsibilities.

The Effects of Occupational Crowding on Female Unemployment

Continued segregation of women in clerical and service occupations, combined with the huge influx of women workers over the past decade, has both pushed wages down and made it more difficult for women to find jobs. Not only is the traditionally female turf overcrowded, but continued discrimination makes it difficult for women to secure jobs usually held by men.

Statistical evidence of overcrowding is quite impressive. In the 1950s and 1960s, for instance, as Table 10 shows, the unemployment rate for clerical workers remained in the range of 2.9 percent to 4.6 percent. Then the clerical unemployment rate crept up from 4.8 percent in 1971 to 6.6 percent in 1975; it dropped to 5.9 percent in 1977. Clerical workers as a percentage of all unemployed workers (men and women) rose from 9.1 percent in 1958 to 10 percent in the early 1960s, and then rose well above 14 percent after 1968. Although in relative terms average clerical wages declined, the market for clerical workers was still unable to absorb the enormous increase in job seekers.

Similar trends are observed among nondomestic service workers, whose share in total unemployment rose from 9.5 percent in 1958 to 15.2 percent in 1977. In 1958, men and women were about equally represented in this sector. By 1977, women had increased their relative representation by 40 percent.

Because the jobs women traditionally have held have often com-

---

10. Allyson Sherman Grossman, *The Labor Force Patterns of Divorced and Separated Women*, U.S. Department of Labor, Bureau of Labor Statistics, Special Labor Force Report No. 198 (Washington, D.C.: U.S. Government Printing Office, 1977).

Table 10

UNEMPLOYMENT TRENDS IN SELECTED OCCUPATIONS

Year	Economywide Unemployment Rate (percent)	Clerical Workers		Service Workers (Except Domestic)		Blue-Collar Craft Workers	
		Unemployment Rate (percent)	Percentage of Unemployed	Unemployment Rate (percent)	Percentage of Unemployed	Unemployment Rate (percent)	Percentage of Unemployed
1958	6.8	4.4	9.1	7.4	9.5	6.8	13.4
1965	4.5	3.3	11.1	5.5	12.0	3.6	10.2
1970	4.9	4.0	14.2	5.5	11.5	3.8	9.7
1971	5.9	4.8	13.7	6.6	13.0	4.7	10.2
1972	5.6	4.7	14.5	6.6	14.0	4.3	10.0
1973	4.9	4.2	14.6	5.9	14.2	3.7	10.1
1974	5.6	4.6	14.3	6.5	13.9	4.4	10.3
1975	8.5	6.6	13.6	8.9	13.1	8.3	12.7
1976	7.7	6.4	14.6	9.1	14.9	6.9	11.4
1977	7.0	5.9	14.6	8.5	15.2	5.9	10.3

Source: Department of Labor, Employment and Training Administration, *1978 Employment and Training Report of the President*, p. 215.

plemented the jobs men do, it is not possible for women's employment to expand rapidly and for men's to expand less rapidly unless there is some change in the traditional division of labor between men and women in the marketplace. The major avenue for improving women's employment opportunities remains an increase in their representation in the traditionally male sectors of the economy. As a result, a major attack on employment discrimination on the basis of sex must be the central component of any program to reduce female unemployment.

Other Causes of Female Unemployment

Factors other than lack of experience, occupational segregation by sex, and occupational crowding contribute to women's unemployment. Chapter 2 noted that women's underrepresentation in career-ladder jobs, where seniority pays off in higher earnings, depresses the average wages women earn relative to men's wages; this underrepresentation also contributes to women's higher unemployment rates. Seniority and on-the-job training serve as deterrents to job change; because women often are denied both, women are likely to quit or to be laid off more frequently than men are and thus they encounter more unemployment. Within specific industries, women's unemployment rates are higher than men's largely because they are the last hired and first fired. Yet because a high proportion of women's jobs are in the less cyclical sectors of the economy, the overall effect of recessions on women's unemployment is sometimes no greater than their effect on men's unemployment.[11]

Women's relative immobility in terms of relocation not only impedes their opportunities for career development, but also contributes to their unemployment. Wives who relocate because their husbands do may encounter not merely a drop in earnings, but unemployment. A study by Beth Neimi found that a higher proportion of unemployed men than unemployed women move in response to job opportunities in a new location, and that women are far more likely to experience unemployment *after* a move than are men.[12]

---

11. Ralph E. Smith, *The Impact of Macroeconomic Conditions on Employment Opportunities for Women*, U.S. Congress, Joint Economic Committee, Series on Achieving the Goals of the Employment Act of 1946 (Washington, D.C.: U.S. Government Printing Office, 1977).

12. See Beth Neimi, "Geographic Immobility and Unemployment," in Cynthia B. Lloyd, ed., *Sex, Discrimination, and the Division of Labor* (New York: Columbia University Press, 1975).

Policy Considerations

To the extent that female unemployment is related to the sex stereo-typing of jobs and strong barriers between men's turf and women's turf, policy decisions must be aimed at eliminating the occupational segregation of women. Public employment programs, for instance, have become the major instrument for addressing structural unemployment problems in the 1970s. They provide work experience, and in many cases they serve as a bridge between joblessness and private employment for individuals who lack the necessary skills and attitudes. But if these programs train women only in clerical occupations or other female-dominated fields, they just add to the problem by increasing the ranks of job seekers in occupations that are already overcrowded.

Policy makers must recognize that if occupational crowding continues as the female labor force grows, the unemployment situation will become even more intractable. Affirmative action programs to gain access for women in male-dominated fields are absolutely essential, not only to raise the earnings potential of women workers, but also to stem the heavy incidence of joblessness in the female work force. In some cases, new opportunities for women will open up in industries where sex-role stereotypes have not yet been formed. Women seem to be making inroads in computer services, telecommunications, and similar areas. The projected growth of the health services industry also should open up jobs for women.

The main way for women to improve their opportunities, however, is through infiltration of the traditionally male sectors of the economy. A major attack on sex-based employment discrimination must be the central component of any program to reduce female unemployment. The government in particular should avoid stereotypical views of women's work and should attempt to widen women's access to a variety of occupations through its employment and training programs.

At the same time, the special problems of women workers must be taken into account. The fact that women workers are generally less geographically mobile than men are needs to be considered, especially in dealing with unemployed women in depressed areas or in industries impacted by trade liberalization, environmental regulations, and other structural changes in the economy. Similarly, provision of part-time work and flexible working hours will increase the employability of many women with children and other domestic responsibilities. Special counseling programs to meet the needs of women who are just entering or seeking to reenter the job market after a long absence also need to be expanded. Easing the transition of such women into the work force can shorten the initial period of unemployment, help such women find better jobs, and thereby reduce the chances of their quitting—and ultimately reduce the likelihood that they and their children will end up in poverty and on welfare.

Finally, although occupational barriers to women workers and other so-called "structural" factors have been responsible for some of the high unemployment of the 1970s, the persistent slack in the economy over the past decade also has had an adverse effect on the number and quality of job opportunities for women. Affirmative action programs and entry of women into jobs formerly held by men are potentially most effective when there are vacancies to be filled. Ralph Smith has estimated that a strong economic recovery (reducing the overall unemployment rate to 4.5 percent by the end of the decade) would bring about 1 million more women into the labor force than would a weaker recovery (that reduced unemployment only to the 6.3 percent range by 1980). In a strong recovery, women would account for about half the overall increase in employment; the female jobless rate would drop to about 5.4 percent compared with 7.0 percent for a weaker recovery.[13] Further, to the extent that more rapid increases in employment are accompanied by affirmative action and genuine attempts to accelerate the movement of women into formerly male-dominated areas, there should be a general upgrading of the quality of jobs held by women workers and a concomitant narrowing of the male-female earnings gap.

PART-TIME EMPLOYMENT

Part-time employment has already been mentioned in the context of unemployment—people working part time because they cannot find full-time work. Many people today, however, prefer part-time to full-time work in order to accommodate home responsibilities (and perhaps a desire for more leisure than full-time work permits) with the necessity or desire to work for pay.

When most of the female labor force consisted of women without small children, the need for part-time work as a compromise arose

---

13. Smith, *The Impact of Macroeconomic Conditions on Employment Opportunities for Women.*

less often. As popular acceptance of combining a career and family has grown, however, the number of women attracted to part-time job opportunities has increased. Hence one of the consequences of the rapid increase in the number of working mothers of small children has been an increase in the proportion of women voluntarily engaged in part-time work.

This section discusses who makes up the rapidly increasing voluntary part-time labor force, and how the part-time jobs women do (and the pay they receive) differ from the part-time jobs men do (and their pay). We then consider the advantages and disadvantages of part-time work from the standpoint of women and from the point of view of their employers, and discuss the outlook for the future.

The Growing Part-Time Work Force

Between 1965 and 1977, the number of workers on voluntary part-time schedules increased nearly three times as rapidly as the number of full-time workers. As Figure 9 shows, most of the increase in part-time employment was among women. In 1965, 65 percent of the workers on voluntary part-time schedules were women; by 1977, women held nearly 70 percent of the part-time jobs.

The propensity of women to work part time is related to marital status and the presence and age of children. As Table 11 shows, a higher proportion of employed married women than of employed divorced, separated, and widowed women work part time. Among employed married women, those with children under age eighteen are most likely to work part time. The reverse is true among the divorced, separated, and widowed. The proportion of all employed women working part time has increased for most groups since 1967, but this increase may partly reflect the rise in involuntary part-time employment mentioned earlier.

These statistics show that the rapid growth of the part-time work force since the mid-1960s is largely the result of an increase in labor force participation among the group most likely to work part time, that is, married mothers. This finding is consistent with the age-sex breakdown in Table 12 that shows that the most rapid increase in voluntary part-time employment for women since 1965 has been among those eighteen to forty-four years old. Among males, part-time jobs are held primarily by young people and persons over age sixty-five. Although the percentage increases in part-time employment among males in the twenty-five to sixty-four age groups have been quite high, there are still very few "prime age" males voluntarily working part time.

Many part-timers work only part of the year. In 1976, for instance, about 40 percent of the women who worked part time worked twenty-

FIGURE 9

THE GROWTH IN PART TIME EMPLOYMENT FOR
MEN AND WOMEN, 1965-1977

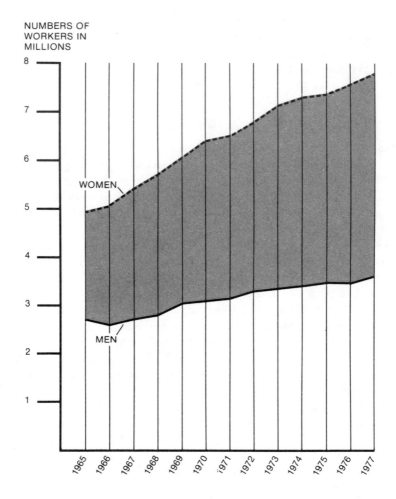

NOTE: Excludes agricultural workers and part-time workers who
          want full-time jobs but cannot find them.

SOURCE: U.S. Department of Labor, Employment and Training
          Administration, 1978 Employment and Training Report
          of the President, p. 226.

Table 11

PERCENTAGE OF EMPLOYED WOMEN ON PART-TIME
SCHEDULES AND LABOR FORCE PARTICIPATION RATES
BY MARITAL STATUS AND PRESENCE AND AGE OF
CHILDREN, MARCH 1967 AND MARCH 1976

	Percentage on Part-Time Schedules		Labor Force Participation Rates (percent)	
	March 1967	March 1976	March 1967	March 1976
Married, husband present	24	29	37	45
No children under age 18	18	23	39	44
Children ages 6–17, none under age 6	29	34	45	54
Children under age 6	30	35	26	37
Divorced, separated, widowed	18	21	39	42
No children under age 18	18	23	NA	NA
Children ages 6–17, none under age 6	20	17	NA	NA
Children under age 6	18	19	NA	NA

Source: Tabulations from the Current Population Survey provided by the U.S. Department of Labor, Bureau of Labor Statistics, 1978.

six weeks or less compared with around 20 percent of full-time workers. For men, 43 percent of all part-time workers worked twenty-six weeks or less, compared with only 14 percent of full-time workers. Only one-fourth of mothers of preschool children who worked during 1975 did so on a full-time basis all year. For mothers of six- to seventeen-year-olds, the percentage was 40 percent.[14]

Nearly half of all women who worked part year gave "taking care of home" as the reason for not working a full year. For men, unemployment and school attendance were the main reasons for part-year work; only around 1 percent gave "taking care of home" as the major reason.[15]

---

14. Howard Hayge, *Marital and Family Characteristics of the Labor Force*, U.S. Department of Labor, Bureau of Labor Statistics, Special Labor Force Report No. 183 (Washington, D.C.: U.S. Government Printing Office, 1976), Table I, p. A25.

15. U.S. Department of Labor, Bureau of Labor Statistics, *Work Experience of the Population in 1976*, Special Labor Force Report No. 201 (Washington, D.C.: U.S. Government Printing Office, 1977), p. 22.

Table 12

WORKERS ON VOLUNTARY PART-TIME SCHEDULES
BY SEX AND AGE, 1965 AND 1977

(Excluding Agricultural Workers)

	1965	1977	Change
	(thousands)		(percent)
Women			
Age			
16–17	860	961	11.7
18–24	639	1,601	150.5
25–44	1,681	2,894	72.2
45–64	1,422	1,887	32.7
65+	350	503	43.7
All females	4,952	7,859	58.7
Men			
Age			
16–17	1,103	984	−10.8
18–24	662	1,235	86.6
25–44	190	423	122.6
45–64	266	377	41.7
65+	434	572	31.8
All males	2,662	3,580	34.5

Source: U.S. Department of Labor, Employment and Training Administration, *Employment and Training Report of the President, 1977* (p. 182), *1978* (p. 226).

Note: Numbers may not add to totals shown because of rounding.

Part-Time Job Opportunities and Pay Rates

Some jobs are part time by nature—school crossing guards and cafeteria workers and peak-load shift workers in restaurants and retail trade, for example, are needed only a limited number of hours a day. In other cases, part-time work can be accomplished by splitting the schedules in jobs normally requiring full-time shifts. Depending on the number of hours worked, freelance work may qualify as another category of part-time work.

Women traditionally have dominated the first type of work involving limited hours. Generally such jobs pay little, offer no opportunity for advancement, and have no job security or fringe benefits. People who hold these jobs are usually assumed to be intermittent workers without career ambitions, and the labor market has been structured accordingly.

People in the other two categories are harder to define. They may have higher pay and better opportunities for advancement, but they probably pay a high price for their freedom in reduced job security and fringe benefits, if they have them at all.

In 1977, 70 percent of all female part-time workers were in sales, clerical, and nondomestic service occupations. As Table 13 shows, the median part-time pay rates are well below the median full-time rates for each occupational category.

Comparison with male part-time workers is revealing. Although the male part-time work force is more evenly distributed among occupations than is the female part-time work force, more than half the men are working in sales, nonfarm labor, and nondomestic service. It is interesting to note that part-time pay rates for men are about on a par with rates for women, undoubtedly reflecting the fact that most male part-timers are either younger-than-average or older-than-average workers. In 1977, for instance, 68 percent of male part-time workers were under twenty-two years of age or over fifty-five. For women, only 42 percent were in those age categories.

Despite the facts that part-time pay rates are generally lower than rates for full-time work and that fringe benefits, where they exist at all, are also usually lower, studies comparing adult part-time workers with full-time workers have generally shown part-timers' hourly productivity to be higher, and turnover and absenteeism rates much lower.[16] This comparison suggests that there is an untapped potential that might be developed by expanding part-time job opportunities in sectors that in the past have offered only full-time work.

Outlook for the Future: Some Policy Considerations

Opinions vary as to the wisdom of a woman's taking a part-time job. Some think that a woman's working part time contributes to the view that household responsibilities prevent her from a serious career commitment. Further, the part-time aspect of work strengthens traditional attitudes about women as secondary earners. Yet part-time work may be the only way some women can maintain employment continuity, particularly during childbearing years.

There is no question that there will continue to be a growing number of women with a permanent commitment to the labor force who

---

16. See, for example, U.S. General Accounting Office, *Part-time Employment in Federal Agencies* (Washington, D.C.: U.S. Government Printing Office, 1976).

Table 13

EARNINGS OF PART-TIME VERSUS FULL-TIME
WORKERS BY OCCUPATION AND SEX, 1977

Women

Occupation*	Percentage of the Work Force on Part-Time Schedules	*Median Hourly Earnings*		Part-Time Earnings as a Percentage of Full-Time Earnings
		Full-Time	Part-Time	
All workers	29	$3.85	$2.87	74
Sales	54	3.05	2.64	86
Clerical	24	3.91	3.06	78
Services (nondomestic)	47	2.95	2.59	88

* The detailed occupations shown include 70 percent of all female part-time workers.

Men

Occupation**	Percentage of the Work Force on Part-Time Schedules	*Median Hourly Earnings*		Part-Time Earnings as a Percentage of Full-Time Earnings
		Full-Time	Part-Time	
All workers	11	$5.88	$2.87	49
Sales	13	5.87	2.70	46
Nonfarm labor	25	4.56	2.77	61
Services (nondomestic)	28	4.19	2.50	60

** The detailed occupations shown include 51 percent of all male part-time workers.

Source: Unpublished tabulations from the Current Population Survey provided by the U.S. Department of Labor, Bureau of Labor Statistics, 1978.

Note: Data for part-time workers include persons who usually work from 1 hour to 34 hours per week. Data for full-time workers include persons who usually work at least 35 hours per week.

are seeking part-time work, for a time or permanently. If they can find work only in the traditionally female sector, their added partici- pation will contribute to the overcrowding problem. Yet the figures in Table 13 do not suggest that, at present, women will find better part- time opportunities in the male sector of the economy.

The fact that female occupations have been structured under the assumption that employees will be intermittent workers may explain the prevalence of part-time opportunities in the traditionally female occupations, but this assumption is no longer consistent with reality. If jobs typically held by men were restructured to permit part-time work, more women would be attracted to nontraditional fields. Such restructuring also would provide opportunities for men who prefer not to work in traditionally female jobs to reduce their working hours.

As the number of working wives increases, both spouses will have more incentive to reallocate their time between paid employment and nonmarket work. Although there are socially acceptable mechanisms that permit wives to increase their working hours, husbands find it far more difficult to reduce their working hours without a severe loss of income and status. As men begin to realize that their wives' income would enable them to slow their work pace and to direct some of their energies elsewhere, employers may begin to take seriously the possibility of providing part-time job opportunities for their male employees, even for those in senior positions. Such a trend would surely facilitate the entry of women into better-paying positions and also diminish the distinctions between male and female jobs. Moreover, if employers offered attractive, well-paying, part-time employment, not only would they be able to tap a much larger pool of potential workers, but also they might find that overall worker morale and productivity improved.

Resistance on the part of employers to providing part-time job opportunities stems in part from a lack of information about the availability and commitment of part-time job seekers. Moreover, employers incur some genuine economic penalties in hiring part-time workers. The Social Security system, as well as many private benefit structures, presupposes that all workers are full time. For instance, under current Social Security regulations, employer contributions will be higher for two part-time workers earning $15,000 each than for one full-time worker earning $30,000.

There are compelling social and economic reasons for improving the job market prospects of part-time workers and for eliminating the economic penalties connected with hiring and being hired for part-time work. The part-time work force no longer consists primarily of in-school youths and wives looking for "pin money." Many of those seeking part-time work are female household heads with small children. For these women, the availability of a part-time job may mean the difference between work or welfare. Further, the availability of fringe benefits, particularly health and hospitalization insurance, may be crucial, especially when the jobs pay low wages. Because welfare recipients are eligible for free medical care under the Medicaid program, welfare is often more beneficial than part-time work in jobs without fringe benefits.

Any program designed to promote equal employment opportunity for men and women must include action to improve the part-time job market. The availability of well-paying, part-time employment is essential to a general reallocation of hours in paid employment between husbands and wives. Part-time work also must be available to serve as an incentive for women to remain in the labor force when small children are present in the household. Affirmative action programs should include as a priority the provision of part-time jobs for men and women in high-paying professional categories. And disincentives to part-time work must be eliminated if the part-time job seeker is to compete fairly with the full-time worker.[17]

FLEXIBLE WORK SCHEDULES

An issue closely related to improving part-time job opportunities concerns the growing practice of allowing workers—both full-time and part-time—some flexibility in scheduling their working hours. Many considerations favor flexible scheduling—better utilization of public transportation, improved job satisfaction, and the like—but the rise in two-earner and female-headed households provides a particularly strong argument for this approach. Many workers see flexible hours as a way to combine their careers with parenthood, to reduce child care costs, and to spend more time with their children.

Although the mechanics of flexible scheduling vary from place to place, the basic idea is to allow employees some choice in the hours they work. One pattern is to establish core hours during which everyone must be present—perhaps from 9:30 A.M. to 4:00 P.M.—and then to allow workers to arrive as early as 7:30 A.M. or to leave as late as 6:00 P.M. This type of arrangement allows one parent to remain at home until the children begin school or until preschool children have finished breakfast, while freeing the other to be with the children in early afternoon after school and to prepare the evening meal. Other plans put all workers on a four-day, forty-hour week, or permit employees the option of extending their daily working hours in exchange for a free day every week or two. The first arrangement is most applicable to office or factory shift work, while the second is best suited to work in retail trade, hospitals, and service institutions like libraries where long hours and continuous coverage are necessary.

---

17. A strong disincentive to part-time employment in the federal government and in many state and local governments has been hiring freezes and mandated personnel ceilings associated with reorganization plans and efforts to reduce government spending and make government more efficient. When agencies are limited to a stipulated number of employees (without regard for cost or profitability), they will usually prefer full-time to part-time employees. One way to circumvent this problem would be to express personnel ceilings as full-time equivalent positions.

In the past, most opportunities for flexible scheduling occurred in retail trade, in some consumer service industries, and in some professions. With the exception of the professions, in which individuals have traditionally had more control over their working conditions, flexible working hours were available only in the low-paying female sector. The growth of the female labor force, and especially in the number of working mothers, however, has provided an impetus to experimentation with "flexitime" in a wide range of establishments.

The use of flexitime has become quite popular in some European countries, but its introduction in the United States is more recent and experimental. Although one authority has estimated that only several hundred thousand persons were working under flexitime arrangements as of 1977,[18] other studies indicate that a wide range of firms have at least experimented with flexitime. In 1975 the Business and Professional Women's Foundation estimated that about 16.5 percent of public and private establishments had used some sort of rearranged work week.[19] Further, the National Council for Alternative Work Patterns found that of thirty-four state governments which responded to its survey in 1977, eighteen had used alternative work schedules.[20]

Legislation has been introduced to encourage adoption of flexitime programs in federal agencies, as well as to provide more part-time opportunities in the federal government. Several agencies have adopted flexitime on a three-year experimental basis to enable the federal government to evaluate its effects.[21] Despite these initiatives, however, relatively few organizations have adopted flexitime systematically and permanently.

Although flexitime raises some complicated legal issues, such as the rights of workers to overtime and shift differentials, and the possibility that employers might pressure workers to "volunteer" for a longer day or week, most studies report favorable results from flexitime experiments. The Business and Professional Women's Foundation found substantial reductions in tardiness, absenteeism, and turnover among firms experimenting with flexitime, along with a general increase in

---

18. John D. Owen, "Flexitime: Some Management and Labor Problems of the New Flexible Hour Scheduling Practices," *Industrial and Labor Relations Review* 30 (January 1977): 152–61.

19. Business and Professional Women's Foundation, *Hours of Work When Workers Can Choose* (Washington, D.C., 1975), p. 16.

20. Maureen McCarthy, "Federal and State Activities: Report of a Survey of Alternative Work Schedules in State Governments," in a Resource Packet for the National Conference on Alternative Work Schedules, Chicago, March 1977.

21. National Council for Alternative Work Patterns, "Summary of Alternative Work Schedule and Related Legislation Pending Before the 95th Congress," in a Resource Packet for the National Conference on Alternative Work Schedules, Chicago, March 1977.

productivity.[22] A 1977 Bureau of Labor Statistics study of three large establishments that had adopted flexitime reported "generally positive results," but cautioned that "general conclusions must await more rigorous studies based on more extensive experience."[23]

Another 1977 study compared the activities of male, blue-collar workers on four-day work weeks with similar workers on traditional five-day schedules.[24] Four-day workers expressed greater satisfaction with their use of free time than did men on five-day schedules, and four-day workers did not show a greater tendency to work much overtime or take a second job. According to the study,

> The primary benefits gained from working a 4-day week appear to be in its effect on time allocated to activities within a family setting. (Although) . . . 4-day workers as a group do not seem to help their wives by taking on more of the routine housework, they were found . . . to spend additional time doing major household chores such as gardening, errands, and repair work. Of probably greater significance, 4-day workers allocated more than five times as many minutes to . . . child care. The opportunity to so engage oneself appears to be a principal advantage of working a 4-day week.[25]

As the flexitime trend continues, it will be extremely important to monitor the availability of flexitime and part-time employment opportunities to ensure that they are not limited to the traditionally female sector and to ensure that they provide the same opportunities for upward mobility as do jobs with more rigid hours requirements. If flexitime is to be a mechanism for women to move into better-paying jobs and for men to participate more fully in family life, it cannot at the same time serve as a subtle mechanism for keeping women segregated in the traditionally female sector or for limiting their training opportunities and chances for upward job mobility.

WOMEN IN FEDERAL EMPLOYMENT PROGRAMS

This chapter has identified a number of special factors that contribute to women's unemployment. Occupational segregation of women coupled with rapid growth of the female labor force has made jobs

22. Business and Professional Women's Foundation, *Hours of Work When Workers Can Choose*, p. 20.

23. Janice Neipert Hedges, "Flexible Schedules: Problems and Issues," *Monthly Labor Review* 100 (February 1977): 62–64.

24. David Mark Maklan, "How Blue-Collar Workers on 4-Day Workweeks Use Their Time," *Monthly Labor Review* 100 (August 1977): 18–26.

25. Ibid., p. 26.

in traditionally female occupations especially difficult to find. Moreover, the greater propensity of women to move into and out of the work force means that women have to look for jobs more frequently than men do. Finally, women may be more likely than men are to have competing demands on their time, and hence may have special job requirements, such as flexible or part-time working hours, or geographic restrictions, that make finding employment more difficult.

The federal government has a strong commitment to policies that will provide work for all who want it. Recognizing that macroeconomic fiscal and monetary policies are capable only of stimulating demand across a broad range of industries rather than of creating jobs in particular occupations or for workers with special disadvantages, the government has established various programs to provide jobs for individuals unable to find work in the private sector or in regular government employment.

Many of these programs were consolidated in the Comprehensive Employment and Training Act of 1973 (CETA). CETA provides public service jobs, training, and other services leading to unsubsidized employment for economically disadvantaged, unemployed, and underemployed persons.[26] In 1977, outlays for general training and employment programs under CETA exceeded $5.8 billion; the Office of Management and Budget projects outlays under CETA at $12.5 billion by 1980.[27]

Another employment program, the Work Incentive Program (WIN), is designed to place welfare recipients—persons receiving Aid to Families with Dependent Children (AFDC)—in jobs or training. Although WIN is much smaller than CETA (budget outlays in 1977 were $361 million and are not expected to increase by 1980),[28] it is an important source of job placement and training for poor female household heads. The next section examines how well the federal government, through CETA, WIN, and other employment programs, has met the needs of unemployed women.

Historical Evolution of CETA

During the 1974–75 recession, public service employment under CETA was used largely to alleviate unemployment among workers laid off for

---

26. U.S. Department of Labor, Employment and Training Administration, *Employment and Training Report of the President, 1978* (Washington, D.C.: U.S. Government Printing Office, 1978), p. 39.

27. *The Budget of the United States Government, Fiscal Year 1979* (Washington, D.C.: U.S. Government Printing Office, 1978), p. 165.

28. Ibid.

cyclical reasons. The emphasis was on keeping people at work during the temporary downturn in economic activity rather than on providing new skills and work experience for persons who would have difficulty finding jobs even in relatively tight labor markets.

In 1975 and 1976 the CETA program grew rapidly and the Carter administration made it the centerpiece of its overall labor market policy. By fiscal year 1978 the number of positions authorized for CETA had increased by more than 50 percent; in that year about 725,000 persons were in public service employment (Titles II and VI). As recovery from the recession reduced cyclical unemployment, CETA shifted its emphasis toward workers with various disadvantages—the so-called structurally unemployed. Included as target groups were minorities, youths, veterans, and women.

Although CETA is a federal program, funds are channeled through state and local "prime sponsors," usually state and local government agencies or nonprofit organizations. The National Commission for Manpower Policy notes that federal guidelines for CETA eligibility often contain conflicting objectives and that the multiplicity of target groups gives the local prime sponsors considerable leeway in actually implementing the program.[29]

Table 14 compares the characteristics of CETA participants in public service employment with the characteristics of the unemployed during the period 1975–77. Most CETA participants are white males between the ages of twenty-two and forty-four with twelve or more years of education. Although racial minorities have participated in the public service employment program in a greater proportion than their representation among the unemployed, women have not. In 1977, for instance, women were only 35.7 percent of CETA Title VI (Emergency Jobs Program) participants and 40.1 percent of Title II (Public Employment Programs) participants, even though they were 47.7 percent of the unemployed.

*Why Women Are Underrepresented in
Federal Employment Programs*[30]

One reason for women's underrepresentation in federal employment programs is that women, especially married women, are commonly

29. This point is emphasized in National Commission for Manpower Policy, *An Interim Report to the Congress*, vol. I (Washington, D.C., March 1978).

30. Many of the ideas and information in this section are taken from Lorraine A. Underwood, *Women in Federal Employment Programs* (Washington, D.C.: The Urban Institute, 1979).

believed to need jobs less than men do. This view has led to the formulation of policies that explicitly favor husbands or limit jobs to the "principal earner" in a family. Although policies favoring male family heads are often promulgated at the local level by CETA prime sponsors, some are actually written into federal law. For instance, federal guidelines in the WIN Program give explicit priority to male family heads. Although in 1976 female family heads were 90 percent of AFDC recipients and hence of the WIN target population, they accounted for only 73 percent of the WIN participants and only 65 percent of the number who eventually found jobs (see Table 15).

Public service employment programs other than WIN do not explicitly favor men, but the family income limit for eligibility has the same effect. For example, any woman with an employed husband whose earnings exceed the family income limitation would not be eligible for one of these jobs. Men with employed wives are more likely to be eligible, because more women than men will have earnings below the family income ceiling.

In 1977 the Carter administration proposed a comprehensive welfare reform program called "The Program for Better Jobs and Income" (PBJI) that eliminated any uncertainties about the view that men should get preferential treatment. The intent of the PBJI program was to provide jobs for the poor. According to the Department of Labor,

> Only one job or training opportunity will be offered to each family. That opportunity will be available to the sole parent or, if there are two parents, to the family's usual "principal earner." The principal earner is defined as the parent who either has worked the most hours or had the highest earnings in the past 6 months.[31]

Although the language is carefully worded to appear sex neutral, the facts that women's earnings are typically far below those of men's and that only about 10 percent of wives earn more than their husbands exclude most wives from the category of "usual principal earner." Here is an example of a recent policy proposal reflecting a much-outdated view of family support systems—the idea that there is a principal breadwinner with a wife who is either a secondary earner or a nonworker. This unfortunate provision would not even allow husband and wife to determine which would take the job, because the government has already decided it should be the one with the higher previous earnings, in most cases the husband.

---

31. *Employment and Training Report of the President, 1978*, p. 129.

Table 14

COMPARISON OF CHARACTERISTICS OF PARTICIPANTS IN CETA TITLES II AND VI
AND OF U.S. UNEMPLOYED, 1975–77

Characteristics	CETA Participants						U.S. Unemployed Annual Averages		
	Title II			Title VI					
	FY 1975	FY 1976	FY 1977	FY 1975	FY 1976	FY 1977	1975	1976	1977
	(percent)			*(percent)*			*(percent)*		
Sex:									
Male	65.8	63.8	59.9	70.2	65.1	64.1	56.0	54.4	52.3
Female	34.2	36.2	40.1	29.8	34.9	35.9	44.0	45.6	47.7
Age:									
Under 22 years	23.7	21.9	20.4	21.4	22.0	20.3	33.0	33.6	34.4
22 to 44 years	62.9	64.1	64.3	64.8	64.1	64.8	38.5	38.1	38.6
45 years and over	13.4	14.1	15.3	13.8	13.9	14.8	28.5	28.3	27.0
Education (UN data exclude teenagers)									
8 years and under	9.4	8.0	7.2	8.4	8.1	8.2	14.2	13.5	12.3
9 to 11 years	18.3	17.9	15.1	18.2	17.7	18.9	20.4	20.0	20.6
12 years and over	72.3	74.1	77.7	73.3	74.2	72.8	65.5	66.6	67.1
Economically disadvantaged	48.3	46.5	48.3	43.6	44.1	66.5	NA	NA	NA

Races:									
White	65.1	61.4	71.5	71.1	68.2	66.3	81.3	80.3	78.4
Black and other	34.9	38.6	28.5	28.9	31.8	33.7	18.6	19.7	21.6
Hispanic origin	16.1	12.4	13.5	12.9	9.9	12.0	6.3	6.6	6.4
Limited English-speaking ability	8.0	4.3	2.1	4.6	3.3	2.9	NA	NA	NA
Veterans:									
Vietnam era	11.3	10.1	7.4	12.5	8.7	6.5	7.2	6.9	6.9
Other	12.6	11.4	15.6	14.6	12.0	18.4	10.8	9.9	8.7

Source: National Commission for Manpower Policy, *An Interim Report to the Congress,* vol. I (Washington, D.C., March 1978), p. 54.

Note: Totals may not add to 100 percent because of rounding.

Table 15

WIN PROGRAM DATA

Fiscal Year	Federal Obligations ($ millions)	New Enrollees (thousands)	Percentage Female	Number of Enrollees Who Found Employment Through WIN (thousands)	Percentage Female	Number Able to Leave Welfare by Finding Employment Through WIN	Percentage Female	Hourly Entry Wage		Women's Wage as a Percentage of Men's
								Men	Women	
1977	$370	NA	75[a]	203,000[a]	61[a]	94,000[a]	NA	$3.70[a]	$2.73[a]	74
1976	230.1	445,200	73	186,062	65	86,668	47	3.50	2.57	73
1975	199.9	360,400	75	170,641	65	51,627	56	2.94	2.42	82
1974	250.1	353,100	72	177,300	69	52,000	49	2.72	2.07	76
1973	208.8	238,500	70	148,200	69	34,373	41	2.58	1.87	72
1972	174.8	120,600	60	NA	NA	NA	NA	2.92	2.11	72
1971	64.1	112,200	64	19,100	NA	NA	NA	NA	NA	NA
1970	78.8	92,700	71		NA	NA	NA	NA	NA	NA
1969	100.8	80,600	60		NA	NA	NA	NA	NA	NA

a. 1977 data for first three quarters only.

Sources: Department of Labor Press Release, November 10, 1977; 1969–76 WIN Annual Reports, *Employment and Training Reports of the President, 1977*, 1976, *Manpower Reports of the President, 1970–75*.

Other factors also share responsibility for women's underrepresentation in federal employment programs. Veterans' preference is a prime example. Veterans accounted for about 17 percent of the unemployed during the 1970s, but they held between 24 percent and 47 percent of the public service jobs.[32] There are few female veterans.

Many programs within CETA simply ignore the needs of women. The Job Corps—modeled after the all-male Civilian Conservation Corps of the Depression—has been one of the federal government's major programs to alleviate problems of unemployed teenagers. Apparently, when the program planners thought of disadvantaged and unemployed youth, they visualized males, because the original plans included no provision for women at all. Although Job Corps centers for women eventually were included in program specifications at the insistence of Congresswoman Edith Green, the centers were sex-segregated prior to 1977. In 1976, although 45 percent of unemployed teenagers were female, only 29 percent of Job Corps participants were female. The Carter administration has announced its intention to increase female participation in Job Corps, but it is clear that the effort will be to patch up a program originally designed for teenage males rather than to incorporate women into the basic program structure. A similar criticism can be leveled at the Young Adult Conservation Corps, formed in 1977, that emphasizes heavy physical labor. Unless special recruiting efforts are made, women's participation will undoubtedly be limited.

Federal employment and training programs are a potentially powerful tool for improving the economic status of women in the labor force. To the extent that women are underrepresented, the usefulness of these programs in dealing with joblessness among women is disproportionately limited. Moreover, underrepresentation of women means that they are not receiving their fair share of the billions of federal dollars spent for programs to reduce unemployment.

Sex Stereotyping

Not only are women underrepresented in CETA, but almost all of those who do participate are engaged in traditionally female jobs—clerical work, health services, library work, elementary school jobs, and the like. Training opportunities are, for the most part, in these same general areas. Although lip service is paid to training and placing women in nontraditional jobs, action in this direction seems to be moving at a snail's pace.

---

32. Underwood, *Women in Federal Employment Programs*, p. 30.

Although WIN has a small training component, the emphasis is on job placement. According to the Labor Department, more than half of all female WIN participants in 1977 were placed in clerical and service jobs compared with less than one-fifth of the male WIN participants.[33] In general, men who obtained jobs were much less concentrated in a single occupation. Further, only about a third of the men were placed in jobs paying less than three dollars per hour, compared with three-fourths of the women who were placed in such jobs. As a consequence, women constituted less than half of all participants who were able to leave welfare as a result of finding a job.[34]

Despite the shortcomings of current employment programs for women, there is growing recognition among policy planners that continued crowding of women into traditionally female jobs only exacerbates women's unemployment problems. Not only must women be encouraged to seek a broader range of career opportunities in the private sector, but also government as a model employer should take the lead in offering nontraditional training and job options for women in its employment programs. In cooperation with the Labor Department's Women's Bureau, the Employment and Training Administration has sponsored a few experimental programs to encourage women to enter the skilled trades. In 1974 the Bureau of Apprenticeship and Training in the Labor Department's Manpower Administration initiated a pilot project to place women in apprenticeable and nontraditional occupations. In addition, the bureau has changed the language in all its apprentice outreach contracts to include women and to encourage special recruiting efforts to attract women into apprenticeship programs.[35] The Women's Bureau, recently elevated to the Office of the Secretary of Labor, has exhibited a strong commitment to this approach. If progress is to be made in substantially reducing women's unemployment and upgrading women's earnings and occupational status, however, far more resources will have to be devoted to moving women into nontraditional jobs than have been spent in the scattered and small-scale pilot projects conducted to date.

---

33. *Employment and Training Report of the President, 1978*, p. 54.

34. Ibid., pp. 54–55.

35. U.S. Department of Labor, Employment Standards Administration, Women's Bureau, *1975 Handbook on Women Workers* (Washington, D.C.: U.S. Government Printing Office, 1976), p. 234.

Chapter 4

WOMEN'S EMPLOYMENT AND MARRIAGE

SANDRA L. HOFFERTH and KRISTIN A. MOORE

Women have always worked, but the employment of married women, particularly mothers, outside the home has typically been viewed at best as an unfortunate necessity and often as a tragedy. Even though this perspective continues to be prevalent in some circles in the United States, we have seen that a dramatic increase has occurred in the labor force participation of women of all income levels, including married women who traditionally have felt no economic need to work. In the past twenty years the overall female employment rate has risen by more than 50 percent, and the rate for married women, with children, living with their husbands has doubled. During the same period, birthrates have dropped by 40 percent, divorce rates have doubled, and cohabitation outside marriage has become widespread. Many people have been alarmed by these trends, because they interpret them as indications of the probable demise of marriage and the family. Yet female employment rates continue to increase. What does the future hold for our society?

The traditional notion of the family has certainly been changing. What are these changes and to what extent has the increased employment of women outside the home been responsible for the changes? How have these changes affected the stability and happiness of marriage? What further developments can be expected? What can be done to ease the problems that families face during this transition period? This chapter addresses these questions.

Concern over women's employment has often centered on the welfare of children. The well-being of children is, of course, critical to any society, and children are the focus of the next chapter. Women's employment, however, has important consequences for adults as well, both as individuals and as members of families. The mental and physical health of individual adults are vital to any society, and family health is important to individual health. Marital satisfaction is a critical predictor of individual happiness for both married men and women.[1] Therefore it is important to consider the effects of increased female employment on both the individuals themselves and on the interactions of individuals within the family.

Contemporary Marriage

Although pessimists cite falling birthrates, increasing divorce rates, and the rising proportion of the population delaying marriage or living together without marriage as proof that family life is dying, if not already dead, the numbers do not really support that claim. On the contrary, most adults still marry; most families have children; and most children are raised in families.[2]

Changes in Marriage. Despite social, economic, and political upheavals, the marriage rate (number of marriages per thousand population) has, with the notable exception of the post-World War II boom, hovered at about the same level since 1900 (see Figure 10). Because this measure includes not only first marriages but remarriages (which rise in number as the divorce rate rises), the proportion in different generations who have ever been married should also be considered.

About 95 percent of contemporary American women are expected to marry at some time in their lives.[3] This proportion represents a slight increase over the figures for the early part of the century. For

---

1. Norval D. Glenn, "The Contribution of Marriage to the Psychological Well-Being of Males and Females," *Journal of Marriage and the Family* 37 (August 1975): 594–601.

2. Paul C. Glick and Arthur J. Norton, "Marrying, Divorcing, and Living Together in the U.S. Today," *Population Bulletin* 32 (1977): 3–39.

3. Paul C. Glick, "Updating the Life Cycle of the Family," *Journal of Marriage and the Family* 39 (February 1977): 3–15.

FIGURE 10

MARRIAGE AND DIVORCE RATES (PER 1,000 POPULATION), U.S., 1890-1978

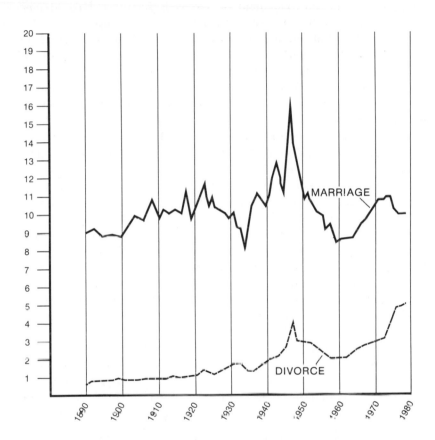

Sources: U.S. Department of Health, Education, and Welfare, Public Health Service. "100 Years of Marriage and Divorce Statistics, United States, 1867-1967." *Vital and Health Statistics,* series 21, no. 24, December 1973.

U.S. Bureau of the Census, *Statistical Abstract of the United States, 1977* . Washington, D.C.: U.S. Government Printing Office, 1977.

U.S. Department of Health, Education, and Welfare, Public Health Service. "Births, Marriages, Divorces, and Deaths for June 1978." *Monthly Vital Statistics Report,* vol. 27, no. 6, September 12, 1978.

example, only 92 percent of the women born in the 1900s had married by the time they reached their forties.

Although the proportion of the entire population that reaches age forty without marrying is currently at an all-time low, an increasing proportion of the under-thirty age group has never been married. This trend may signal postponement of marriage, but also it could mean that a larger proportion of recent generations will never marry. One study forecasts that among women born in the 1950s the proportion never married by age forty will rise to 7 percent,[4] but this group still will represent a small minority.

Then too, "never married" does not mean "never cohabitated." Census Bureau data indicate that the proportion of males and females under age forty-five who reported themselves as sharing a household with one other unrelated person of the opposite sex doubled between 1970 and 1976.[5] Although the actual numbers involved are small—about 2 million—the trend is striking. Whether "living together" represents a new life-cycle stage or a more permanent family form is not yet known. Nor are the implications of cohabitation for childbearing and child rearing known.

The commitment of Americans to marital living arrangements is also illustrated by the frequency of remarriages following divorce. Four of every five persons whose first marriage ends in divorce eventually remarry, half within five years.[6]

Changes in the Family Life Cycle: The Relative Importance of Childbearing and Marriage. Since the turn of the century, fundamental changes in the life cycles of families have been occurring. The child-rearing period—that time between birth of the first child and departure of the last from the household—has been narrowed by approximately three years.[7] As life expectancy has increased, the average age of an individual at the death of a spouse has risen to such a degree

4. Ibid.

5. U.S. Department of Commerce, Bureau of the Census, "Marital Status and Living Arrangements: March 1976," *Current Population Reports*, series P-20, no. 306, 1977.

6. U.S. Department of Commerce, Bureau of the Census, "Number, Timing and Duration of Marriages and Divorces in the United States: June 1975," *Current Population Reports*, series P-20, no. 297, 1976.

7. The average time span between the birth of the first child and the birth of the last one has declined to about seven years; the median age of the mother at the birth of her first child has risen to about twenty-two, while her age at the birth of her last child has declined to slightly under thirty. Glick, "Updating the Life Cycle of the Family."

that a marriage can be expected to remain intact for about thirteen years following the departure of the last child. Thus the *relative* length of the period of child rearing in an individual's life has declined and may decline even further. The period during which preschool children are present in the household now averages only about one-third of a typical married life span (thirteen of forty-four years).[8] Women can no longer expect to spend all their adult lives in child rearing. The rapidly increasing rate of participation of women, especially married women, in the labor force suggests that more of women's lifetimes will be spent in employment. For this reason it is becoming more and more worthwhile for women to invest in training for such activities.

Changes in the Causes of Marital Disruption and Family Composition. The divorce rate has been the most worrisome indicator of change in marriage throughout the past decade. As Figure 10 shows, between 1967 and 1977 the divorce rate rose from 2.5 per thousand population to 5.0. Although there is evidence that the rapid increase has begun to slow, the divorce rate is at an historic high.

Yet a high rate of marital disruption is not new. At the turn of the century, 29 percent of all children under the age of eighteen lived in households that had been broken by divorce, separation, or the death of one parent. Of the children born between 1941 and 1960, the proportion experiencing family disruption averaged about 25 percent. Of children born around 1970, between 32 percent and 40 percent are forecast to experience some family disruption before they reach age eighteen. The causes of disruption, of course, have changed. In 1900 the primary cause was the death of a parent; in the 1970s it is divorce or separation. The low point in the 1940s occurred because death rates had declined while divorce rates, although rising, remained low.[9]

The increased divorce rate has been cited as a major cause of the increase in families in which no adult male is present, a family form that is statistically likely to be poor. Because the proportion of families experiencing disruption has risen less dramatically than the proportion of female-headed families, however, causes other than disruption must be identified. One reason for the rise in single-parent households is that an increased proportion of women now establish their own households following separation or divorce. In 1940 only 44 percent of women with children but without husbands headed their own fam-

---

8. Ibid.

9. Mary Jo Bane, *Here to Stay: American Families in the Twentieth Century* (New York: Basic Books, Inc., 1976), Table A-4.

ilies; the figure today is 80 percent.[10] Although the proportion of
children living with *both* parents has declined, the proportion living
with at least one parent has risen. In fact, in 1976 some 97 percent of
all children lived in families with at least one of their natural parents,[11]
compared with 90 percent in 1940.[12]

The Various Effects of Wives' Employment on Marriage

As home production has become less efficient relative to industrial
production, families have relied increasingly on money to purchase
goods and services. Because participation in the labor force provides
both men and women with the money to substitute purchased goods
and services for home-produced ones, dependence on the family as an
economic unit has diminished. Employment outside the home, therefore, has an "independence" effect and may increase the odds of
divorce by enabling spouses to support themselves if the marriage
breaks down. Conversely, the income produced by two working members of a family may add to marital stability, because the combined
income increases the family's standard of living and hence the benefits
of marriage.

Employment of a wife may change not only the economic structure
of the family but also the social and psychological rewards families
gain from marriage. A wife who once obtained satisfactions such as
social contact, feelings of competence, prestige, and the like from
marriage and family may obtain these satisfactions outside the family.
At the same time, satisfaction of other members of the working-wife
family may decrease. Women working outside the home have less time
to care for children and to do housework. Working wives may come
to demand a greater role in family decision making. If expectations
of appropriate behavior and task assignment within the family do not
change, overload on the part of the working wife plus frustration and
dissatisfaction on the part of all family members seem likely. Terms
such as "role strain," "exchange imbalance," and "inequity" are often
used to describe conditions in affected households.

---

10. Phillips Cutright, "Components of Change in the Number of Female Household Heads Aged 15–44: United States 1940–1970," *Journal of Marriage and the
Family* 36 (November 1974): 714–21. Children whose households were disrupted in
an earlier day might have gone to live with relatives, gone to work, or been sent to
an orphanage.

11. U.S. Department of Commerce, Bureau of the Census, "Marital Status and
Living Arrangements," p. 6.

12. Bane, *Here to Stay*, p. 13.

Alternatively, if husbands view their wives' increasing willingness to shoulder part of the burden of supporting the family as a relief rather than a threat, the husbands may begin to share in the household work while enjoying a higher total income. As a result, the rewards of family life may increase for everybody.

Since most women work outside the home at some point in their lives,[13] it seems likely that the effects of employment on marriage vary with the number of years worked, the life-cycle stage during which the woman works, the concentration of time worked (part or full time), the type of jobs obtained, the wage or salary, the reason for working (economic necessity, choice, or both), and the attitude of the woman's husband toward her work.

The following sections discuss in some detail the effects that the employment of wives has had on the incidence of marriage and marital dissolution, on the household work of families, on the development of husbands and wives as individuals, and on marital relationships. We will attempt to specify where possible, and speculate where it is impossible to specify, what it is about women's working outside the home that has these effects. Finally, we will consider what can be done to help couples cope with the problems that result.

Unfortunately, this task is made more difficult by a shortage of relevant research. Few studies have attempted to grapple directly with the changes that occur when women who have been full-time homemakers begin working outside the home. Such analyses are rare partly because few studies have followed individuals over time. Most studies deal principally with correlates of behavior such as divorce at a particular time.

From the fact that women with relatively high family incomes are less likely to divorce than are women with lower incomes, for example, we cannot necessarily conclude that as the mean income of the population increases the divorce rate will fall. In fact, just the opposite has been the case. Over the past half-century, divorce rates and living standards have risen together.[14] The difficulty of inferring consequences of societal changes is especially severe in studying marriage-related variables such as satisfaction, inasmuch as over time we might expect

---

13. Sandra L. Hofferth and Kristin A. Moore, "Age at First Childbirth: Labor Force Participation and Earnings," The Urban Institute Working Paper 1146–4, Washington, D.C., 1978.

14. For example, see Robert T. Michael, "Factors Affecting Divorce: A Study of the Terman Sample," National Bureau of Economic Research Working Paper No. 147, Stanford, Calif., 1976.

unhappy couples to have divorced, leaving, presumably, only the more compatible couples still married.

Our discussion in the next section focuses on the few longitudinal studies that do permit tracing causal sequences, but our inferences about future trends are necessarily limited by lack of appropriate data.

THE FORMATION AND DISSOLUTION OF MARRIAGES

The most important events in the life cycles of families are those that bring them into being, cause them to grow, and dissolve them. We begin here, therefore, with a discussion of the impact that the employment of women has had on marriage, divorce, and death. (Effects on childbearing are discussed in Chapter 5.)

Family Formation: Marriage

Are working women more likely than nonworking women to marry late or not at all? There is evidence that working women are more likely to postpone marriage, but little that they tend not to marry at all. Employment has several competing types of effects: On the one hand, women who are working may not marry because they have their own means of support and personal satisfaction (the "independence" effect). On the other hand, women who are working may be more likely to marry because a young couple can more easily afford to marry when both partners are working (an "income" effect), because working women's earning ability makes them more attractive (a "dowry" effect), or because working women have more opportunities to meet eligible men (an "access" effect). We can identify the positive and negative effects of working on marriage, but the relative importance of the different factors has not been documented.

A number of researchers have found associations between working and marriage. One pair found that among women ages twenty-two to twenty-four with attractive employment opportunities, a relatively large proportion had not been married. They interpreted their findings as supporting the "employment as an alternative to marriage" hypothesis.[15] These results, of course, do not necessarily mean that the proportion of "never-married" among these women will remain low as they grow older.

A study relating to the period 1968 to 1972 found that type of income had an effect on whether female household heads under age

---

15. Samuel H. Preston and Alan Thomas Richards, "The Influence of Women's Work Opportunities on Marriage Rates," Demography 12 (May 1975): 209–22.

fifty-five with children younger than age eighteen remarried. Other factors being equal, women with relatively high total household incomes tended to remarry, while women with significant assets were less likely to remarry. Receiving income from welfare may also have an "independence" effect similar to that of income from employment, since women on welfare also tended not to remarry.[16]

Other researchers have failed to find simple associations between several measures of employment and income and the probability of marrying over a given period.[17] It is possible that various effects cancel each other out. There may also be an interaction effect. For example, although one group did not find an overall relationship between the receipt of income maintenance payments and marriage rates, they did find that both black and white women who had been single for less than four years when they began receiving income supplements had a lower probability of remarriage than did a comparable group of women who had not received payments. Women in the income supplement program who had been single longer than four years at enrollment had a higher probability of remarriage than did controls. The authors interpreted these results as indicating an independence effect of income maintenance among the recently single, whereas an income-dowry effect operated among those who had been single longer (that is, women who presumably had already experienced "independence").[18] Others found that receipt of welfare severely depressed remarriage during the first two years after the termination of an earlier marriage; this negative effect wore off somewhat after two years, but it was not entirely eliminated.[19]

These results support the notion that employment leads to postponement, but not necessarily rejection, of marriage. Employment may serve as an alternative for younger women but as a "dowry" for older women, particularly among women with children who contem-

---

16. Isabel V. Sawhill, Gerald E. Peabody, Carol A. Jones, and Steven B. Caldwell, "Income Transfers and Family Structure," The Urban Institute Working Paper 979–03, Washington, D.C., 1975.

17. Greg J. Duncan, "Unmarried Heads of Households and Marriage," in Greg J. Duncan and James Morgan, eds., *Five Thousand Families*, vol. 4 (Ann Arbor: Institute for Social Research, University of Michigan, 1976); and Nancy Brandon Tuma, Lyle P. Groeneveld, and Michael T. Hannan, "First Dissolutions and Marriages: Impacts in 24 Months of the Seattle and Denver Income Maintenance Experiments," research memorandum, Center for the Study of Welfare Policy, Stanford Research Institute, 1976.

18. Tuma et al., "First Dissolutions and Marriages."

19. Sawhill et al., "Income Transfers and Family Structure."

plate remarriage.[20] Marriage rates cited previously indicate that the proportion never married is rising among those under age thirty and dropping among those over age thirty. Further evidence for this interpretation was found in a study of 1957 high school graduates. For females, but not for males, high occupational aspirations in high school were associated with delayed marriage. For both sexes, higher educational attainment was associated with later marriage.[21]

To the extent that the incomes of employed women allow them to support themselves, increased employment of women is likely to push the marriage age upward. Employment does not, however, seem to lead women to develop tastes or lifestyles that preclude eventual marriage. Only a slight increase—from 5 percent to 7 percent—in the proportion of women who never marry is expected among those who turned twenty during the 1970s. Rather than indicating a rejection of marriage, this increase will probably reflect both the inability among some of those who postpone marriage to find a suitable partner when they are ready for marrage, and some increase in cohabitation.

Marital Dissolution: Divorce

As with marriage, the impact of women's employment on divorce can be either positive or negative. On the one hand, a woman with a job has an alternative means of support if her marriage is unsatisfactory. On the other hand, a wife's working can raise the couple's joint standard of living—and perhaps improve their quality of life—thereby increasing the benefits of remaining in the marriage. Because of these competing effects, we should not expect clear-cut evidence that employment of wives outside the home itself causes divorce.

One research team was unable to detect any effect of wives' employment on marital stability.[22] Another researcher concluded on the basis of a literature review that couples in which the wife is employed are no more likely to separate or divorce than are those in which the wife is not employed, although lower-income working-wife families do reveal evidence of greater stress.[23]

---

20. Valerie Kincade Oppenheimer, "Divorce, Remarriage, and Wives' Labor Force Participation," paper presented at the annual meeting of the American Sociological Association, September 1977.

21. Paul Voss, "Social Determinants of Age at First Marriage in the United States," unpublished dissertation, University of Michigan, 1975.

22. Saul Hoffman and John Holmes, "Husbands, Wives, and Divorce," in Duncan and Morgan, eds., *Five Thousand Families*, vol. 4, pp. 23–76.

23. F. Ivan Nye, "Husband-Wife Relationship," in Lois Wladis Hoffman and F. Ivan Nye, eds., *Working Mothers* (San Francisco: Jossey-Bass, 1974), pp. 205–06.

Evidence of the "independence" effect of working outside the home has been found. In one study, wives with relatively high earnings in 1968 were found to be more likely than were those with lower earnings to separate or divorce by 1972.[24] If it is true that working causes marital dissolution because working allows women to support themselves, receipt of or expectation of receipt of welfare payments should also predict possible marital breakup. Two different research teams have reported that under certain conditions receipt of welfare or income maintenance payments decreased marital stability.[25]

Theoretically, the size and dependability of total family income or husband's income should affect marital stability. Yet one study failed to find that total household income had any effect on divorce.[26] Another study found divorce generally less likely as the husband's income increased, but at the highest income levels, the likelihood of divorce rose again.[27] Which spouse earns most of the family income also affects stability. Two studies found a greater probability of divorce or separation among couples in which the wife earned most of the household income than when the situation was reversed.[28] Finally, the stability of that income is important. Women who perceived an improvement in their family finances over a five-year period have been found to be less likely than others were to experience divorce.[29] Another study found that families in which husbands had experienced unemployment were relatively unstable.[30] One study that analyzed divorce rates since the turn of the century suggests that the employment of women appears to be not a cause of divorce but rather a response to increased marital instability brought about by greater

24. Isabel V. Sawhill et al., "Income Transfers and Family Structure."

25. Hoffman and Holmes, "Husbands, Wives, and Divorce"; and Michael T. Hannan and Nancy Brandon Tuma, "Income and Marital Events: Evidence from an Income-Maintenance Experiment," *American Journal of Sociology* 82 (May 1977): 1186–1211.

26. Sawhill et al., "Income Transfers and Family Structure."

27. Gary S. Becker, Elizabeth M. Landes, and Robert T. Michael, "Economics of Marital Instability," National Bureau of Economic Research Working Paper No. 153, Stanford, Calif., October 1976.

28. Kristin A. Moore, Linda J. Waite, Sandra L. Hofferth, and Steven B. Caldwell, "The Consequences of Age at First Childbirth: Marriage, Separation and Divorce," The Urban Institute Working Paper 1146–03, Washington, D.C., 1978; and Andrew Cherlin, "The Effect of Children on Marital Dissolution," *Demography* 14 (August 1977): 273–84.

29. Frank L. Mott and Sylvia F. Moore, "The Socioeconomic Determinants and Shortrun Consequences of Marital Disruption," paper presented at the annual meeting of the Population Association of America, St. Louis, April 20–22, 1977.

30. Sawhill et al., "Income Transfers and Family Structure."

control over conception. Couples with small families are more likely to divorce than those with large families, and divorced women are more likely to work.[31]

There is, then, no clear-cut body of evidence indicating that in individual couples employment of the wife leads to divorce or separation. Thus, although we know that employment of women is linked in certain ways to divorce, to predict whether increased employment will bring about even higher divorce rates is premature.

Marital Dissolution: Death

To suggest sickness and death as consequences of female employment may seem farfetched, but because women have traditionally made nurturing and home production their principal concerns, some people might fear that the loss or diminution of these services would lead to poorer health among family members. Of course, women who opt for the working world expose themselves to job tensions, commuting accidents, and occupational hazards; as a consequence, their mortality may rise.[32] Given a picture of overwork and strain in households with two full-time earners plus children, it seems possible that parents will pay less attention to their own diet and rest. Parents cannot afford to take the time to relax or to be ill, so their physical health may deteriorate. Two-job couples may consequently have shorter life spans.

Yet the higher incomes of families with employed wives may provide the wherewithal for an adequate diet and preventive medical care. Husbands who are freed from omnipresent concern with supporting their families may enjoy lower blood pressure and have fewer heart attacks. Moreover, such husbands may be able to turn down overtime or leave a job that is harmful to their long-term health. These benefits from women's rising labor force participation might lengthen the average life span, particularly among men.

At this time, no studies are known to have addressed this issue. If increased female employment should prove to extend men's longevity, the frequency and length of widowhood would be lessened. Fewer retired people might be unmarried. If, however, the strains experienced by two-earner families are found to increase the incidence of sickness and early death, the importance of flexible and part-time employment becomes self-evident. Either way, pension systems and health care services would be greatly affected. Clearly this topic merits research attention.

Our speculation at this point is that the long-term effect of women's working will be to equalize life spans, lengthening men's lives but

31. Michael, "Factors Affecting Divorce."
32. I. Waldron, "Why Do Women Live Longer Than Men?" *Social Science and Medicine* 10 (August 1976): 349–62.

shortening women's. To the extent that both sexes reject the aggressive, competitive model of employment, the shortening of women's life span will be less likely.

Summary

Americans do not appear to have given up on marriage. Couples are marrying later—sometimes after an initial period of cohabitation—and women's employment seems to be a factor in the delay of marriage. Divorce is certainly more frequent now, but data implicating women's employment are not conclusive. Although employment of the wife may create problems of overwork and strain in traditional roles and make marital break-up more economically feasible, the added income may make marriages happier and more stable. Moreover, the rising age at first marriage may result in establishment of more mature and considered marriages, which would have a lower probability of divorce. The effect of women's employment on the incidence of sickness and death is not known. Overwork, strain, and job-related accidents may produce increases in sickness and earlier death among females. At the same time, sharing the burden of supporting a family with their wives may lengthen husbands' life spans. To date, no research has specifically addressed this question.

In sum, the principal known effect of women's labor force participation on the formation and dissolution of marriage is to delay formation. Other effects may exist, but they have not been documented. A wife's employment seems likely to affect numerous aspects of the couple's marital relationship. The next section therefore considers the effects of women's employment on individuals and on their relationships.

THE HOUSEHOLD WORK OF FAMILIES

Although most household goods and many services are now purchased or carried out with the help of machines, the time spent in domestic activities has not declined over the past decades. Estimates of the time that full-time homemakers today devote to household work range from thirty-five hours per week[33] to sixty hours per week.[34]

---

33. Sharon Nickols, "Work and Housework: Family Roles in Productive Activity," paper presented at the annual meeting of the National Council on Family Relations, October 19–23, 1976, New York; and Martin Meissner, Elizabeth W. Humphreys, Scott M. Meis, and William J. Scheu, "No Exit for Wives: Sexual Division of Labour and the Cumulation of Household Demands," *Canadian Review of Sociology and Anthropology* 12 (1975): 424–39.

34. Joann Vanek, "Time Spent in Housework," *Scientific American* 231 (November 1974): 116–20; and Kathryn E. Walker, "Household Work Time: Its Implication for Family Decisions," *Journal of Home Economics* 65 (October 1973): 7–11.

Yet between one-quarter[35] and two-thirds[36] of husbands in the United States reportedly do no housework at all. Husbands who do any of the regular household work are estimated to put in somewhere between six[37] and eleven[38] hours per week. Each child between the ages of six and eleven is estimated to contribute one-half hour per day, and each teenager about one hour per day.[39]

Mothers spend additional time in direct care of children—one research group estimates eleven hours a week per child.[40] This figure varies inversely with the child's age, dropping from about two hours a day for children under age three to perhaps thirty minutes for older children.[41] Of course, mothers spend much more time (from four to seven hours per day) in the company of their children. Fathers reportedly spend between two and three hours per day in the company of their children, and contribute six to twenty minutes to child care on weekdays, plus thirty minutes a day on weekends.[42]

Adding up, we estimate the weekly burden of work in the average household to be between forty and seventy hours. If household work is this time consuming, what happens when a wife goes to work outside the home?

Effects of a Wife's Employment on Time Spent in Housework

Complete substitution of paid help would be prohibitively expensive for most families.[43] The options that remain are (1) to rely on non-

---

35. Harriet B. Presser, "Female Employment and the Division of Labor Within the Home: A Longitudinal Perspective," paper presented at the annual meetings of the Population Association of America, St. Louis, Mo., April 20–23, 1977.

36. Nickols, "Work and Housework."

37. Ibid.

38. Walker, "Household Work Time"; and Meissner et al., "No Exit for Wives."

39. Walker, "Household Work Time."

40. Meissner et al., "No Exit for Wives." Direct care is defined as (a) care of babies, (b) care of older children, (c) supervision of school work, (d) reading of stories, (e) indoor games, (f) outdoor games, (g) medical care, and (h) travel. See Philip J. Stone, "Child Care in Twelve Countries," in Alexander Szalai, ed., *The Use of Time* (The Hague: Mouton, 1972).

41. Ibid.

42. Ibid., and Stone, "Child Care in Twelve Countries."

43. The value of the services provided by a full-time homemaker, priced at the minimum wage for a family with two children, the youngest under age six, has been estimated at $7,000 per year (1973 dollars) by Walker in "Household Work Time." The median income of women (full-time civilian workers age fourteen and above) was only $6,335 in 1973. U.S. Department of Commerce, Bureau of the Census, "A Statistical Portrait of Women," *Current Population Reports*, series P-20, no. 58, 1976.

paid help from spouse, relatives, and friends, (2) to reduce house-keeping standards, (3) to become more efficient at household work, and (4) to work part time.[44] Working women typically use some combination of these options.

Several researchers have found that although women who enter the labor force continue to spend considerable time in housework, they do reduce their hours of housework by about half—to about twenty-six hours a week.[45]

Unlike household work, which can be done at any time, however, many of the needs of children cannot be put off until a convenient time can be found. Moreover, cutting back on standards of child care is an unacceptable alternative for most parents, although a 1976 Census survey indicated that 13 percent of the seven- to thirteen-year-olds with mothers in the labor force are sometimes left to care for themselves.[46] Becoming more efficient is not the solution to child care that it can be to housework, either, given children's need for continual care, supervision, and teaching. Consequently, as might be expected, a large proportion of employed mothers pay for child care—far larger than the proportion who pay for household help.[47]

Effects of a Wife's Employment on Household Division of Labor

A number of researchers have hypothesized that female employment will result in more sharing of family functions by both spouses.[48]

---

44. Meissner et al., "No Exit for Wives."

45. Ibid.; Vanek, "Time Spent in Housework"; and Nickols, "Work and Housework."

46. U.S. Department of Commerce, Bureau of the Census, "Daytime Care of Children: October 1974 and February 1975," *Current Population Reports*, series P-20, no. 298, 1976.

47. Shirley S. Angrist, Judith R. Lave, and Richard Mickelson, "How Working Mothers Manage: Socioeconomic Differences in Work, Child Care, and Household Tasks," *Social Science Quarterly* 56 (1976): 631–37. This team found that of a group of employed women surveyed in 1973, 69 percent of those in clerical and 94 percent of those in professional-managerial positions paid for child care. None of the clerical but 38 percent of the professional-managerial women had paid household help.

48. W. Silverman and R. Hill, "Task Allocation in Marriage in the United States and Belgium," *Journal of Marriage and the Family* 29 (May 1967): 353–59; Robert O. Blood, Jr., and Donald M. Wolfe, *Husbands and Wives: The Dynamics of Married Living* (New York: Free Press, 1960); Lois Wladis Hoffman, "Effects of the Employment of Mothers on Parental Power Relations and the Division of Household Tasks," *Marriage and Family Living* 22 (February 1960); and K. S. Powell, "Family Variables," in F. Ivan Nye and Lois Wladis Hoffman, eds., *The Employed Mother in America* (Chicago: Rand McNally, 1963); and others.

Although there is evidence that between 1960 and 1970 the number of husbands participating in housework and the share of housework handled by husbands generally increased, we find little evidence that task sharing is linked to having a working wife. According to one study, husbands whose wives were in the labor force in 1976 but not in 1973 helped more in 1976 than they had in 1973, while those whose wives were employed in 1973 but not in 1976 helped less in 1976.[49] Yet, husbands whose wives were in the labor force in both years decreased their participation in household tasks; those whose wives did not work either year increased their participation. Because the group with wives who worked in neither year is the largest, the upward shift in husbands' participation predominates in the entire sample of couples. Increased participation in household tasks, therefore, may be less a response to the wife's employment than to historical or generational shifts in norms and attitudes regarding the appropriate allocation of tasks between spouses.[50]

When the total time spent on housework by husband and wife is considered, however, the husband's *share* of the total workload has been found to decline with his wife's employment and with the presence of a child under age ten.[51] The reason, of course, is that the *total* workload increases faster than the husband's contribution rises. One researcher found that husbands of employed wives without children spent only about six additional minutes per week on regular household work, while husbands of employed wives with a child under age ten worked one hour per week more than husbands of comparable nonworking wives did.[52] Another researcher was unable to find that a wife's working had any real impact on the amount of time her husband spent in housework. Husbands whose wives increased their time spent in paid work increased their own housework time by an average of only eighteen minutes per week.[53]

It seems clear that working-wife households must reduce the time spent on housework, whether it be because they are more efficient, because they are less thorough about their housework, or because time-intensive tasks like making bread are relegated to the status of

---

49. Presser, "Female Employment and the Division of Labor."

50. See, for example, Karen Oppenheim Mason, John L. Czajka, and Sara Arber, "Change in U.S. Women's Sex Role Attitudes 1964–1974," *American Sociological Review* 4 (August 1976): 573–96.

51. Meissner et al., "No Exit for Wives."

52. Ibid.

53. Nickols, "Work and Housework."

luxuries. Even so, employment of a wife outside the home seems to result in a substantial increase in the woman's work week. One researcher estimates that when both partners work full time, the work week of wives (job plus housework) averages sixty-six to seventy-five hours and exceeds that of husbands by about eight hours.[54] Another research team estimates that women who work do so at a sacrifice of fourteen hours a week from other activities such as gardening, visiting, eating, sleeping, and television viewing.[55] Although we have noted that the number of men who help with household tasks seems to have increased over time, the average husband's investments still tend to be very small, and seem unaffected by the number of hours his wife works. Thus when a wife goes out to work, she usually continues to do most of the work that gets done at home. Wives who work full time make up most of their housework on weekends, thereby cutting down what had been their free time. The result, certainly, is overload for wives.

It is possible that women's own attitudes explain, in part, their husbands' lack of participation in household work, for many women apparently share men's view that housework is women's responsibility. For example, 47 percent of a sample of women interviewed in 1970 did not agree that "men should share the work around the house with women, such as doing dishes, cleaning and so forth."[56] Among black working-wife couples, wives have favored sharing household tasks more than husbands have; in contrast, among Chicano couples, wives have proved to favor the traditional division of labor more than their husbands have.[57]

Husbands generally appear to be willing and interested in the care of children,[58] but housework has few rewards—it is not very appealing, it is rarely finished, and it offers little sense of accomplishment. Many women may find it easier to do the tasks themselves than to nag or cajole their husbands into doing them. Other women may prefer to do everything themselves than to accept what they feel are the

---

54. Walker, "Household Work Time."

55. Meissner et al., "No Exit for Wives."

56. Karen Oppenheim Mason and L. L. Bumpass, "U.S. Women's Sex Role Ideology, 1970," *American Journal of Sociology* 80 (1975): 1212–19.

57. Ruth Cronkite, "Determinants and Changes in Normative Preferences of Spouses." Research memorandum, Center for the Study of Welfare Policy, Stanford Research Institute, Menlo Park, Calif., 1977.

58. Walter McIntire, Gilbert D. Nass, and Donna L. Battistone, "Female Misperceptions of Male Parenting and Expectancies," *Youth and Society* 5 (1974): 104–12.

clumsy efforts of inexperienced "house-husbands." To even the burden, not only husbands but also wives may need to change their
attitudes. Whether public policy can affect such issues is a question
to be considered later, but basically this battle is one that must be
fought over individual vacuum cleaners and kitchen sinks.

As women's work outside the home inevitably has an impact on
the work inside the home, both will affect family relationships and
satisfactions. These effects are discussed next.

WIVES' EMPLOYMENT AND THE
HUSBAND-WIFE RELATIONSHIP

Given the strength of traditional sex roles and the burden of housework, the increasing employment of wives outside the home might be
expected to put enormous strain on the husband-wife relationship.
The first topic to be considered in this section is the change in the
nature of this relationship, especially with respect to decision making.
The second issue is the satisfaction of the partners with the marriage.

The Power Structure

One of the most interesting characteristics of a marriage is its power
structure—that is, the way decisions affecting the family are made.
Although most decisions affect all members to some extent, individuals
are not typically affected in the same way by any one decision. The
greater the difference in the effect, the greater the possible disagreement in decision making. Employment of a wife may increase disagreement, for example, when a job-related move is being considered.
As more women become committed to employment, spouses may find
decision making increasingly problematic.

Traditionally, power has been measured by studying the actual
decisions couples make; the person whose preference determines the
decision is said to have greater power. This method of measurement,
however, works only when there is disagreement. To explain decision
making as a process, we need to examine the sources of bargaining
power. According to resource theory, power is based on the comparative resources of family members, so decision-making power is allocated
on the basis of relative resource contribution to the family. From this
perspective the two major questions are (1) what are resources and
(2) how is their value determined?

According to the earliest proponents of resource theory, a resource
is "anything that one partner may make available to the other, help-
ing him satisfy his needs or attain his goals," for example, income,

education, occupation, and organizational membership.[59] Other researchers have pointed out additional types of resources: homemaking ability, attractiveness, social skills, and so on.[60] (Children are usually ignored in the discussion of family power structure, although they have been found to have increasing power as they grow older and acquire resources. Their resources may include helpfulness, academic achievement, and eventually even earnings.)

It is far easier to list potential resources than to determine their value. Although the earliest researchers of this theory refer to the value of resources within the family,[61] others have valued resources in market terms—that is, by their dollar value to others outside the marriage. One researcher argues that although wives' services are essential to family members, the low value placed on these services outside the family is reflected in a low social evaluation of housework and child rearing.[62]

Because money talks, it has been hypothesized that by working, wives would increase their overall decision-making power. Data gathered by numerous researchers support this hypothesis.[63] Yet other studies indicate that whether working wives gain power varies with the area of decision making studied and with the characteristics of the couple, such as socioeconomic position, residence with relatives, subcultural norms, and race.[64]

Although the weight of evidence indicates that employed wives enjoy greater influence than full-time homemakers do in decision making, recent critics have questioned the adequacy of decision-making

---

59. Blood and Wolfe, *Husbands and Wives*, p. 12.

60. David M. Heer, "The Measurement and Bases of Family Power: An Overview," *Marriage and Family Living* 25 (1963): 133–39; and Constantina Safilios-Rothschild, "The Study of Family Power Structure: A Review 1960–1969," *Journal of Marriage and the Family* 32 (November 1970): 539–52.

61. Blood and Wolfe, *Husbands and Wives*.

62. Among others, Heer, "The Measurement and Bases of Family Power."

63. Among others, ibid.; Blood and Wolfe, *Husbands and Wives*; Hoffman, "Effects of Employment of Mothers"; Constantina Safilios-Rothschild, "A Comparison of Family Power Structure and Marital Satisfaction in Urban Greek and French Families," *Journal of Marriage and the Family* 29 (May 1967): 345–52; R. H. Weller, "The Employment of Wives, Dominance, and Fertility," *Journal of Marriage and the Family* 30 (August 1968): 437–42; F. Ivan Nye, "Marital Interaction," in Nye and Hoffman, eds., *The Employed Mother in America*, pp. 263–81; Olivera Buric and Andjelka Zecevic, "Family Authority, Marital Satisfaction and the Special Network in Yugoslavia," *Journal of Marriage and the Family* 29 (May 1967): 325–36.

64. Maximiliane E. Szinovacz, "Role Allocation, Family Structure and Female Employment," *Journal of Marriage and the Family* 39 (November 1977): 781–91; and Cronkite, "Determinants and Changes in Normative Preferences of Spouses."

studies for describing family structures.[65] Not only have the decision-making studies failed to define the conditions under which the relationships hold, but none of the studies has measured the wife's power before employment. Consequently, we have no evidence that in households in which the wife begins working, she also begins taking a greater role in family decision making. Thus it is possible that wives who are more dominant in decision making for other reasons may also tend to work outside the home.

In addition, societal changes seem to have made many studies obsolete. One researcher found evidence that role preferences of individual couples are becoming less traditional; that is, over time spouses have liberalized their role preferences as they adjusted to the preferences of the other person. Because this trend has occurred regardless of background characteristics, life-cycle stages, and economic factors, the researcher concluded that the shift to less traditional division of labor within marriage reflects broader societal changes.[66] This increasing blurring of traditional roles, coupled with increasing employment of wives outside the home, should increase the power of women in marriage.

Marital Satisfaction

Research indicates that marital satisfaction is the most important component of life satisfaction for married men and women.[67] Because the issues of who does the housework, who is responsible for providing the family's livelihood, or how family members spend their days necessarily impinge on evenings and weekends, marriages in which the wife is a full-time homemaker are inevitably different from those in which the wife works away from the home.

Wives. How does working outside the home affect the satisfaction of wives with their marriages? The evidence is mixed. Several studies indicate that working wives are less satisfied than nonworking wives.[68]

---

65. See, for example, Safilios-Rothschild, "The Study of Family Power Structure: A Review 1960–1969"; David H. Olson and Carolyn Rabunsky, "Validity of Four Measures of Family Power," *Journal of Marriage and the Family* 34 (May 1972): 224–34; and R. Cromwell and D. C. Olson, eds., *Power in Families* (New York: John Wiley [Halstead], 1975).

66. Cronkite, "Determinants and Changes in Normative Preferences of Spouses."

67. Glenn, "The Contribution of Marriage to the Psychological Well-Being of Males and Females."

68. Blood and Wolfe, *Husbands and Wives*; A. Michel, "Comparative Data Concerning the Interaction in French and American Families," *Journal of Marriage and the Family* 29 (May 1967): 337–44; Buric and Zecevic, "Family Authority, Marital

A larger number, however, indicate no difference in satisfaction,[69] and several recent studies suggest that working women are happier than nonworking ones.[70]

It seems likely that a working/nonworking dichotomy is too simplistic. Whether employment affects satisfaction depends upon various factors, of which educational level of the wife appears to be most important. Early studies found no difference in marital satisfaction between highly educated full-time housewives and highly educated working wives; however, less-educated full-time housewives were found to be much more satisfied than were less-educated working wives,[71] perhaps because well-educated women work more from choice and have better jobs. More recent studies indicate that highly educated working wives are significantly more satisfied with their marriages than are comparably educated full-time housewives.[72]

The effect of family income per se in moderating the effect of working on marital satisfaction is not clear.[73] Nor is the effect of high or

Satisfaction"; and Safilios-Rothschild, "A Comparison of Power Structure and Marital Satisfaction."

69. S. Feld, "Feelings of Adjustment," in Nye and Hoffman, eds., *The Employed Mother in America*; F. Ivan Nye, "Personal Satisfactions," in ibid.; Robert O. Blood, "The Husband-Wife Relationship," in ibid.; F. L. Nolan, "Rural Employment and Husbands and Wives," in ibid.; K. S. Powell, "Family Variables," in ibid.; Harvey J. Locke and Muriel Mackeprang, "Marital Adjustment and the Employed Wife," *American Journal of Sociology* 54 (May 1949): 536–38; and Graham L. Staines, Joseph H. Pleck, Linda J. Shepard, and Pamela O'Connor, "Wives' Employment Status and Marital Adjustment: Yet Another Look," University of Michigan, Institute for Social Research, 1978.

70. Myra Marx Ferree, "Working Class Jobs: Housework and Paid Work as Sources of Satisfaction," *Social Problems* 23 (April 1976); 431–41; and Ronald J. Burke and Tamara Weir, "Relationship of Wives' Employment Status to Husband, Wife and Pair Satisfaction and Performance," *Journal of Marriage and the Family* 38 (May 1976): 278–87.

71. Nye, "Personal Satisfactions," in Nye and Hoffman, *The Employed Mother in America*; Feld, "Feelings of Adjustment," in ibid.

72. Burke and Weir, "Relationship of Wives' Employment Status;" and J. A. Birnbaum, "Life Patterns, Personality Style and Self Esteem in Gifted Family Oriented and Career Committed Women," unpublished Ph.D. dissertation, University of Michigan, 1971.

73. Feld, "Feelings of Adjustment"; Blood, "The Husband-Wife Relationship"; H. Feldman and M. Feldman, "The Relationship Between the Family and Occupational Functioning in a Sample of Rural Women," Department of Human Development and Family Studies, Cornell University, 1973; David A. Gover, "Socioeconomic Differential in the Relationship Between Marital Adjustment and Wife's Employment Status," *Marriage and Family Living* 25 (November 1963): 452–56; and Ferree, "Working Class Jobs."

low work commitment clear.[74] It does appear, however, that wives who work from choice rather than economic necessity,[75] those whose husbands are favorable toward their employment,[76] and those who work part time[77] are happier with their marriages than are full-time housewives.

Clearly, working is a significantly different proposition for the educated woman with interesting work that she can pursue part time from choice, often with domestic help, from what it is for the woman working full time from necessity at a job that is often not inherently interesting or pleasant. Even if neither husband helps with housework, the woman described first has more time and resources to expend on her household, on her family, and on herself than does the second.

There are several possible reasons that no clear picture of marital satisfaction has emerged. First, marital satisfaction is obviously not easily measured with statistics. Moreover, a number of components, both positive and negative, make up satisfaction. For example, it may be that working wives report both greater tensions and greater satisfactions than do nonworking wives. Employed wives may experience work overload, particularly when husbands do not pitch in. Yet even wives with relatively uninteresting and unchallenging jobs report that their work provides them with a feeling of competence, a sense of contact with society, and a sense of self-determination.[78] These feelings may of themselves enrich the marital relationship.

Husbands. According to one study, husbands of working wives have reported lower marital satisfaction, greater job pressures, and lower mental and physical well-being than have husbands of full-time housewives. The researchers explain this reaction as a result of the husband's loss of dominance and power as well as their increased burden

---

74. For example, see Carl A. Ridley, "Exploring the Impact of Work Satisfaction and Involvement on Marital Interaction when both Partners are Employed," *Journal of Marriage and the Family* 35 (May 1973): 229–37; Constantina Safilios-Rothschild, "The Influence of the Wife's Degree of Work Commitment Upon Some Aspects of Family Organization and Dynamics," *Journal of Marriage and the Family* 32 (November 1970): 681–91.

75. Susan R. Orden and Norman M. Bradburn, "Working Wives and Marriage Happiness," *American Journal of Sociology* 74 (January 1969): 392–407.

76. Artie Gianopulos and Howard E. Mitchell, "Marital Disagreement in Working Wife Marriages as a Function of Husband's Attitude Toward Wife's Employment," *Journal of Marriage and the Family* 19 (November 1957): 373–78.

77. Orden and Bradburn, "Working Wives and Marriage Happiness"; Nye, "Personal Satisfactions"; and Ferree, "Working Class Jobs."

78. Ferree, "Working Class Jobs."

of household responsibilities.[79] This study, however, made no distinction between families in which wives were working from economic necessity and families in which wives worked from choice. Although this distinction is often artificial, because many women work for both reasons, sorting wives on this basis seems to matter. In a different study, husbands of wives who worked by choice reported greater marital satisfaction, as well as lower tension, than did husbands of full-time housewives.[80]

Why should female employment differentially affect the marital satisfaction of husbands and wives? The seeds for this discrepancy are apparent in a study of males in their senior year on a liberal college campus in 1969–70. Only 7 percent of these young men expressed willingness to significantly modify their own career and domestic roles in order to "facilitate their future wives' careers."[81] The remainder of the men expected to be the family breadwinners and qualified their acceptance of a wife's career with the expectation that it not interfere with their own careers or with the efficient operation of their homes. A majority assumed that a wife would be at home while preschool children were in the home, and the males were often explicit that the wife's career should be secondary in importance and in level of success. Given such assumptions even among well-educated males, it is not surprising that men are often somewhat discontented with the realities of life with an employed wife.

Evidence from other studies suggests that many husbands accept their wives' work grudgingly; that men may have more trouble than women do adapting to nonstereotypical roles; and therefore that men experience greater difficulties resolving the resulting stress.[82] Other researchers note that in going to work a woman is frequently expanding into a familiar role, one that is higher in status than that of homemaker, while a husband who assumes homemaking functions is adopting a role of lower status—a role that may strain not only his sense of status and identity but his feeling of competence as well.[83] Furthermore, a busy wife may not be able to provide the same level of physical and emotional support that a full-time homemaker can, so a husband may well come to feel he is losing out on all fronts.

79. Burke and Weir, "Relationship of Wives' Employment Status."

80. Orden and Bradburn, "Working Wives and Marriage Happiness."

81. Mirra Komarovsky, *Dilemmas of Masculinity* (New York: W. W. Norton and Co., 1976).

82. Rhona Rappoport, Robert Rappoport, and Michael Fogarty, *Sex, Career, and Marriage* (Beverly Hills, Calif.: Sage, 1971); and Ferree, "Working Class Jobs."

83. Burke and Weir, "Relationship of Wives' Employment Status."

Yet it can be argued that the strains of having both spouses employed are offset by numerous advantages, the most obvious of which is a second income. For many families, a wife's income raises the family to the middle-class status. A second salary may also provide a family with a cushion against the firing of the principal earner. A wife's income can provide a man the freedom to take time out to seek a better job, to return to school, to start his own business, or to be a full-time father for a while. A wife's income also can permit a man to decline to work overtime or to refuse a transfer. Removing sources of anxiety, frustration, and overwork from men's lives could, as already noted, even improve men's health or lengthen their life span. These advantages might compensate for some of the disruptions and tensions that are so often discussed.

Whether the overall effect is positive or negative probably varies greatly from man to man and from couple to couple. The one study that looks at the overall *balance* of satisfaction and tensions finds that husbands as well as wives are more satisfied if the wife is working by choice than they are if she is working out of necessity or if she is a full-time housewife.[84] Hence the net effect of having a working wife appears to be positive, under certain conditions.

Summary

The picture reported here is rather troubling—unequal participation in both the physical and emotional work of the home, employed wives taking on more responsibility and doing more work, but husbands not proving particularly responsive to wives' increased loads. Yet working wives seem to be at least as satisfied in their marriages as full-time housewives are, while husbands with working wives tend to be less satisfied in their marriages than husbands with nonworking wives are. Marital satisfaction for both partners seems to be enhanced by employment of the wife when she works by choice, works part time, or works when children are no longer of preschool age. Of course, a wife's working full time from economic necessity poses numerous strains to the family, in addition to the problem of work overload for the wife. Because economic support of a family is still more fundamental to a husband's role than to a wife's role, a husband's failure to provide an adequate income may mark him as inadequate, either in his own eyes or in his wife's eyes. A working wife may feel resentment if her husband does not do a share of the housework. These fac-

---

84. Orden and Bradburn, "Working Wives and Marriage Happiness."

tors may help explain the higher incidence of divorce among couples with a working wife.

Dissatisfied couples do not always divorce, however; nor are heavily overloaded wives always dissatisfied in their marriages. Clearly the situation is extremely complex. More sources of satisfaction than those that have been measured by social scientists, as well as more sources of solidarity, must be available to couples. Until the satisfactions and tensions provided by work and those provided within marriage are better understood, a complete picture of the effect of working on marital satisfaction will continue to elude researchers.

SUMMARY, POLICY IMPLICATIONS, AND CONCLUSIONS

Employment of women outside the home turns out to be neither a universal destroyer of marriage nor its universal salvation. The true situation is complex. On the one hand, young women who are working are likely to postpone marriage. This may have a positive effect. When they do marry, they will probably be more economically secure, more mature, better prepared for marriage, and hence less prone to divorce. On the other hand, statistics indicate that employed women have a higher probability of divorce, for reasons that are not clear. Employment may increase strain to the point that marriages break up. Or employment may provide persons contemplating divorce the possibility of self-support and self-respect, and thereby ease the path to divorce. A happily married working woman can share the economic burden of the household and substantially increase her family's economic well-being. Although husbands are increasingly sharing the burdens of decision making with their working wives, there is little evidence, unfortunately, that husbands are responding to their wives' employment by sharing the burden of household work.

Over the next decade marriage may not be easy, but there is no indication that individuals will avoid it. At some point in our lives nearly all of us will marry, and those of us who divorce will probably remarry.

Marriage is a private institution, and its burdens do not lend themselves to bureaucratic resolution. There are, however, some actions that the government could take to help reduce the strains experienced by two-earner couples. To the extent that women bear most of the burden at home because of their lesser earning power, equal pay and equal job opportunity for both men and women are absolutely essential. Increased availability of part-time jobs and flexible work schedules without loss of benefits, seniority, and prestige would enable men to participate more fully in family life, women to participate more fully in work life, and the two activities to be judged equal in importance. The increased representation of women in unions, in the skilled trades, in government training programs, and in important government positions might also bring about changes in attitudes toward women's and men's work. Changing the Social Security system to recognize wives' contributions in one-earner couples (through such policies as earnings sharing) would probably lead couples to think more carefully about their division of labor. Finally, a system of individual taxation would equalize the impact of each partner's earnings in contributing to the family's financial well-being. Once women's employment is viewed as appropriate and important and once wives' earnings are comparable to husbands' earnings, it will be less "natural" to simply assume that in a two-earner couple the wife should make all of the adjustments and accommodations.

The employment of women outside the home can benefit their husbands, their families, and the women themselves. Will these potential benefits be fully realized over the next decade? Certainly many couples have already learned to enjoy their increased incomes and the sharing of family roles. Moreover, evidence of increased flexibility and of some attitude change is starting to surface. Whether change will be general is hard to predict, but the pressures to change behavior, if not ideology, are real. We anticipate that these pressures will, for many individuals, eventually combine with their desires for compatible and happy marriages to produce greater satisfaction and harmony.

Chapter 5

WOMEN AND THEIR CHILDREN

KRISTIN A. MOORE and SANDRA L. HOFFERTH

The rearing of children is one of the principal tasks of any society. Since women traditionally have been the child rearers, the influx of mothers into the labor force has generated great concern over the care and nurture of children whose mothers work. Of all the issues associated with the increasing participation of women in the labor force, questions about the upbringing of the next generation have caused some of the most intense controversy and unresolved anxiety.

There is widespread recognition of the challenge implicit in combining child rearing with the workload of a two-earner household, and the demands on single parents who work are even greater. Given these heavy demands, questions have been raised as to whether working parents find time to interact with their children and share their concerns, much less play with them. As the birthrate has dipped below replacement level, some people have even worried that women are rejecting motherhood entirely in favor of other roles. The possible effects of women's increasing employment on fertility rates and family

125

size concern not only would-be grandparents but also business and government leaders attempting to plan for the future. In view of the difficulty of simultaneously fulfilling two such demanding roles as worker and parent, it would not seem surprising if an increasing number of young people "opt out" of parenthood, or if some working parents perform inadequately as parents. A major question to be considered here, therefore, is whether there is any evidence that either of these trends is occurring.

Another question relates to the kinds of day care working parents rely on and the degree of satisfaction parents have with the care their children receive. The supply of high-quality day care services relative to the number of children who will need those services should be an issue of concern to everyone who does not want to see children placed in marginal child care arrangements.

Perhaps the most emotional issue of all relating to maternal employment is that of the effects of day care on children. Policy makers and parents alike worry that employment of mothers may have negative consequences for their children's development. Indeed, the effects and adequacy of day care are issues with a very large constituency, ranging from parents and feminists to child development specialists and officials attempting to make work requirements part of the welfare system. What are the effects of maternal employment in general and day care in particular on children? Are there particular circumstances under which maternal employment is bad for children? Are there policies that can or ought to be implemented by government or business to improve life for working parents and their children? This chapter addresses these important questions, and associated issues.

CHANGES IN CHILDBEARING PATTERNS

Except for the decade following World War II, the birthrate in the United States has been declining steadily throughout this century (see Figure 11). Rather than indicating a trend toward childlessness, however, declining birthrates appear to reflect preferences for smaller family sizes. Women born in 1880 had three or four surviving children, compared with the two-child average expected for women born in 1950. Although contemporary families are small, nearly all women express a desire for some children.[1] The proportion of women who remain childless to age forty has dropped from 22 percent among women born in the 1880s to 10 percent among those born in the 1930s. This change is probably the result of the greater fecundity of recent

1. U.S. Department of Commerce, Bureau of the Census, "Fertility of American Women: June 1976," *Current Population Reports*, series P-20, no. 308, 1977, Table 5.

FIGURE 11

BIRTHRATE (PER 1,000 POPULATION), U.S. 1890-1977

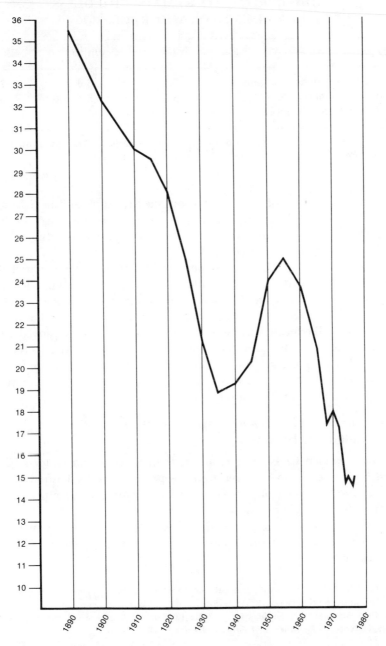

Source: Statistical Abstract, 1975 .
         Vital Statistics, 1975, 1977 .

Table 16

PERCENTAGE OF WOMEN AGES 18–34 REPORTING
THEY EXPECT TO REMAIN CHILDLESS,
BY EDUCATION AND RACE, 1976

Education	Total	White	Black
Not a high school graduate	6.9	6.9	7.6
High school graduate	8.5	8.7	6.6
College, 1 year or more	14.4	14.4	11.4

Source: U.S. Bureau of the Census, "Fertility of American Women: June 1976," *Current Population Reports*, series P-20, no. 308, 1977, Table 5.

generations (a result of better nutrition, medical care, and health) and of the fact that a larger proportion of women have married. Only a slight increase in voluntary childlessness is expected for those born in the 1950s and marrying in the 1970s.[2]

Since the turn of the century, better-educated women in particular have been more likely to be childless than have women with less schooling[3] and it does not appear that young, well-educated women today will differ from their predecessors in this respect (see Table 16).

Because well-educated women are more likely to be employed than are their less highly educated age peers, it may be the perceived conflict between market and home work that has in part produced this association. What effect might increasing rates of female employment have on fertility in coming years?

The Relationship between Employment of Women and Childbearing Patterns

Working women have fewer children than nonworking women have. This basic association has been found repeatedly in the United States. Family size between groups may differ, but within each group working women have smaller families. For example, fertility varies with women's age and race, but within each age-race category working women have lower fertility than nonworking women have, as Table 17 illustrates.

---

2. Paul C. Glick, "Updating the Life Cycle of the Family," *Journal of Marriage and the Family* 39 (February 1977): 3–15.

3. Paul Matessich, "Childlessness and Its Correlates in Historical Perspective: A Research Note," *The Journal of Family History*, 1978.

Table 17

CHILDREN EVER BORN TO WOMEN AGES 25–44
IN 1976, PER 1,000 WOMEN

	White	Black
Women ages 25–34		
In labor force	1,273	1,837
Not in labor force	2,151	2,658
Women ages 35–44		
In labor force	2,642	3,356
Not in labor force	3,142	3,998

Source: U.S. Bureau of the Census, "Fertility of American Women: June 1976," *Current Population Reports*, series P-20, no. 308, 1977, Table 5.

While this association can be readily documented, it is not so easily explained. Four principal explanations have been proposed, and some evidence can be marshaled to support each. (1) It has been argued that it is the presence of children that makes women less able or willing to take employment outside of the home.[4] (2) Conversely, it has been contended that women restrict childbearing if they want to be more involved in paid employment.[5] (3) Another line of reasoning suggests that some outside or antecedent factor, such as family background or attitudes, actually explains both employment and the number of children a woman bears.[6] (4) Most persuasively, some researchers have explored the idea of mutual causation. According to this thesis, women (or couples) make decisions about employment and childbearing at the same time.[7]

Which of these explanations for the association between women's employment and childbearing finds acceptance is not a trivial issue.

4. Ronald Freedman, Pascal K. Whelpton, and Arthur A. Campbell, *Family Planning, Sterility, and Population Growth* (New York: McGraw Hill, 1959).

5. Judith Blake, "Demographic Science and Redirection of Population Policy," *Journal of Chronic Diseases* 18 (1965): 1181–1200.

6. Jacob Mincer, "Market Price Opportunity, Costs, and Income Effects," in C. F. Christ, ed., *Measurement in Economics: Studies in Mathematical Economics and Econometrics in Memory of Yehuda Grunfeld* (Palo Alto: Stanford University Press, 1963), pp. 67–82.

7. Linda J. Waite and Ross M. Stolzenberg, "Intended Childbearing and Labor Force Participation of Young Women: Insights from Nonrecursive Models," *American Sociological Review* 41 (April 1976): 235–52.

Only if it is found that paid employment for women has an important impact on how many children women have can we infer that the increased employment of young women might have an impact on future U.S. population size and age structure. Furthermore, the reason for the relationship between employment and fertility is as important as the fact of an association. For example, if employment and motherhood are seen as inherently incompatible, perhaps because of the drain on emotional energy and time that each entails, then increased female employment is much more likely to lead to reduced rates of childbearing than would be the case if the link were simply due to inadequate child care facilities or social disapproval of working mothers.

The reasons suggested to explain an association between women's employment and childbearing rates are both legion and susceptible to change. The reasons noted by one researcher range from the heavy time demands of child care and the lack of help received from other household members to tastes acquired while working at nonfamilial activities, and the power over decision making that an income-earning wife exercises.[8] Although new, easy-care models of children are not known to be in the development stage, other changes may reduce the perceived incompatibility of parenthood with maternal employment.

Trends toward further mechanization of housework, greater participation in housework and child rearing by fathers, flexible scheduling of work hours, the availability of part-time employment, and paid parental leave after childbirth may make employment more manageable for mothers. The increasing acceptance of convenience foods, restaurant meals, apartment or condominium living, and day care for young children may also make motherhood and paid employment more compatible. These changes suggest that the increasing employment of women is not likely to result in further declines in birthrates.

Actually, there are many reasons why working women and their husbands will continue to want children. Children provide variety, joy, purpose, novelty, and even feelings of power and creativity in ways that most jobs do not. To the extent that employment and success may threaten women's feelings of femininity, motherhood provides a way to restore that image. Thus, it seems very unlikely that the advent of generally available and effective fertility control will divide women into childless workers and homemaker brood mothers. Most young women expect to have children and most also expect to

---

8. Robert Weller, "Wives' Employment and Cumulative Family Size in the United States, 1970 and 1960," *Demography* 14 (February 1977): 43–65.

Table 18

PERCENTAGE DISTRIBUTION OF WOMEN AGES 18–34 BY NUMBER OF LIFETIME BIRTHS EXPECTED, BY RACE

	Total	White	Black
None	10.1%	10.3%	7.9%
One	12.3	11.6	18.5
Two	46.7	48.2	34.8
Three	19.8	19.7	21.6
Four or more	11.0	10.3	17.2

Source: U.S. Department of Commerce, Bureau of the Census, "Fertility of American Women, June 1976," *Current Population Reports*, series P-20, no. 308, 1977, Table 5, p. 15.

work. Only 3 percent of the seventeen-year-old girls surveyed in the National Assessment of Educational Progress in 1973–74 selected housewife as their first choice for a career,[9] and only about 10 percent of young women expect to be childless[10] (see Table 18). Apparently young women are planning to combine the two roles. This suggests that future couples probably will have families, but small families, which is exactly what young women are telling Census Bureau survey-ors. Nearly 80 percent of all young women ages eighteen to thirty-four in 1976 said they expected to have between one and three children, with 47 percent expecting two children.

Yet fertility differentials by employment status are not likely to vanish. For a variety of reasons some families will choose to "specialize" in childbearing, and their desire for children will affect the mothers' labor force participation. Similarly, women with especially good jobs—interesting work and high pay—are likely to have a stronger commitment to work, because employment is more satisfying for them than for women with less attractive jobs. If such careers re-quire long hours and much responsibility, and penalize women for any time stolen from career for family, then career women will probably continue to have smaller families.

In sum, although changes are always possible, the Census Bureau

9. I. V. Mullis, S. J. Oldefendt, and D. L. Phillips, *What Students Know and Can Do: Profiles of Three Age Groups* (Denver: National Assessment of Educational Progress, 1977).

10. U.S. Department of Commerce, Bureau of the Census, "Fertility of American Women: June 1976," *Current Population Reports*, series P-20, no. 308, 1977.

fertility projections seem highly reasonable. Most people will have children, but they will have relatively small families. Fertility differentials may continue to decrease, but they seem unlikely to disappear altogether. To the extent that employment and child rearing remain incompatible, working women will probably tend to have somewhat smaller families than nonworking women have; but the increased employment of women does not seem likely to usher in an era of childlessness. Women's employment will, however, affect the way in which children are reared and this topic is discussed in the next section.

DAY CARE

Using Census Bureau projections, it is possible to develop estimates of the number of children who will have employed mothers in 1990—in other words, the number of children who will need some kind of alternate care. A substantial increase in such children is likely. Even though the fertility of individual women has been declining, the number of preschool children with working mothers is likely to continue to increase throughout the 1980s, for two reasons: First, the number of mothers will increase as the large baby boom generation of the 1950s and early 1960s enters its peak childbearing years. In addition, because the labor force participation rates of mothers are expected to continue to increase, the proportion of children who need care will increase. In 1977, there were an estimated 17.1 million preschool children (under age six) in the United States, of whom 6.4 million had working mothers (Table 19). How are children of working mothers being cared for now? What changes should be anticipated and planned for?

What we know about the care of the children of today's working mothers can help us project the day care needs of the nearly 10.5 million children who may have working mothers by 1990. Unfortunately, we know very little about day care today. Surveys have been notoriously poor in ferreting out the kinds of arrangements on which parents rely. Many working mothers, for example, depend on several types of arrangements. Some do not consider nursery schools as day care, even though nursery schools may serve that purpose as well as others. Other working mothers maintain that they themselves remain the principal caretakers for their children, even when others are temporarily in charge. The best estimate is that between 10 percent and 15 percent of all preschool children of working mothers are cared

Table 19

NUMBERS AND PERCENTAGES OF CHILDREN UNDER AGE 6 WITH MOTHERS IN THE LABOR FORCE

(Estimated for 1970, 1975, and 1977; projected for 1990)

	1970	1975	1977	1990
		(in thousands)		
Number of total children under age 6	19,606	18,134	17,117	23,331
Number of children under age 6 with mothers in the labor force	5,590	6,512	6,431	10,453
Percentage of children under age 6 with mothers in the labor force	28.5%	35.9%	37.6%	44.8%

Note: The projected number of children under age 6 with mothers in the labor force in 1990 is based on the projections of the number of mothers in the labor force reported in Table 1 and the assumption that the average number of children under age 6 among working mothers with any children under age 6 will not change. In 1977, this figure was approximately 1.2 for mothers with husbands present and 1.1 for other mothers.

Sources: Estimates of the total number of children under age 6 and the number of children under age 6 with working mothers from 1970 to 1977 are from the Current Population Surveys, taken by the Census Bureau in March of each year. These are reported in the following publications: For 1970–75: Allyson Sherman Grossman, "Almost Half of All Children Have Mothers in the Labor Force," *Monthly Labor Review* 100 (June 1977): 41–44. For 1977: Allyson Sherman Grossman, "Children of Working Mothers," *Monthly Labor Review* 101 (January 1978): 30–33. Projections of the total number of children under age 6 are taken from U.S. Department of Commerce, Bureau of the Census, "Projections of the Population of the United States: 1977 to 2050," *Current Population Reports*, series P-25, no. 704, 1977.

for in day care centers.[11] The rest are cared for individually or in small groups in their own homes or in the home of a caretaker who may or may not be related to the child.

Although 10 percent to 15 percent is a relatively small proportion of all preschool children, this figure represents an approximate doubling of the use of day care centers over the past decade. In 1965 fewer than 6 percent of the preschool children of working mothers were cared for in day care centers.[12]

---

11. U.S. Department of Health, Education, and Welfare, *The Appropriateness of the Federal Interagency Day Care Requirements: Report of Findings and Recommendations* (Washington, D.C.: U.S. Government Printing Office, 1978).

12. Seth Low and Pearl Spindler, *Child Care Arrangements of Working Mothers in the United States* (Washington, D.C.: U.S. Government Printing Office, 1968).

These figures, however, are deceptive. One problem is that, because few centers and no nursery schools accept children under the age of three, the relevant population is probably not all preschool children but only the three- to five-years-olds. In 1977 there were approximately 18,300 day care centers in the United States, with total enrollment estimated at 900,000 children.[13] This figure amounts to half the number of the three- to five-year-old children of working mothers in 1977 (about one-quarter of all three- to five-year-olds). Of course not all children in center care have working mothers; nor are all children in center care between three and five years of age. Day care centers do, however, provide care for a substantial portion of the three- to five-year-old children of working mothers at the present time.

A second problem with traditional estimation techniques is that nursery schools are not generally recognized as a form of day care. Enrollments in nursery schools and kindergartens have grown substantially during the past decade. In the mid-1960s, fewer than one-third of all three- to five-year-olds were enrolled. In 1976 almost half were enrolled for at least part of the day in a nursery school or kindergarten—26 percent of the three-year-olds, 48 percent of the four-year-olds, and 82 percent of the five-year-old children of working mothers.[14] Even though working mothers may not acknowledge what preschools provide as "day care," preschool attendance by their children may help some working mothers solve their day care problems. The substantial increase in preschool enrollments that these figures represent indicates widespread change in the care of children. The increase in preschool attendance of children, however, appears to have had little connection with the increased employment of women outside the home. Children of working and nonworking mothers are equally likely to be enrolled, although the children of working mothers are more likely to be enrolled for the full day than are children of non-working mothers.

Thus the trend throughout the past decade has been toward increased group care, often with an educational component, for three- to five-year-olds. In the next decade, group care of even younger children—already relatively common in other countries—may come

---

13. Abt Associates, "National Day Care Study: Preliminary Findings and Their Implications," Cambridge, Mass., 1978, p. 21.

14. U.S. Department of Commerce, Bureau of the Census, "Nursery School and Kindergarten Enrollment of Children and Labor Force Status of Their Mothers: October 1967 to October 1976," Current Population Reports, series P-20, no. 318, 1978.

of age in the United States.[15] What factors have contributed to the increased use of group care for the three- to five-year-olds and what factors can be expected to affect the use of group care, especially for the under-threes, in the future?

Day Care's Cost and the Relationship of Cost to Kinds of Care Available

The relative costs of various kinds of care constitute the most important factor in determining both demand for and supply of child care facilities. The day care choice of parents with relatively high incomes appears to be full-time care in their own homes; therefore, we assume that most parents would purchase such care if they could, at least for their youngest children. Although the cost of day care in general has not increased beyond the average rate of inflation in the economy (see Table 20), the subsidization of care in centers since the late 1960s has lowered the relative cost of such care to parents, no doubt contributing to its use. Care priced on a sliding scale can relieve even middle-income parents from paying the full cost of care, so more of them are turning to group care for their children.

The apparently increased difficulty of locating individual day care providers at reasonable cost may also have contributed to the increasing use of group care. Little is known about these providers who work within their own homes or go to the homes of their clients; most are probably not licensed, and their clientele is usually located by word of mouth. Thus it is impossible to know how many of these individual providers there are, what their motivations are, how profitable child care is, or what type of care is being provided. The providers' pay, however, appears to be low.[16] Hence women who have been providing child care at home—their own homes or their clients'—may view participation in the formal labor force as a promising alternative to their previous activity. As women enter the labor force in increasing numbers, the pool of day care providers may decline or their price may rise above the level mothers are willing or able to pay.[17] The wages

---

15. Sheila Kamerman and Alfred J. Kahn, "European Family Policy Currents: The Question of Families with Very Young Children," Columbia University School of Social Work, preliminary draft, 1976.

16. Arden Hall and Samuel Weiner, "The Supply of Day Care Services in Denver and Seattle," Center for the Study of Welfare Policy, Research Memorandum 33, Stanford Research Institute, Menlo Park, Calif., June 1977.

17. Richard L. Shortlidge, Jr., and Patricia Brito, "How Women Arrange for the Care of Their Children While They Work: A Study of Child Care Arrangements, Costs, and Preferences in 1971," Center for Human Resource Research (Columbus: Ohio State University, January 1977).

Table 20

DAY CARE ARRANGEMENTS: MEAN PAYMENT BY HOUSEHOLDS PAYING FOR CHILD CARE BY TYPE OF ARRANGEMENT AND SURVEY YEAR IN WHICH DATA WERE COLLECTED

(*$ in Year of Data Collection*)

Type of Arrangement	1964 (Low and Spindler, 1968) Weekly	1970 (Westat, 1971) Weekly	1974 (Hall and Weiner, 1977) Seattle Weekly	Seattle Hourly	Denver Weekly	Denver Hourly	1975 (Unco, 1975) Weekly	1975 Hourly
Relative:								
Child's home	—	—	—	—	—	—	$10.52	$0.34
Other's home	—	—	—	—	—	—	14.24	0.38
Nonrelative:								
Child's home	$5–$9	—	$ 7.63	$0.46	$ 6.52	$0.45	7.78	0.52
Other's home	5–9	—	—	—	—	—	16.07	0.55
Unlicensed	—	—	16.22	0.54	14.73	0.47	—	—
Licensed	—	—	18.86	0.54	17.22	0.47	—	—
Day care center:								
Nonprofit	10+	$13	—	—	—	—	19.56	0.60
Private	—	—	10.98	0.47	7.37	0.33	—	—
Public	—	—	13.85	0.63	10.21	0.48	—	—
For profit	—	16	15.62	0.50	11.98	0.60	—	—
Nursery school	—	—	—	—	—	—	14.59	0.67

Sources: Low and Spindler, *Child Care Arrangements of Working Mothers in the United States*; Westat Research Inc.; "Day Care Survey 1970: Summary Report and Basic Analysis," Westinghouse Learning Corporation, 1971; Arden Hall and Samuel Weiner, "The Supply of Day Care Services in Denver and Seattle," Center for the Study of Welfare Policy, Research Memorandum 33 (Menlo Park, Calif.: Stanford Research Institute, June 1977); Unco Inc., *National Childcare Consumer Study: 1975*, 4 vols.

of working women, the cost of informal child care, and the relative cost of group care will be important in determining what kind of care children will receive during the next decade.

Other Factors Affecting Demand for and Availability of Child Care

Several factors other than cost have affected and appear likely to affect the demand for different types of child care and the availability of such care during the next ten years. First are demographic factors, particularly changes in family structure and birthrates. Employment conditions, attitudes of parents, and public policies also have offsetting or multiplying effects on the need for and the availability of day care.

Demographic Factors. Female-headed families and small families are more likely to use licensed centers and homes than are two-parent and large extended families.[18] There has been an enormous increase in the number of families headed by one parent (usually the mother) in the last decade.[19] As a result, the proportion of children living with both parents has declined. In 1968, for example, 87 percent of all children under age six were living with both natural parents (Table 21). By 1977 that proportion had dropped to 81 percent. These figures mask enormous race differences. Fewer than half (44 percent) of all black preschool children were living with both natural parents in 1977, compared with 87 percent of white preschoolers. Most of these black and white children living with only one of their natural parents were living with their mothers. In 1977, 15 percent of all preschool children were in female-headed families (10 percent of whites, 41 percent of blacks). Fewer than 1 percent were in families headed by single males.

Most of the increase in the number of families headed by women has been found to be attributable to divorce and separation, with a small part due to out-of-wedlock childbearing.[20] In recent years the divorce rate has slowed its rapid rise, but future trends in divorce are, of course, unpredictable. At present, 40 percent of all new marriages are expected to end in divorce, and from one-third to one-half of all children born in the 1970s are expected to spend at least a few years in a family with no adult male present before they reach the age of eighteen.[21]

---

18. Hall and Weiner, "The Supply of Day Care Services in Denver and Seattle."

19. Heather Ross and Isabel V. Sawhill, *Time of Transition: The Growth of Families Headed by Women* (Washington, D.C.: The Urban Institute, 1975), pp. 21–24.

20. Ibid.

21. Paul C. Glick and Arthur J. Norton, "Marrying, Divorcing and Living Together in the U.S. Today," *Population Bulletin* 32 (1977): 5.

Table 21

FAMILY RELATIONSHIP AND PRESENCE OF PARENTS,
CHILDREN UNDER AGE 6, BY RACE, 1968 AND 1977

All Races	1968		1977	
	Number	Percentage	Number	Percentage
Total	22,932	100.0	18,620	100.0
In families	22,809	99.5	18,509	99.4
Living with both parents	19,918	86.8	15,018	80.6
Living with mother only	2,138	9.3	2,745	14.7
Living with father only	109	0.5	128	0.5
Living with neither parent	645	2.8	619	3.3
Not in families	123	0.5	111	0.6
White				
Total	19,129	100.0	15,332	100.0
In families	19,050	99.6	15,263	99.5
Living with both parents	17,591	91.9	13,388	87.0
Living with mother only	1,178	6.2	1,546	10.1
Living with father only	67	0.3	102	0.7
Living with neither parent	213	1.1	226	1.5
Not in families	79	0.4	69	0.4
Black				
Total	3,487	100.0	2,845	100.0
In families	3,450	98.9	2,809	98.7
Living with both parents	2,069	59.3	1,237	43.5
Living with mother only	916	26.3	1,162	40.8
Living with father only	42	1.2	26	0.9
Living with neither parent	424	12.1	385	13.5
Not in families	37	1.1	36	1.3

Sources: U.S. Bureau of the Census, "Marital Status and Family Status, March 1968," *Current Population Reports*, series P-20, no. 187, 1969; and U.S. Bureau of the Census, "Marital Status and Living Arrangements: March 1977," *Current Population Reports*, series P-20, no. 323, 1978.

Children in female-headed families, as in other families, are most in need of day care if the mother works outside the home. In 1977, more than half of all female family heads were in the work force.[22]

22. Beverly L. Johnson, "Women Who Head Families, 1970–77: Their Numbers Rose, Income Lagged," *Monthly Labor Review* 101 (February 1978): 32–37.

Therefore, factors affecting the growth of families headed by women should affect the growth in the number of preschool children of employed female family heads. If the divorce rate fails to decline, the demand for centers and licensed homes should continue to rise, as single-parent families are more likely than two-parent families are to use such care for their young children.

There has also been a trend toward smaller families. Census Bureau projections are based on the assumption that current generations of young women will bear an average of 2.1 children by the time they finish their childbearing.[23] A much smaller proportion of families in the future will have three or more children than was the case in the past. If in addition to being fewer in number the children are closely spaced, it is unlikely that both preschool and adolescent children will be present at the same time. The likelihood of using in-home care is reduced if adolescent children are not available to care for their younger siblings before and after school. Parents can also better afford tuition or fees if they have only one or two children. For all these reasons, we might expect an increase in the use of centers and licensed homes to result from declining family sizes.

Families are small also because they are less and less likely to consist of more than parent and child generations. In 1969, for example, about 89 percent of all families with their own children were "nuclear" families; fewer than 7 percent consisted of three or more generations.[24] The increasing popularity of separate residences for the elderly removes a traditional source of child care for mothers, and greater geographic mobility separates them from kin even as neighbors. Continued trends toward the nuclear family structure will probably result in greater reliance on center and other types of group care.

Demographic changes are likely to affect the supply of caretakers of various ages at the same time that those changes affect both the number of school-age children in need of care and parental preferences as to the type of care. As birthrates decline, the proportion of elderly persons increases relative to younger age groups. The increased number of senior citizens coupled with the increased participation of young women in the labor force may result in a shift toward older caretakers both as individual care providers and as day care center workers. Of course, the large number of young women and men in their twenties

23. U.S. Department of Commerce, Bureau of the Census, "Projections of the Population of the United States: 1976 to 2050," *Current Population Reports*, series P-25, no. 601, 1975.

24. U.S. Department of Commerce, Bureau of the Census, "Family Composition," *1970 Census of Population, Subject Reports*, no. PC(2)-4A, 1972.

and thirties available for employment may make it harder for older or younger persons to get a job of any sort; so this competition for employment may increase the attractiveness of being an individual day care provider. In addition, the decreased number of school-age children has made it difficult for teachers to find work, a situation that is expected to become worse, not better.[25] The surplus of trained and certified teachers may be increasingly funneled into day care or into "preschool education." At present, certification levels for licensed day care providers are being upgraded, and some states (Maryland, for example) are already providing a half-day of formal schooling for four-year-olds.

Employment Conditions. Changes in the structure of work have been slow to develop, but they would have substantial impact on the need for day care. Mothers working part time are much less likely to use day care centers than are mothers employed full time.[26] Increased flexibility of work hours (flexitime) and increased access to part-time employment would allow parents in two-earner families to share child care. Cooperative day care arrangements among neighbors, friends, and relatives would also be facilitated.

The impact that flexible scheduling of work hours would have on the use of day care by two-earner families depends on the willingness of fathers to share in child care. There is some evidence that fathers do take a larger share of the care of their children when wives are employed. In 1965 almost half the young children of working mothers who were cared for principally by a parent were cared for by the father while the mother was working.[27] Analysis of more recent data indicates that in 1973 in one-quarter of all two-earner families the parents split the care of their children during work hours.[28] The impact of flexible scheduling on one-parent, one-earner families is less clear-cut. Flexible scheduling may help female family heads arrange day care and take care of emergencies, but the same number of hours of care would be needed as the number of hours of work.

---

25. Susan Abramowitz and Stuart Rosenfeld, eds., *Declining Enrollments: The Challenge of the Coming Decade* (Washington, D.C.: National Institute of Education, 1975).

26. Low and Spindler, *Child Care Arrangements of Working Mothers*; and U.S. Department of Commerce, Bureau of the Census, "Daytime Care of Children: October 1974 and February 1975," *Current Population Reports*, series P-20, no. 298, 1976.

27. Low and Spindler, *Child Care Arrangements of Working Mothers*.

28. Katherine Dickinson, "Child Care," in Greg J. Duncan and James Morgan, eds., *Five Thousand Families*, vol. 3 (Ann Arbor: Institute for Social Research, University of Michigan, 1975).

Increased wages for women working outside the home might encourage some women to move out of marginal employment as home day care providers. In addition, creation of part-time and flexitime job opportunities or provision of day care at the work place may encourage more women to work outside their homes rather than to provide in-home care for other people's children. Increased employment opportunities also would serve as an incentive to switch from informal to formal market work.[29]

Attitudes and Ideology. The importance of attitudes and ideology in determining both labor force participation and choice of day care arrangements should not be underestimated. Changes in attitudes regarding the desirability of center care for young children, the father's role in child rearing, and the relative roles the family and other institutions should take in the rearing of the young can be expected to affect the demand for group versus individual care. Attitudinal change has been very slow, but demographic changes influence attitudes. As female family heads and women with fewer children become more numerous, for example, their views (presumably favoring group day care modes) may become more influential.

Along with changes in economic incentives and disincentives for women to select various occupations, attitudes regarding the appropriate caretakers for children and the appropriate roles for women may affect providers. Working in another's home, for example, may be seen as demeaning, whereas working in a formal day care center at competitive wages may be perfectly acceptable. Such attitude changes would reduce the supply of care provided by baby-sitters, housekeepers, and maids. A logical result might be the professionalization of child caretakers, and concomitant increases in their wages and salaries.

Public Policies. Direct federal expenditures on child care amounted to some $2.5 billion in fiscal year 1977, but public policies also affect demand and supply in ways other than direct expenditures. Public policies that lower the cost to the parent and raise the quality of group care are likely to increase the use of such care. Welfare policies that require women to work or that provide benefits below minimum living

---

29. In Sweden, for example, good job opportunities and good wages coupled with subsidized day care have made it more desirable for women to move into the labor force, even if women have to pay for the day care, than to work as in-home day care providers outside the formal labor force. However, women in Sweden have been encouraged to work. Social attitudes may encourage both working and collective day care, and discourage even the wealthy from hiring housekeepers. See Siv Gustafsson, *Cost-Benefit Analysis of Early Childhood Care and Education* (Stockholm: The Industrial Institute for Economic and Social Research, 1978).

standards will force women to work and also increase the need for day care. Conversely, policies that promote flexible scheduling of work and extended pregnancy or parental leave for women and men may decrease the demand for group modes of care. Besides direct regulations and requirements, such as for the receipt of welfare benefits or food stamps, various government policies can encourage mothers of young children to enter or stay out of the labor force. Policies that provide a public service job only to the principal earner in two-parent families (as in proposed welfare reform legislation) or that offer generous maternal work leave while children are young (as in some European countries) should reduce demand for all types of day care. Finally, tax policies that allow deductions for expenditures on certain types of day care and not others will increase the reliance on the specified types of care.

Federal funds serve as the principal source of support for research and evaluation. Decline of federal interest in (and funding for) early childhood educational programs coincided with the failure of various research efforts to find lasting benefits from Head Start.[30] Recent research that indicates considerable long-term benefits of early education may once again raise interest in such programs and increase demand by parents for such care.[31]

On the supply side, public funding has been very important in the development of nonprofit day care centers, and the subsidization of low-income families continues to support such centers. The direction of future funding will be critical to the future supply of such care. The federal role in setting standards for facilities and qualifications of staff members also affects the cost and price of group care, and the willingness and ability of providers to enter or remain in the field. Rigorous enforcement of licensing requirements may raise the price and lower the current supply of low-cost care in day care homes as well.

Social Security, income tax, and welfare rules can also affect the supply of in-home providers. Earnings limits for recipients of Aid to Families of Dependent Children (AFDC) restrict the amount of money such women might earn by baby-sitting or by providing home day care. Older individuals who might serve as caretakers would find their Social Security benefits considerably reduced; as a result, these people would be discouraged from providing day care.

---

30. Gilbert V. Steiner, *The Children's Cause* (Washington, D.C.: Brookings Institution, 1976).

31. U.S. Department of Health, Education, and Welfare, *The Persistence of Preschool Effects: A Long Term Follow-Up of Fourteen Infant and Preschool Experiments* (Washington, D.C.: U.S. Government Printing Office, 1977).

Conversely, one of the advantages to provision of in-home day care is that it is an activity through which individuals may evade income taxes and Social Security tax payments. As long as a person cares for only a few children and does not advertise, the chances that anyone will question his or her tax status are minimal. Many married women may find no short-term economic advantage in working outside their homes, especially if they must pay for child care and if the extra income brought into the household increases the family's total tax burden. Moreover, the present Social Security system is so structured that the benefits most married women would accrue based on their own earnings outside the home are lower than those they would receive as wives or widows without any contribution to the system at all. Given recent legislation which will substantially increase Social Security withholdings over the next several years, the benefits of formal labor force participation may decline even further. Thus, the advantages of staying out of the formal labor force may increase as time passes. Increased surveillance by the Internal Revenue Service and crackdown on small-income recipients, though unlikely, would greatly decrease the supply of low-cost day care arrangements.

Summary

The number of young children needing day care is expected to increase both because more babies are being born and because more mothers are working. Even if finding day care for their children does not seem to be a major barrier deterring mothers from entering the labor force now, day care may become a problem in the future, when parents will probably place increasing reliance on group forms of care. The availability and quality of such care will depend in part on public policy over the next decade.

As a result of these trends, it has become increasingly important that the effects of maternal employment and the different types of day care on children be studied. The next section provides an overview of the research that has been done in this field and suggests some factors that might help determine the effects of day care on the children of working mothers.

THE EFFECTS OF MATERNAL EMPLOYMENT AND DAY CARE ON CHILDREN AND FAMILIES

There has been considerable debate over the effects of maternal employment and day care on children. Early researchers suggested that the well-being of children inevitably suffers whenever their mothers become employed, a conclusion that was widely accepted for some years. The limitations of the research on which this conclusion was based, however, have recently been recognized. Documentation of apathy and retardation among institutionalized children[32] was inappropriately extrapolated to the children of women who merely left their children each day to go to work. Routine day care in a familiar setting with familiar people should not be expected to have the same consequences as custodial care in a residential institution, and it does not. Much of the work done on the consequences of child care has been similarly misdirected or crudely done. But we now have a substantial number of studies that are relatively consistent in their findings.

The essential answer to the query "Does maternal employment—and day care—harm children?" seems to be "No, not typically; but it depends." The caveat is important, because it acknowledges that the last word is not in, and emphasizes what should be obvious: children, families, and types of day care vary enormously.

The effects of substitute care on children depend, first, on the quality of that care. Second, they depend on the mother's reasons for working; for example, the child of a restless, unhappy homemaker is likely to be better off being cared for by a substitute, with the mother employed outside the home, while just the opposite may be true with respect to the child of a dissatisfied working mother.[33] Third, the effects probably depend on characteristics of the child, although we have little evidence on this matter. (An especially sickly or aggressive child, for example, might be rejected by caretakers and bounced from one to another; as a result, such a child might have difficulty in forming attachments.) Fourth, a family's social milieu may influence the effects of day care; a mother whose husband, relatives, and community continually criticize her for working may feel guilty about her job. To suggest that those in her environment ought to be more supportive

---

32. J. A. Bowlby, "Some Pathological Processes Engendered by Early Mother-Child Separation," in M. Senn, *Infancy and Childhood* (New York: Josiah Macy, Jr. Foundation, 1953); and R. A. Spitz, "Hospitalism: An Inquiry into the Genesis of Psychiatric Conditions in Early Childhood," *Psychoanalytic Studies of the Child* 11 (1945): 53–74.

33. One study that differentiated between homemakers and employed mothers who were either satisfied or dissatisfied emphasized the importance of distinguishing between women on the basis of their preferences. They found that dissatisfied homemakers scored lowest on adequacy of mothering, while satisfied homemakers scored highest; working mothers scored in between. See M. R. Yarrow, P. Scott, L. DeLeeuw, and C. Heinig, "Child-rearing in Families of Working and Nonworking Mothers," *Sociometry* 25 (1962): 122–40.

ignores the impact that the lack of support can have. The mother may come to resent her children's presence, whereas the children may come to believe that their mother would not work if she really loved her children.

Another factor that forces us to qualify our conclusion is the inadequacy of the available research. Some research studies have used poor research methods; samples have been small and controls too inadequate with regard to factors such as class, sex of child, mother's type of job, mother's reasons for working, hours worked, and so on. Because any employment effects almost certainly vary by class, parents' work schedule, and family structure, results should not be extrapolated without extreme caution. Moreover, it should be noted that most studies published to date have been based on research done before the recent revolutionary changes in attitudes and behavior. Whether greater acceptance of maternal employment has produced relaxed parents or lax parents is not yet known.

These cautions, and presumably others, should temper our desire to offer the last word on a complex subject. Having thus hedged, however, we can report that the overwhelming consensus of different studies is that most children of working mothers seem to develop normally and well.[34] The several differences that have been found will be emphasized here, so *it should be understood that most studies find very few differences.*

Quantity versus Quality of Parental Care

According to one researcher, employed mothers spend about an hour a day in direct, physical care of their children under age three, and only about twenty minutes per day for children over age three. This total amounts to about half the time full-time housewives are reported to spend in direct care of their children. Employed mothers are also estimated to spend about half the total amount of time that full-time housewives spend in the company of their children—which means about three hours total per day for working mothers when the children are under age three, slightly less time for older children. On weekdays, working women's husbands are reported to spend twice

---

34. Gail Howrigan, "Effects of Working Mothers on Children," Center for the Study of Public Policy, Cambridge, Mass., August 1973; Claire Etaugh, "Effects of Maternal Employment on Children: A Review of Recent Research," *Merrill Palmer Quarterly* 20 (1974): 71–98; Lois Wladis Hoffman, "Effects of Maternal Employment on the Child: A Review of the Research," *Developmental Psychology* 10 (1974): 204–28; and Allison Clarke-Stewart, *Child Care in the Family: A Review of Research and Some Propositions for Policy* (New York: Academic Press, 1977).

as much time on child care as do husbands of full-time housewives; but on weekends, husbands of employed women apparently make up for their additional help during the week by doing less (spending an estimated three-fifths of the time husbands of full-time housewives spend with their children on weekends).[35]

Although in an absolute sense employed mothers undoubtedly spend less time with their children than nonworking mothers do, it is not at all clear that the number of hours spent with a parent is the critical determinant of a child's development. Characteristics of parent-child interaction—for example, the appropriateness of the parent's stimulation to the child's developmental maturity, the variety of the stimulation, and responsiveness to the infant's behavior[36]—are more important to child development than is the sheer quantity of interaction or stimulation.

Furthermore, the quantity of time spent with a child or children does not seem to differ so much by maternal employment status as is often assumed. Contrary to the imaginings of many guilt-ridden working mothers, full-time homemakers do not spend most of their days in stimulating or affectionate play with their children.[37] The amount and kind of stimulation afforded a child may vary more by the educational level of the parent, for example, than by the mother's employment status.

Finally, one frequent fear relating to children of working mothers seems to have been happily put to rest. One of the primary concerns of researchers has been that infants with working mothers might not form normal attachments to their mothers, but infants of working mothers do appear to establish normal attachment relationships.[38]

How Children and Families Vary According to Maternal Work Status

Although a child's attachment to its mother and the child's general development do not seem to be impaired by the mother's employment, several other differences in children and families have appeared con-

---

35. Philip J. Stone, "Child Care in Twelve Countries," in Alexander Szalai, ed., *The Use of Time* (The Hague: Mouton, 1972).

36. Clarke-Stewart, *Child Care in the Family*.

37. Ibid.

38. J. Conrad Schwartz, "Social and Emotional Effects of Day Care: A Review of Recent Research," paper presented to the Society for Research in Child Development Study Group on the Family, Ann Arbor, University of Michigan, October 1975; Howrigan, "Effects of Working Mothers on Children"; Barbara Wallston, "The Effects of Maternal Employment on Children," *Child Psychology* 14 (1973): 81–95.

sistently when children of working women have been compared with children of nonworking women. Children of working mothers do more housework than do children of full-time homemakers. Also, daughters of women who work tend to have less traditional views of marriage and sex roles than do daughters of nonworking women.[39] For example, ninth-grade black students whose mothers worked viewed female employment as less threatening to a marriage than did black students whose mothers were not employed.[40] In addition, one research team found that maternal employment did not affect daughters' evaluations of how warm and expressive women are, but that daughters of working women did view women as more competent than did daughters of nonworking women.[41]

In another study, college students were found to evaluate an article attributed to a female author less positively than they evaluated the same article attributed to a male author, regardless of topic.[42] When the study was replicated comparing the reactions of daughters of employed women and those of daughters of full-time homemakers, working women's daughters were significantly less likely than the others to devalue articles attributed to women.[43]

These findings are significant because they suggest the movement of women into the labor force will have continuing effects on the attitudes of coming generations. Perhaps the current generation of employed mothers will raise sons as well as daughters who value women's work role, who know how to do housework, and who accept maternal employment as a natural part of life.

It is important, though, to keep in mind that numerous factors mediate the effects of maternal employment. For example, the effects

---

39. Shirley Matile Miller, "Effects of Maternal Employment on Sex Role Perception, Interests, and Self Esteem in Kindergarten Girls," *Developmental Psychology* 11 (May 1975): 405–06; Aletha Houston Stein, "The Effects of Maternal Employment and Educational Attainment on the Sex Typed Attributes of College Females," *Social Behavior and Personality* 1 (1973): 111–14; Wallston, "The Effects of Maternal Employment on Children."

40. Karl King, Thomas J. Abernathy, and Ann H. Chapman, "Black Adolescents' Views of Maternal Employment as a Threat to the Marital Relationship," *Journal of Marriage and the Family* 38 (November 1976): 733–37.

41. Inge Broverman, S. R. Vogel, D. M. Broverman, F. E. Clarkson, and P. S. Rosenkrantz, "Sex Roles Stereotypes: A Current Appraisal," *Journal of Social Issues* 28 (1972): 59–78.

42. Phillip A. Goldberg, "Are Women Prejudiced Against Women?" *Transaction* 5 (May 1968): 28–30.

43. G. K. Baruch, "Maternal Influences Upon College Women's Attitudes Toward Women and Work," *Developmental Psychology* 6 (1972): 32–37.

may differ with the family's income level. The earnings brought home by the working wife of a low-income husband may bring the family into the middle class. The salary of a single parent is also essential to family well-being. In such instances, the family may view the mother's employment very favorably. Conversely, in some families the mother's contribution may undermine the position of the father in his children's eyes, so that while the mother is viewed more positively by virtue of her employment, the father is viewed as inadequate.[44] In some families in which the mother works for reasons other than economic need, however, the mother's employment may be viewed as a rejection of her maternal role.

Another important variable affecting the impact of maternal employment is the amount of time the mother works—part time or full time. Considering the minimum amounts of time all mothers have been estimated to spend in child care described earlier in this chapter, plus the time mothers are estimated to spend in housework (Chapter 4), working mothers have very full weeks, even without adding in commuting time. It is not surprising that many mothers now work part time, or would prefer to work part time if they could find good part-time jobs. Numerous studies suggest that part-time employment is an accommodation that greatly eases the strain often experienced by employed mothers.[45]

The Effects of Day Care

It has been found that young children cared for in groups tend to get more colds and flu than other young children do.[46] Several studies have also found that children in day care become more peer-oriented and more physically active and aggressive than do other children.[47] Such a tendency might be explained by too large a group or too low a ratio of adults to children. The quality of the particular day care facility needs to be examined before a judgment about day care in general is warranted.

Other effects attributed to day care are hard to document. One researcher has suggested that some negative effects attributed to day

---

44. E. Douvan, "Employment and the Adolescent," in F. Ivan Nye and Lois Wladis Hoffman, eds., *The Employed Mother in America* (Chicago: Rand McNally, 1963).

45. Lois Wladis Hoffman and F. Ivan Nye, eds., *Working Mothers* (San Francisco: Jossey-Bass, 1974).

46. Anna-Beth Doyle, "Infant Development in Day Care," *Developmental Psychology* 2 (September 1975): 655–56.

47. See Schwartz, "Social and Emotional Effects of Day Care."

care experiences may actually be rooted in hostility or detachment on the part of the mother that antedates the child's birth.[48]

Several studies have shown that while intelligence test scores of lower-class children reared in their own homes or in family day care tend to decline over time, intelligence scores of lower-class children in center care remain constant.[49] It is not clear, however, that day care centers are more intellectually stimulating than is the home care provided by well-educated, middle-class parents. Several researchers have reported that sons of working mothers, especially among middle-class families, have lower grades or lower intelligence scores than do sons of nonworking middle-class mothers. Conversely, daughters of working mothers of all classes and sons of lower-class working mothers have been found to have better academic performances and higher educational aspirations than do children of nonworking mothers.[50] Of course, a positive association between educational plans and maternal employment may reflect either higher aspirations on the part of the children or the greater ability of two-income families to provide for the education of their children. Until more detailed analyses are completed we cannot be sure of the explanation. Inasmuch as both the meaning of maternal employment and the effects of day care might differ by socioeconomic level as well as by sex of a child, multivariate analyses seem to be the crucial next step before these findings can be accepted as really meaningful.

Unanswered Questions for Research

In addition to a need for better research, there is a strong need for research attention to topics that have been relatively ignored to date. Surprisingly little is known about the characteristics of fathers and of substitute caretakers, but clearly both have an enormous impact with respect to children and mothers who rely on them. The willingness of a father to participate in substantial child care and housework, the hours he works, and the attitudes he holds about his wife's employment will undoubtedly affect the quality of the family's life. Equally important are the values, educational level, and background of the care provider. Child care by a professional with a teaching orientation, for example, may provide a more intellectually stimulating environ-

---

48. Ann D. Murray, "Maternal Employment Reconsidered: Effects on Infants," *American Journal of Orthopsychiatry* 45 (October 1975): 773–79.

49. Carnegie Corporation, "Average Day Care: Harmful or Beneficial?" *Carnegie Quarterly* 25 (Summer 1977): 5–6.

50. Lois Wladis Hoffman, "Effects of Maternal Employment on the Child," in Hoffman and Nye, eds., *Working Mothers*, pp. 126–66.

ment but less warmth to a child than does care by an older woman who has turned to day care after rearing her own family. A neighbor mother who is staying home to rear her children because she feels that good mothers do not work may transmit her prejudice against maternal employment to children for whom she baby-sits, while a woman who comes into a child's home to baby-sit and do housework may provide considerable warmth but little intellectual stimulation for a child. In the absence of research, these thoughts are highly speculative, but the range of differences in care providers and their potential importance are obvious.

Much of the research to date has concentrated on the consequences of maternal employment on children. The mother's feelings about her child have been ignored. Do women who continue working full time even when their babies are small develop as close a relationship with their children as do nonworking mothers? Because most women work from necessity and because paid maternity leave on most jobs is very short, mothers may increasingly return to work soon after childbirth. The consequences of different leave patterns for a mother's feelings about her baby should be explored because we know nothing about the impact on the mother of an early return to employment.

Study also might be done on the impact of paternity leave on father-child relationships. Perhaps having the experience of intensive interaction with their infants that most women have had would produce stronger bonds between the father and the child. This bond could have an impact on the father's participation in child care, his attitudes about divorce, and even his willingness to provide child support in the event of marital disruption.

Single parents merit particular attention. Coping with both employment and child rearing with little or no support from the absent parent would strain even the most motivated adult. The poverty that female-headed families so often experience[51] makes them a particularly vulnerable group. Ways to assist single parents deserve far more attention than they have received to date.

One other comment needs to be made about the limitations of the research that has been done. Most studies were conducted when only a minority of women were employed and mothers often felt guilty about their employment. Ignoring for the moment the gains to women of overcoming such guilt, let us consider the impact of maternal concern on children. Mothers who felt great concern, even guilt, over

---

51. Ross and Sawhill, *Time of Transition*, pp. 9–10.

the effects of their employment on their children may have compensated for their absence at work very effectively—more effectively, in fact, than women do who take everything in stride. Yet guilt is not a positive motivation, so the mitigation of guilt may mean that mothers nowadays are engaging in more voluntary, enthusiastic interaction with their children (especially if the mothers decided on both motherhood and careers voluntarily). Clearly there is a need for more up-to-date research on this subject.

Summary

The research literature is unanimous in finding that high-quality child care does not harm children, but this conclusion does not mean we can breathe a sigh of relief and turn to other issues. First, not all children receive high-quality care. Second, children with special problems or needs may require the kind of attention that only parents may be motivated to provide; as a result, they may not flourish in group settings.

In addition, multiple problems may arise if those mothers who, for various reasons, are better off not working respond to pressures to be employed and take jobs anyway. Some families do not have the physical or emotional energy to have two earners in the labor market, particularly full time. Some women will not have the help with child care and housework that they need from their husbands. Some women will not have husbands to rely on at all. Others will not be able to locate employment with reasonable hours. Further, fathers who may be required to work long hours and to travel leave a gap that mothers need to fill. Whatever opinions outsiders may have about a particular father's home role and the value of women's work, individual women rearing children in the real world face situations that often limit their ability to cope adequately, much less ideally.

Unquestionably, the development of children who are physically, emotionally, and intellectually healthy is important to every society. If women are drawn into the labor force regardless of their preferences, their families' situations, or their inability to pursue successfully several roles simultaneously rather than consecutively, inadequate child rearing and unhappy families may result.

Most working women, however, could not afford to quit working, even if maternal employment were found to be harmful under some circumstances. Only a minority of women are working solely because they enjoy it rather than because they need the money, so most could not drop out of the labor force to enhance the development of their children. In recognition of this fact, the next section discusses ways to ease the burden of working parents.

POLICY IMPLICATIONS AND CONCLUSIONS

To work and to raise children simultaneously is a challenging task for working couples as well as for single working parents. Clearly, the difficulties and satisfactions of combining the two roles are best handled by those who are voluntarily involved in both. Therefore, the most basic, if not the most obvious, policy implication is that individuals should have control over whether and when they become parents. Untimely pregnancies both precipitate marriage between people who might not otherwise have chosen to marry and place heavy economic and emotional demands on couples who may not be ready to assume them. Clearly couples who wish to focus their energies solely on employment and have no children, and those who want to limit their family size, should have these options. This argument implies that family planning services and sex education should be widespread and readily available to people of all ages.

As already noted, however, most young American women intend both to have children and to be employed. Unfortunately, many families in which the woman is employed, especially those with children, are experiencing a difficult period of change in American society. Despite a general lack of services and social support, most of these families are performing remarkably well. Children from such homes seem to compare well with other children. Given the strains experienced by parents trying to juggle several demanding roles, though, it seems important to consider ways to ease their burdens. What policies can be pursued by families, employers, day care providers, and others that might improve the day-to-day lives of individuals and their families over the next decade?

As the United States tries to formulate a coherent set of policies, the experience of European countries may be instructive. Leave from work after childbirth is generally accepted and subsidized in European countries; for example, governments provide maternity leave ranging from three to six months at full salary and cash or in-kind benefits at birth.[52] In the United States, most health benefit plans connected with employment provide inadequate maternity benefits and leave allowances, or none at all. After giving birth, many employed mothers therefore must choose between resuming work, regardless of whether

52. Kamerman and Kahn, "European Family Policy Currents."

they are physically or emotionally ready, or giving up their jobs. An increasing number of women work during most of their pregnancy and return to work while their children are young.[53]

The fact that in this country benefits to working mothers stop at the end of maternity leave presents many parents with another dilemma. Although programs for three- to five-year-olds have expanded enormously over the past decade, mothers who wish to work or have to work encounter serious problems finding adequate and affordable care for infants and toddlers. Moreover, a substantial number of mothers are committed to returning to work but do not want to do so while their children are very young. If they remain at home, however, they are certain to lose their jobs as well as their seniority and benefits.

In most European countries, government benefits to working mothers do not stop with maternity leave. Some of the programs with which various countries are experimenting include monthly cash benefits until the child reaches age two or three (Czechoslovakia, Hungary, and France), extended leave with partial or no pay but maintenance of job and seniority (Hungary and Poland), social insurance credit (West Germany and Hungary), and substantial paid leave to care for sick children (all countries). Only in France are benefits tied to income. Most benefits in most countries, however, are available only to women who were working prior to childbirth. In addition, day care for the very youngest children (under age three) is widely available (though perhaps inadequate in quantity) in East Germany and France.[54]

In contrast, the United States provides no government subsidy for maternity leave, unless AFDC benefits are counted, but these benefits are tied to income rather than to employment. Federal employees do not have the benefit of formal maternity leave; instead they must depend on accrued sick leave and vacation time or take leave without pay. Private industry is under no legal obligation to provide any benefits at all. In Europe the option to be full-time subsidized parents while children are young is more generally available, and in Sweden men also have the option.

Many mothers, because they are single parents or because their husbands earn low wages, are working to support their families; the size of the woman's paycheck is critical to the well-being of these

---

53. U.S. Department of Health, Education, and Welfare, "Pregnant Workers in the United States," Public Health Service: National Center for Health Statistics, no. 11, September 1977; Frank L. Mott and David Shapiro, "Work and Motherhood: The Dynamics of Labor Force Participation Surrounding the First Birth," in *Years for Decision*, vol. 4 (Columbus: Ohio State University, 1977), pp. 65–111.

54. Kamerman and Kahn, "European Family Policy Currents."

families. It is important, of course, to ensure equality of pay and job opportunity to all people as a matter of law and principle. Ways to bring about equal opportunity through extensive changes in the structure of occupations and in the process of occupational choice have already been discussed in Chapters 2 and 4.

There is enormous concern in the United States with the effects of income supplement and welfare programs on the stability of families. Our review of the evidence in the last chapter indicated that, like income from employment, income supplement payments may in some instances encourage divorce at least in the short run, because they provide women in unhappy marriages with the means to support themselves. In contrast, programs that provide jobs for husbands may promote stability, because such jobs permit husbands to maintain their traditional position as wage earner in the eyes of their wives and their communities. The problem with such programs is that if the marriage does end, the wife is left without job skills or experience. Provision of two part-time jobs might be a better way to foster economic independence without lowering stability. If only one job is available per family, it may be wise to permit the couple to decide who will work, rather than to assume the husband should get the job. In the long run, society may benefit most, in terms of reduced public assistance, if the woman works. A woman whose marriage breaks up (an event predicted for nearly half of new marriages) is better able to care for herself and her children if she has some work experience, some training, and a job.

For those mothers (and fathers) who do work, increasing the availability of rewarding part-time work seems to be a vital first step toward reducing the problems of work overload, marital strain, and day care scheduling. Part-time paid employment at the same level as full-time employment, including employee benefits, would go far to mitigate the problems families currently face. For example, parents working full time typically find it hard to be home when their children return home from school. Time-consuming tasks, such as taking a small child to the doctor, use up precious vacation days or go undone. Doing shopping, cooking, and cleaning solely on evenings and weekends necessarily reduces time for family interaction and leisure, making life something of a treadmill. Even highly committed career workers can find such a schedule wearing and, as a result, they may not be able to perform well or even adequately at the work place or in the household. Yet they may cling to full-time work because they cannot locate well-paid, secure, or interesting part-time work. Many women prefer to drop out of the labor force rather than work full time, or they may exhaust themselves at full-time employment from necessity rather than choice. Men also might benefit from a shorter work week. But currently, it is exceptionally difficult for either women or men to find good part-time work.

To illustrate the costs associated with inflexible hours, consider the case of a husband and wife, each of whom earns $10,000, who are expecting their first child. If both partners were to work only four days a week they could still earn 80 percent (before taxes) of their previous combined income. Further, they could take different days off, thereby reducing their need for day care to three days a week. In the absence of such employment options, both husband and wife may choose to work full time and cope as best they can. If, however, the husband keeps his job and the wife gives up paid employment, as often happens in such cases, the family income is reduced to $10,000, unless the wife is able to pick up occasional or part-time work close to home. Whether the wife leaves her full-time job for full-time homemaking or part-time work, she loses her seniority, and, depending on the nature of any part-time work she finds, her occupational skills may deteriorate. As a result, not only is current family income lower, but also future family income will probably be lower. In addition, the wife has had to sacrifice the job which she preferred and for which she presumably was trained, while her husband has had to give up the prospect of leisure and the chance to spend more time with their child. Furthermore, should the marriage break up, the woman may not be able to contribute to the support of herself and the child adequately and may require welfare assistance.

The moral of this illustration is that if families were provided the opportunity to make real choices about work versus family and dollars versus hours, both family adjustment and earnings would probably increase, in the short and the long run. Certainly federal and state governments can take the lead in providing good part-time jobs, and incentives might be offered to private industry to do the same.

The greater availability of "flexitime"—the flexible scheduling of work hours—would also help two-earner families. As already indicated, if parents can stagger their working hours, they can reduce the number of hours their children spend in day care and take turns being home when children return from school. By avoiding rush hour traffic, parents can reduce their commuting time, thereby adding time to their productive day. For couples who cannot or do not want to reduce their earnings by working part time, flexitime might facilitate child care.

Although part-time work and flexible scheduling of hours will help parents resolve their child care needs, many couples will still need to

rely at least occasionally on day care, as must single parents. The goal
of concerned policy makers should be to facilitate maximum choice
and quality with minimum cost and red tape.

Several points need to be made with regard to setting day care policy.
First, there is no typical child or typical parent. Day care needs and
preferences of children and parents differ from family to family. As
has already been pointed out, some parents use day care primarily as
a means of supervision and care while they are working, while others
view day care primarily as educational or developmental. In fact, many
nonworking mothers send their children to nursery schools because
of this conviction. In view of this variation, whether all care should be
governed by standardized regulations is a difficult question. Certainly
there is no immediate threat of government investigation into the
millions of unlicensed baby-sitters and caretakers. Policy makers might
consider establishing minimum standards for various types of care,
rather than setting the same standards for all care. It might be useful,
also, to educate parents about what constitutes high-quality care and
how to distinguish it from poor-quality care. Of course, recognition of
high-quality care is of little use if such care is not available or is too
expensive. Persons particularly likely to be affected by any decrease in
supply or increase in cost are low-income mothers who do not want
to be on welfare but who cannot really afford to work if they must
pay the full cost of day care. Ways to increase the supply of quality
day care and to make it affordable, perhaps using sliding scales, will
be an important topic over the coming decade.

Although we have reviewed the prospects for day care of children
of working mothers over the next decade given current trends and
policies, it is impossible to determine whether there is a shortage of
facilities at present or whether there will be one in the future. There
is simply too little information available on parental needs or on the
availability of different types of care to make an informed judgment.

By 1990, however, it appears that there may be a shortage of family
day care for the millions of children of working mothers who prefer
such care; if such a shortage occurs, more day care centers will be
needed. As we have pointed out, if labor market opportunities continue
to become more attractive, fewer family day care providers may be
willing to remain in what has been found to be a rather poorly paid
occupation except while they themselves have small children. The
supply of such caretakers may be even more seriously affected if the
government should increase its efforts to apply a single set of standards
to all child care providers and incorporate all providers into the formal
labor force. Depending on the demand for women in the labor force,

the market wage, and the enforcement of current laws and regulations, therefore, women may or may not find it profitable to provide low-cost day care to children for even a certain period in their lives.

The possible phasing out of day care by one group of women could coincide with the increasing development of day care provided by senior citizens, and increased reliance on cooperative arrangements and sharing of child care by fathers. Unless there is a reversal in the trend toward entry of mothers of young children into the labor force, however, a substantial increase in the need for center care over the next decade appears inevitable. Even assuming increased availability of part-time work and jobs with flexible schedules, the demand for group care will probably increase because of the increasing number of single parents and small and highly mobile families, and because of the rising cost of individual, in-home care.

*　　*　　*

In conclusion, several important principles to guide decision makers can be listed. Individuals should have freedom of choice in how they design and live their lives. Women should have equal opportunity with men for gainful employment. And last but not least, the next generation should be reared in healthy families by parents who have chosen to be parents and who have time and energy to devote to child rearing. These goals cannot be defined as mutually exclusive. The challenge is to design policies that meet the needs of families while adapting to the changing realities of family life both now and in the future.

Chapter 6

WOMEN'S ECONOMIC CONTRIBUTION TO THE FAMILY

CLAIR VICKERY*

The widespread entry of wives into the labor market in recent years can be viewed as one more step in the family's pursuit of the "good life." Like other manifestations of industrialization that have improved the economic lot of the majority, employment of married women has both advantages and disadvantages for individuals and for society. Because the movement of married women into the paid labor force involves a long-term change in the work roles of both men and women, the transition period is particularly disruptive.

No one can escape the impact of these changes. On the one hand,

* The author wishes to acknowledge the assistance of Russ Jones, who performed the computer programming for this project, and Sean Flaherty, who assisted with the research through the Institute of Industrial Relations, University of California, Berkeley.

the working-wife family must work with and restructure social institutions that evolved during a period when mothers usually did not
work outside the home. On the other hand, the full-time homemaker
family, once the ideal, finds itself under attack as being exploitive of
the wife and consequently outmoded as an appropriate family model.
In addition to confronting social norms that are changing to its disadvantage, the full-time homemaker family is finding that its material
well-being is falling in comparison with the material well-being of the
increasing number of working-wife families. As the standard changes,
a family will find it necessary for both spouses to be employed in
order to maintain the living standards set by two-earner families
headed by adults of comparable age and education.

AN OVERVIEW

The main outcome of a wife's working for pay is a substantial increase in the family's money income. At the same time, the entry of a
wife into the labor market necessarily changes the way her family
lives, because the wife's contribution to her family as a full-time earner
differs substantially from her contribution as a full-time homemaker.
When a wife is employed, her family loses its full-time manager and
caretaker in return for higher money income. A working-wife family
provides less personalized care for its members and gives less time to
parent-child interactions in exchange for increased consumption of
market-produced goods and services and increased financial assets.

This chapter explores how a wife's decision to divide her time between unpaid labor in the home and paid labor in the marketplace
affects the living standard of her family. It examines these major
questions: To what extent does a wife's employment add to her family's material well-being and financial security? And what is the wife's
overall work burden when she takes a job outside the home?

The chapter first notes the increase in the number of two-earner
families in the United States since 1950 and the associated changes
in expenditure patterns. In order to evaluate what these changes mean
for the family's well-being, two economic measures are estimated—
the expenses related to a wife's employment and what her paycheck
buys. Then, in order to compare the living standard of the working-
wife family with that of the homemaker family, the chapter examines
the change that occurs in housework activities when a wife is employed. The chapter concludes with comments on the long-range
outlook for sex and work roles.

The Family's Material Well-Being

The concepts of work and material well-being need precise definition. For purposes of this chapter, wives who work exclusively in the home and receive no earnings will be called homemakers; wives who are employed for pay will be called working wives. This terminology should not detract from the basic facts that all wives work (whether or not they receive earnings) and that all wives engage in homemaking activities. As for the concepts used to indicate standards of living, family expenditures serve as an indicator of material well-being, but the expenditure of money must be coupled with the use of time in order to know the total resources available to the family.

Comparing working-wife families with homemaker families requires comparing housework time as well as expenditures. To differentiate households by their money and time resources, money income (or income) will be used to designate the flow of monetary resources, and housework time will designate all productive activities outside the marketplace. Full income will designate combined time and money resources.

Although a wife's employment increases her family's income, her paycheck is not equivalent to the same lump sum received without her working. It must be reduced by her work-related expenses and the decline in her housework. If two families—one homemaker and one working-wife family—with the same money income are compared, the full income of the homemaker family is higher than the full income of the working-wife family because a working wife spends at least 15 percent of her paycheck, excluding income taxes, on work-related expenses, chiefly for transportation, Social Security, and clothing.

In the absence of a wife's paycheck, a homemaker family's expenditures on clothing, transportation, recreation, and retirement are as much as 50 percent lower, and its expenditures on the basics of food and shelter are slightly lower. A family's savings rate and its financial assets also are lower when the wife is not employed. Except for the work-related expenditures, these differences are what would normally be expected in comparing two families with a 30 percent difference in income. The expenditure patterns of families seem to be little affected by the amount of housework time available to the family.

With an increase in income comparable to a wife's paycheck, a homemaker family would spend more on shelter, food, recreation, and gifts and less on transportation, clothing, and Social Security than a working-wife family would spend. A working-wife family's lower expenditures on shelter reflect its lower full income, compared with the full income of a one-earner family with the same money income. It may also reflect those situations in which a wife's earnings are not counted on to be a constant flow of income, so that the family discounts her earnings in deciding how expensive a house it can afford.[1]

Although working-wife and homemaker families with the same money income do not have the same full income, this discrepancy is not recognized by the current Social Security and income tax systems (as discussed in Chapters 7 and 8). Child care costs are allowed as a work-related expense in the income tax code, but these costs are only a small part of a wife's work-related expenses; the majority of working mothers find informal ways for providing child care within the home or neighborhood, or their children care for themselves. As the number and political power of working-wife families have grown, many countries have adopted individual taxation programs that treat working-wife and homemaker families more equally; subsequently, it becomes less costly for a wife to take a job (and relatively more costly for her to work exclusively at home).[2]

The Family's Financial Security

In the days when an employed wife was the exception rather than the rule, a wife's possible entry into the labor market was viewed as a family insurance policy against temporary hardships or earnings losses. When a husband was unemployed or experienced a loss in earnings, his working-class wife might work temporarily as a waitress or sales clerk. Many women from middle-class homes earned a teacher's certificate in college "just in case" anything happened to their husbands.

But the entry of a wife into the labor force for the major part of her adult life means that she has switched from being the family's income buffer to being a steady source of earnings. With their higher money incomes, two-earner families adopt expenditure patterns that may increase their dependence on the marketplace at the same time

---

1. The lower shelter expenditures for the working-wife family may also reflect the past practice by banks of disregarding the wife's earnings in determining the amount of mortgage a family can carry. This practice has been made illegal by the Equal Credit Act of 1974.

2. By 1977, individual taxation was allowed in seventeen OECD countries and was compulsory in thirteen countries, including Australia, Sweden, and Japan. Organization for Economic Cooperation and Development, *The Treatment of Family Units in OECD Member Countries Under Tax and Transfer Systems*, Paris, 1977, pp. 15–17.

that their flexibility in switching a member's time between paid and unpaid activities diminishes. How a working-wife family's financial security, which comes with its increased assets and its decreased proportion of income spent on current consumption, compares with a full-time homemaker family's financial security, which comes with its ability to send the wife temporarily into the marketplace, is an important question that remains unanswered.

Although the risk of a family's having *no* money income during a period of unemployment declines if the wife is in the labor force, the emergence of the two-earner family brings with it new problems in dealing with spells of unemployment. A family cannot substitute household production for a large part of what it buys with earned income. Consequently, when a husband or wife becomes unemployed, the unemployed person cannot produce at home what the family usually buys with his or her earnings. An unemployed parent may save the family some money by shopping more carefully for food or by taking care of the family's clothing in the home. But other changes are harder to make; for example, taking a child out of a nursery school may be so disruptive to the family's normal living patterns that this alternative would not be undertaken on a short-term basis. Clearly, the flexibility of the two-earner family in temporarily substituting housework time for earnings is limited.

In general, the dependence of people on the marketplace and the government has increased as household production has declined. Because a two-earner family puts more of its work and consumption activities through the marketplace than a one-earner family does, the two-earner family is more susceptible to market swings and relies more on the government to smooth out income fluctuations either indirectly through monetary and fiscal policy or directly through unemployment compensation or job programs.

The fact that employment of wives increases dependence on the marketplace is part of the long-term shift in the production of goods and services from the household to the marketplace. Although in certain areas of housework—child rearing, meal preparation, and clothing care—the household has not been supplanted by the marketplace, expenditures on food and clothing have been taking a declining share of the family's budget. Meanwhile, expenditures on transportation, housing, and utilities (areas in which household production is minimal), along with insurance and retirement contributions, have been taking an increasing share of the budget.

These trends in expenditure patterns will probably continue and be reinforced by demographic trends which will also affect the need for housework activities. The need for child care has dropped with the birthrate, but the aging of the population has increased the need for individualized nursing care. Care for the elderly was once provided largely within an extended family setting, but in recent years this function has been largely transferred to outside institutions. Although the need for care for the elderly will rise sharply in the coming years, the decline in full-time homemakers indicates that the family may be less able to help care for elderly relatives.

The Wife's Work Burden

When a wife is employed outside the home, the family loses little in actual housework services because the wife increases her total hours of work in order to continue doing the bulk of the housework. A major loss is in the wife's leisure time. Why is the wife willing to shoulder such a heavy load when she becomes employed? For one thing, a paycheck increases her own economic independence; this independence has become increasingly important as our economy has become more and more monetized. A working wife may view her paid work as an insurance policy against the loss of income if she is widowed, or her husband becomes disabled, or her marriage breaks down. Although most marriages will last until one spouse dies, the threat of financial insecurity that accompanies the one-third possibility of a broken marriage may make the economic independence symbolized by the wife's earnings important to her. In addition, bringing home a paycheck usually increases a wife's bargaining power within the household. Perhaps these reasons, coupled with the conflicts a working wife feels about possible neglect of household responsibilities, explain her willingness to bear such a heavy work load.

The shift in work patterns has both contributed to and been affected by the increased material well-being of middle-income families. The following review of the period since 1950 focuses on the major trends that have appeared.

LIVING STANDARDS OF FAMILIES DURING THE PAST TWENTY-FIVE YEARS

More Earners per Family

Real per capita income in the United States in 1972 was 60 percent higher than the 1950 level.[3] This affluence has been achieved partly

3. Real per capita income (national income deflated by the implicit GNP price deflator) was $2,892 in 1950 and $4,558 in 1972 dollars. U.S. Department of

through a general increase in the number of members in each family who are working for pay.[4] Only the lowest-income group, which has a disproportionate share of families headed by adults who are either under age twenty-five or over age sixty-five, as well as unmarried women, does not show an increase in the average number of earners per family.

As Figure 12 shows, except for the lowest-income group, the percentage of husband-wife families with wives in the labor force almost doubled between 1950 and 1972. In 1950, 20 percent to 30 percent of the husband-wife families had wives in the labor force; by 1972, 30 percent to 50 percent had participating wives. At the same time, the labor market participation of husbands (and men generally) declined, especially those in the sixty-plus age group.[5]

In 1950, two in three middle-income families (those in the third fifth of the income distribution) had at most one earner, and almost one-half of the upper-middle-income families (those in the top two-fifths) had at most only one earner (see Figure 13). By 1972, middle- and upper-middle-income families with fewer than two earners were in a shrinking minority; 55 percent to 75 percent of such families had more than one earner, and 10 percent to 30 percent of them had more than two earners. Working children (or family members other than the husband or wife) accounted for slightly more than half of the increase in average earners per family between 1950 and 1960, but working wives accounted for the major part of the increase between 1960 and 1972.[6] By 1972, the typical middle-class family had multiple earners, largely because of the wife's employment.

A family's position on the income ladder, traditionally dependent on the education and labor market position of the male, increas-

---

Commerce, Bureau of the Census, *Statistical Abstract of the United States: 1976*, Tables 636 and 630.

4. The average annual earnings of full-time employees in 1970 were about 1.5 times the 1950 average (in current dollars), but the average family income almost doubled during this period as the labor force participation rate of married women increased from 24 percent to 41 percent. U.S. Department of Commerce, Bureau of the Census, *Historical Statistics of the United States, Colonial Times to 1970*, D722, D6374, G31–39.

5. The labor force participation rates of husbands fell from 90.3 percent in 1957 to 81.8 percent in 1977. U.S. Department of Labor, Bureau of Labor Statistics, *Handbook of Labor Statistics, 1967*, Bulletin 1555, Table 4, and *Employment and Earnings* 25 (January 1978), no. 1, Table 4.

6. The increase in wives' labor force participation rates accounted for 40 percent to 50 percent of the increase in the average number of workers between 1950 and 1960, but accounted for 50 percent to more than 100 percent of the gross increase between 1960 and 1972.

FIGURE 12

**WORKING WIVES, BY INCOME GROUP, 1950 AND 1972
(PERCENTAGE OF ALL HUSBAND-WIFE FAMILIES)**

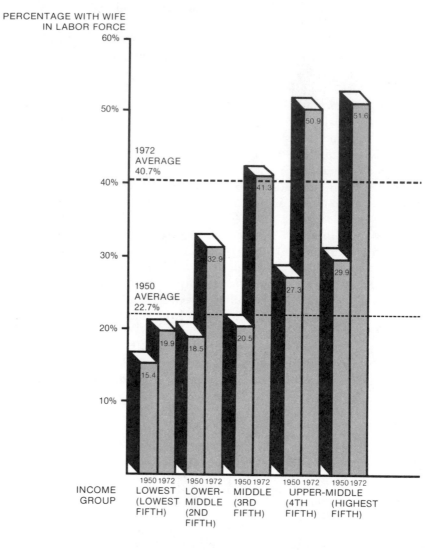

SOURCE: U.S. Bureau of the Census, *Current Population
Reports*, series P-60, no. 80 (Table 12) and
no. 90 (Table 13).

ingly depends on whether and how much the wife works. The American wife's income class is still determined primarily by her husband's earnings, but more and more her family's economic status is being influenced by her own employment decisions. The decision of wives to work outside the home implies that households increasingly have opted for market goods in lieu of some of the housewives' services, and that wives are showing an increased desire to work outside the home. The precise effect that a decrease in a wife's housework and an increase in her market work have on her family's resource position is unclear, because the family's money income grows more rapidly than its full income.

The Wife's Work Decision

The shift of a wife's time toward paid activities reflects her response to three major trends: (1) the growth in productivity in the marketplace relative to the home; (2) the growth in the nation's real income —that is, the greater quantities and more kinds of goods and services available for consumption; and (3) changes in the preferences of households toward purchasing consumption goods in the market. Social customs constrain the direction and force of these trends over time. Expanded economic opportunities affect these customs; at the same time, the customs themselves shape the development of economic opportunities.

The widespread use of modern contraceptives has enabled women to control the number and timing of pregnancies. As childbirth has become more a matter of choice, so have women's decisions about education, marriage, and work. The bearing of fewer children and the availability of public schooling for younger children have shortened the span and lightened the job of mothering. Without young children to care for, many women find that housework does not command all their time and that a lifelong occupation of housewife is unsatisfying.

Theoretically, a husband and wife reach a decision together about how best to divide work time between market and nonmarket activities for the family's well-being. But social custom dictates that a "well-adjusted" husband have a market job and that a "well-adjusted" wife maintain the home and raise children. Within this traditional social context, a wife will decide how she should spend her time by comparing her potential earnings with the impact her employment would have upon her traditional job of running the home and raising children.

FIGURE 13

NUMBER OF EARNERS PER FAMILY
BY INCOME GROUP, 1950 AND 1972

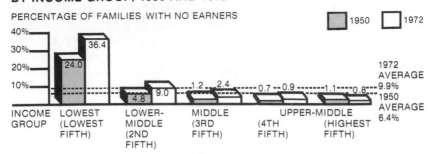

PERCENTAGE OF FAMILIES WITH NO EARNERS

1950   1972

1972 AVERAGE 9.9%
1950 AVERAGE 6.4%

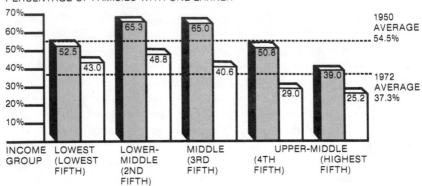

PERCENTAGE OF FAMILIES WITH ONE EARNER

1950 AVERAGE 54.5%
1972 AVERAGE 37.3%

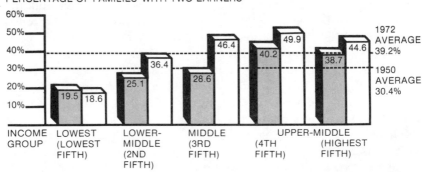

PERCENTAGE OF FAMILIES WITH TWO EARNERS

1972 AVERAGE 39.2%
1950 AVERAGE 30.4%

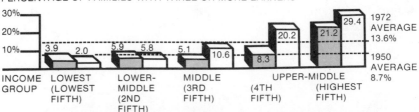

PERCENTAGE OF FAMILIES WITH THREE OR MORE EARNERS

1972 AVERAGE 13.6%
1950 AVERAGE 8.7%

SOURCE: See Figure 12.

A major constraint on a mother's working outside the home is her concern that the children be properly cared for. For the majority of women, proper care seems to mean daytime child care in the home by a parent or relative. In 1975, more than 65 percent of three- to thirteen-year-olds with employed mothers were cared for in the home during the daytime by a parent or relative, and only 20 percent of the three- to five-year-olds with employed mothers were cared for by a nonrelative in someone else's home or in a day care center.[7]

A wife's ability to obtain satisfactory child care within the home or neighborhood, if she has young children, and her willingness to increase her total work hours underlie her decision to work for pay. Furthermore, work decisions are constrained by the characteristics of paid labor (which usually must be provided in blocks of time) and by the characteristics of some housework (such as meal preparation and child care) which must be provided at specific times. Even more fundamentally, market goods and services cannot substitute for some housework activities, such as individualized care of members. Conversely, the household cannot produce some goods and services, such as sophisticated medical care. The relative value a wife and her family place on uniquely market and on uniquely home-produced outputs will influence how the wife allocates her time between paid work and housework. These valuations will shift with the family's life-cycle stage, its experiences over time, and the available options.

Differences in Consumption Patterns

When a wife does take a job, how would we expect her family's expenditures to change? The family will have more money and less time for spending it. Theoretically, the wife will want to buy some of the household services she no longer has time to provide, but realistically such options may be limited.

The most promising areas of household production in which market goods and services may save time or energy are these:

1. *Meal preparation.* A family may eat out more often, or a wife may buy food that is partially prepared. Alternatively, a family may prefer to eat simpler, home-prepared meals that involve fewer dishes and less variety than those the full-time homemaker has time to prepare.

2. *Household operations.* A family may pay someone to clean its home. But some working wives may find the problems of scheduling and supervising substitutes more trouble than the time saved is worth. Buying appliances that aid in cleaning may or may not reduce the

---

7. Calculated from the U.S. Department of Commerce, Bureau of the Census, "Daytime Care of Children: October 1974 and February 1975," *Current Population Reports*, series P-20, no. 298, 1976.

time needed to perform household chores. But the machines may increase the quality of the work or decrease the energy needed to do the job, and thus they may be equally favored by employed and non-employed wives. If a working wife reduces the amount of time spent housecleaning, she may actually use her machines less than the home-maker does.

3. *Child care.* A family may pay others to care for the children while the mother works. But currently most parents do not purchase child care services; whenever possible family members care for chil-dren within the home.

4. *Clothing and clothing care.* A family may pay for laundry and dry cleaning services outside the home. Buying more clothing for each member may decrease the frequency with which clothing has to be cleaned, but it increases shopping time and clothing maintenance decisions.

Besides buying market goods and services that replace some of the wife's housework time, a working-wife family will also incur expenses associated with the wife's employment. These will be mainly for additional clothing and clothing care; for increased transportation needs, perhaps another car for commuting; for the increased costs of meals eaten away from home; and for Social Security payroll taxes and income taxes. In most cases, expenditures to replace housework time and those to cover the wife's work expenses cannot be neatly sep-arated, so these incremental expenditures for food, clothing, clothing care, child care, household operations, transportation, and Social Se-curity taxes will be designated together as work-related expenses.

A household can participate in the nation's income growth by transferring time from housework to market work. As real wages rise, it becomes more expensive for a wife to use her time providing in-dividualized care of family members within the home. Many families have chosen to give up some personalized care in order to gain more market-produced goods and services. The simultaneous expansion in new consumption opportunities and changes in personal preferences are potent forces behind these transitions in women's work.

The reasons for the shifts in work and expenditure patterns in a dynamic world are complex. Technological change and urbanization continually expand and transform the options available to the family. A wife's work decision in such a complicated world is influenced by changes in the way the population as a whole is living—changes that structure her lifestyle expectations.

Technological change offers us increasing amounts and varieties of consumption goods. Since World War II, everyday life has been changed by plastics and synthetic materials, a plethora of electric appliances, television and satellite communication systems, the interstate highway system, air travel, and charge card systems. Advanced medical technology in hospitals has become accessible to a large segment of the population, as has public higher education.

What these changes have meant for most households can be dramatically confirmed with some simple numbers.[8] In 1950, only 65 percent of all housing units had a full bathroom, and 15 percent lacked running water. Only 75 percent of all housing units used gas or electricity for cooking, only 80 percent had a mechanical refrigerator, only 50 percent had central heating, and less than 5 percent had a clothes dryer or dishwasher.

By 1974, only 4 percent of all housing units lacked full plumbing facilities, virtually all households (99 percent) had a gas or electric stove and a refrigerator, 50 percent had air conditioning, 56 percent had a clothes dryer, 37 percent had a dishwasher, and more than 97 percent had an electric coffeemaker, a steam iron, a toaster, and a vacuum cleaner.

Although practically every home had a radio in 1950, only 12 percent had a television set. By 1974, 97 percent of all households owned a television set and 61 percent had a color TV. The percentage of households owning cars increased from 60 percent to 84 percent, and the percentage of families owning more than one car increased dramatically from 7 percent to 45 percent between 1950 and 1974.

The sophisticated and diverse goods that advanced technologies produce and large urban markets make readily available cannot be produced at home. People also find it increasingly difficult or impossible to duplicate in the home the health care available in hospitals and the special education available in public school systems. Many people cannot do their own household repairs. As a result, families need less household production and more income to purchase goods and services.

EXPENDITURE PATTERNS OF HOUSEHOLDS, 1950–73

The aggregate impact of these many and diverse changes just described shows up in families' expenditure patterns, which have registered remarkable shifts since 1950. The expenditures of middle-income

8. U.S. Department of Commerce, Bureau of the Census, *Statistical Abstract, 1950*, no. 979; *Statistical Abstract, 1955*, nos. 976, 978, 979; *Historical Statistics to 1970*, series N240, Q176, Q177, A6; *Statistical Abstract, 1971*, no. 1117; *Statistical Abstract, 1976*, nos. 689, 996, 1273, 1285.

four-person families as recorded in the 1950, 1960–61, and 1972–73 Consumer Expenditure Surveys give the overall impression that the material standard of living has markedly improved (see Table 22).[9] The proportion of after-tax income spent on recorded expenditures dropped dramatically from 111 percent in 1950 to 94 percent in 1972. Expenditures for food, shelter, clothing, and transportation were the most important items in 1950. The most striking change during the period was the decline in the proportion of income spent on food, which dropped from 33 percent in 1950 to 19 percent in 1972. Meanwhile, clothing expenditures declined from 12 percent to 6 percent of after-tax income, and outlay on house furnishings from 7 percent to 4 percent. Together, food and clothing expenditures used up 45 percent of disposable income for the average middle-income family of four in 1950; by 1972, this percentage had dropped to 25.

These declines in the proportion of disposable income spent on food, clothing, and house furnishings were partially offset by the increases in transportation and insurance and retirement payments. Between 1950 and 1972, the proportion of income being spent on transportation became less related to family size and negatively related to income. These trends reflect the large increase in car ownership, the major determinant of transportation expenditures.

---

9. For purposes of comparing the three expenditure surveys made in 1950, 1960–61, and 1972–73, households were divided into four income classes as follows:

Income Class	1950	1960	1972
I. Low			
Before-tax income[1]	$0–$2,059	$0–$3,099	$0–$5,999
Percentage of families (estimated)	25%	23%	22%
II. Lower-middle			
Before-tax income[1]	$2,060–$3,149	$3,100–$5,449	$6,000–$9,999
Percentage of families (estimated)	18%	25%	26%
III. Middle			
Before-tax income[1]	$3,150–$5,399	$5,450–$8,399	$10,000–$14,000
Percentage of families (estimated)	38%	32%	26%
IV. Upper-middle			
Before-tax income[1]	$5,400–$11,000	$8,400–$17,000	$15,000–$25,000
Percentage of families (estimated)	17%	18%	23%

1. Estimated for 1950 and 1960 from after-tax income. Families with incomes above the top incomes shown were not included because of data limitations; they accounted for 2 percent in 1950 and 1960 and 7 percent in 1972.

Table 22

EXPENDITURES OF MIDDLE-INCOME, FOUR-PERSON FAMILIES

	1950	1960–61	1972–73
Income	$4,140	$6,841	$12,427
Taxes	$ 188	$ 629	$ 1,663
Income after taxes	$3,952	$6,212	$10,764
Δ (Assets-liabilities)	−$213	−$27	$897
Percentage owning homes	56.6%	65.4%	72.1%
Recorded expenditures as a percentage of after-tax income	111.2%	108.1%	93.5%
Current consumption	103.6%	98.6%	82.8%
Food, total	33.0	24.9	18.5
Food at home	29.3	21.1	14.8
Shelter	10.8	13.4	12.9
Clothing	12.1	10.6	6.4
Transportation, total	13.3	14.6	17.5
Private auto	11.8	13.5	17.0
Fuel and utilities	4.6	4.8	4.5
Household operations	3.9	5.3	2.9
House furnishings	7.0	4.9	4.1
Recreation	5.0	4.2	5.7
Reading and education	1.6	1.9	1.2
Personal care	2.4	2.9	1.0
Health expenses	5.4	6.3	4.9
Other[1]	4.5	4.9	3.2
Insurance and retirement	5.0%	5.8%	8.1%
Gifts and contributions	2.6%	3.7%	2.6%

1. Includes tobacco and alcohol, and miscellaneous expenditures (such as legal and accounting fees, banking services, expenses connected with investment, property and nonpleasure trips, and funeral expenses).

Sources: 1950 data, *Study of Consumer Expenditures, Income and Savings: Statistical Tables, Urban U.S.—1950*, vol. 18, *Summary of Family Income, Expenditures and Savings, All Urban Areas Combined*, University of Pennsylvania, 1957, Table 2; 1960–61 data, *Consumer Expenditures and Incomes: Cross Classification of Family Characteristics, Urban United States, 1960–61*, Bureau of Labor Statistics Report No. 237–38, Supplement 2-Part A, July 1964, Table 11e; 1972–73 data, *1972–73 Consumer Expenditure Survey*, unpublished tabulations obtained from the Division of Living Conditions, Bureau of Labor Statistics, Department of Labor, Washington, D.C.

Between 1950 and 1972 income and personal property taxes of the average middle-income, four-person family increased from 5 percent to 13 percent of total income. The family's financial position, as measured by the net change in assets minus liabilities, improved from a negative 5.4 percent of after-tax income in 1950 to a positive 8.3 percent of after-tax income in 1972.[10] The improvement in the economic position of these middle-income families is also reflected in the higher home ownership rate, which increased from 57 percent to 72 percent.

Because expenditures reflect both price and quantity changes, the impact of these trends on the standard of living partly depends on the growth of the quantities of goods and services consumed after removing the impact of price changes. In some cases, price changes that were larger or smaller than average concealed the real change in the quantity of an item families actually consumed.[11] The decline in the proportion of income spent on food, for example, occurred because people increased their food consumption less than they increased most of their other consumption expenditures. In contrast, the decline in the proportion of income spent on clothing reflects both lower-than-average price increases and a slower-than-average rate of increase in quantity purchase. The increase in the proportion of income being spent on private automobile transportation reflects the fact that below-average price increases in autos and parts and gas and oil were more than offset by above-average quantity increases. The price of housing grew at the average rate, so the increase in the proportion of income spent on housing reflects above-average growth in the quantity purchased.[12]

---

10. Because of underreporting, the implicit savings should be used only for relative comparisons. In all three surveys, family income appears to be understated more than family expenditures are understated, and savings appear to be understated more than any other item, so that savings are greater than the reported change in assets minus liabilities. See Robert B. Pearl, "The 1972–73 Consumer Expenditure Survey: A Preliminary Evaluation," University of Illinois; Cathryn Dippo, John Coleman, and Curtis Jacobs, "Evaluation of the 1972–73 Consumer Expenditure Survey," U.S. Department of Labor, Bureau of Labor Statistics, both papers presented at the annual meeting of the American Statistical Association, Chicago, August 1977; and Helen H. Lamale, *Methodology of the Survey of Consumer Expenditures in 1950* (Philadelphia: University of Pennsylvania, 1959).

11. In general, prices increased least for durables and energy sources and most for services over this period.

12. Since the 1972–73 Consumer Expenditure Survey was taken, major changes in the price structure have occurred as a result of the oil price increases instituted by OPEC. The United States has not yet absorbed the full impact of the increase in the international price of oil. Although prices increased almost three times

Figure 14 shows changes between 1950 and 1972 in the actual quantities of goods people consumed. These changes must be compared with the 27 percent population growth the country experienced between 1950 and 1972 in order to determine whether a consumption increase implies that the average standard of living improved.

The change in the quantity of food consumed exceeded the population increase but was considerably less than consumption increases in other categories. Consumption of durables, gas and oil, housing, and household utilities increased most rapidly. Fuel oil and coal is the only category to show a decrease in the average per capita consumption.

The higher incomes of American families have enabled them to buy more of all major consumption items; but, as already noted, the proportion of income spent on food and clothing has fallen significantly while the proportion spent on housing and transportation has risen with the increased ownership of homes and automobiles. At the same time, the higher income levels have permitted families to increase their expenditures on nonconsumption items such as pensions and insurance. Although the proportion of income that most families must spend on the traditional necessities—food, shelter, and clothing—has decreased substantially over the past two decades, the proportion of income committed to transportation and insurance has increased, and under modern urban living conditions these payments may seem no less necessary than the payments for food and clothing in an earlier period.

The declining share of the family budget devoted to food and clothing has special significance for women's work patterns. Actions taken by a housewife to decrease household costs through her meal preparation and clothing care efforts made less difference to her family's budget in 1972 than in 1950. Although a dollar saved is still

---

faster than quantities over the 1972–76 period, quantities of personal consumption items still grew 12 percent while the population grew 3 percent.

The price increases of durables were below average while the quantity increases (especially for furniture and household equipment) were above average. The opposite was true for nondurables, which had above-average price increases (especially for gas and oil, fuel oil and coal, and to a lesser extent, food) and below-average quantity increases (with a decrease for fuel oil and coal and almost no change for gas and oil). In general, the price increases for services were above average. But within this group, the increases in the prices and quantities of housing were considerably below average and above average, respectively, and the prices of household gas and electricity increased sharply. Overall, expenditures for energy sources increased much more than average, and food expenditures increased at the same rate as average personal consumption. Except for energy and food, the trends from the earlier period continued between 1972 and 1976.

FIGURE 14

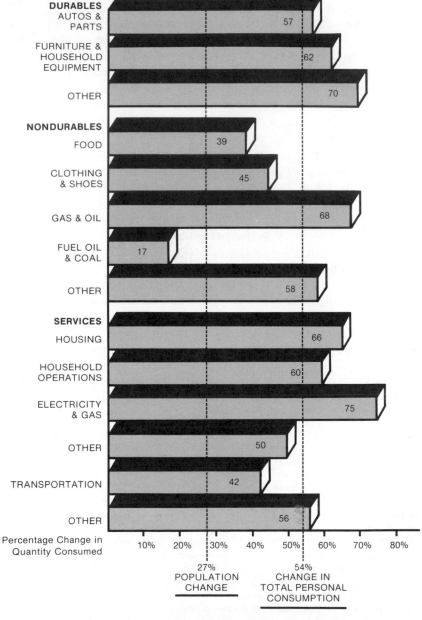

**ESTIMATED QUANTITY CHANGES IN PERSONAL
CONSUMPTION EXPENDITURES, 1950-1972**

SOURCE: Calculated from U.S. Department of Commerce,
Survey of Current Business, January 1976, Part II.
These proportions give the estimated difference
between 1972 and 1950 levels divided by the 1972 level.
Therefore, they should be read as "quantities were X
percent lower in 1950 than in 1972."

a dollar earned, such money-saving activities have become relatively less valuable as a proportion of a family's total expenditures.

Families can use their rising real incomes in any combination of three ways: they can consume more goods and services, they can increase their financial assets (or reduce their debts), or they can have more leisure (nonpaid) time. The data indicate that most American families have chosen the first two ways but not the third.

What the Wife's Paycheck Buys

To calculate the actual contribution of the wife's market work to the household, a two-step procedure will be followed. First, expenditures associated with a wife's working will be estimated; then, the actual increase in expenditures for market goods and services the wife's earnings make possible will be measured. Together, these calculations should answer the question of how the living standard of a household changes when the wife becomes employed.

A close examination of the 1972 Consumer Expenditure Survey reveals the differences in the ways that working-wife and homemaker families spend their money. Cross-tabulations of households provide an impression of the overall outcome of individual decision making about how to form households, how many children to have, how to use time in paid and unpaid work, and how to spend income. Households are divided into four income groups: low ($2,000–$5,999), lower-middle ($6,000–$10,999), middle ($11,000–$16,999), and upper-middle ($17,000–$34,999).[13]

Comparison of Working-Wife and Homemaker Families

Homemaker and working-wife families are compared only for the middle-income groups. There are few working wives among low-income families; in fact, a low-income wife's entry into the labor market normally would raise her family's income above the low-income level of $6,000. In the survey sample, the labor force participation rates of the wives are 36 percent for the lower-middle-income group, 47 percent for the middle-income group, and 58 percent for the upper-middle-income group (see Table 23). On average, the working wife's earnings account for approximately 30 percent of her family's income, and working-wife families have $2,600 more income than homemaker families.

---

13. Because the following analysis of the 1972–73 Consumer Expenditure Survey is based on the data tape of the individual households rather than the published tabulations used in the first part of the paper, the income categories have been slightly modified. The estimated distribution of families is 18 percent (low), 27 percent (lower-middle), 27 percent (middle), and 22 percent (upper-middle). Detailed data on households with incomes below $2,000 or above $34,999 are not available. Households other than husband-wife families were not analyzed.

Table 23

WIFE'S LABOR FORCE STATUS AND EARNINGS IN
1972 SAMPLE

	Number of Families in Group	Percentage of Families with Working Wives	Average Working Wife's Earnings	Wife's Earnings as a Percentage of Family Income (average)
I. Income (low) $2,000–$5,999	334	23	$1,261	29
II. Income (lower-middle) $6,000–$10,999	1,016	36	$2,650	30
III. Income (middle) $11,000–$16,999	1,527	47	$3,871	28
IV. Income (upper-middle) $17,000–$34,999	1,402	58	$6,225	28
Average income:			$14,516	
Working-wife families' income			$15,914	
Wife's earnings			$ 4,520	
As percentage of family income			28%	
Homemaker families' income			$13,325	

Note: A wife is classified as employed if she worked at least 14 weeks in the preceding year or earned at least $900. The sample is based on 4,324 husband-wife families which had incomes between $2,000 and $34,999 and in which the husband was between 25 and 64 years old. Forty-six percent of the wives in this group were in the labor force.

Source: 1972–73 Consumer Expenditure Survey (CEX) interview tapes.

Table 24 shows that the financial resources of homemaker families differ from those of working-wife families in several significant ways. These differences demonstrate that merely comparing the money income of households will exaggerate the full income of working-wife families relative to the income of homemaker families. For a given income group, the estimated savings, the market value of financial assets, and the net change in assets minus liabilities are generally higher for a homemaker family than for a working-wife family. In addition, homemaker families have higher rates of home ownership, and the average value of a homemaker family's home is higher. These differences in wealth or assets result from the fact that, when income is held constant, a working-wife family's full income is less than a homemaker family's because the former has given up some home-produced services and has more work-related expenses. Although minor variations exist, working-wife and homemaker families do seem to spend their incomes in similar ways.[14] In the middle- and upper-income groups, the working-wife family spends less on nondurables; and in all three groups, the working-wife family spends more on finance charges, insurance, and retirement.

Many of the differences in the wealth and expenditure patterns of working-wife and full-time homemaker families are a result of differences in household characteristics rather than in the wife's work status. For this reason, a more detailed expenditure comparison was made, one that took into account a family's assets, the number and age group of its children, the life-cycle stage of the head of the family as well as the work status of the wife and the family's after-tax income.[15]

---

14. Myra H. Strober, "Wives' Labor Force Behavior and Family Consumption Pattern," *American Economic Review*, February 1977, pp. 410–17, found the proportion of income spent on durables was the same for working-wife and full-time homemaker families and the proportion of income spent on consumption was higher for working-wife than for full-time homemaker families. She also found that homemaker families had greater assets than working-wife families did, and that the latter spent more on cars. Myra H. Strober and Charles B. Weinberg found that family purchases of time-saving durables, other durables, hobby and recreation items, vacations, and college education were influenced by family income but not by the wife's labor force behavior. See their "Working Wives and Major Family Expenditures," *Journal of Consumer Research*, December 1977, pp. 141–47.

15. This analysis was based on a multivariate regression equation using data from the 1972–73 Consumer Expenditure Survey. The functional relationship estimated was:

$$\text{EXP}_i = \alpha_0 \prod_i X_i^{\alpha_i} \, e^{\beta_1 \text{PT}} \, e^{\beta_2 \text{FT}}$$

where EXP_i is expenditures on item i; X is a vector of explanatory variables representing after-tax income, assets, number of family members, and their age groupings; FT and PT are dummy variables signifying full-time work (usually thirty-five or more hours at least thirty-two weeks during year with earnings of at least $400) and part-time work (not full-time work but at least thirteen weeks of work and with at least $400 in earnings) for the wife, respectively. Items for which the wife's work status was not significant are not included (house furnishings, furniture and appliances, health expenses). Sample size is 5,996 households. In 40 percent of the families, the wife was in the labor force, and 60 percent of the employed wives were classified as full-time workers.

Table 24

COMPARISON OF FOUR-PERSON HOMEMAKER AND WORKING-WIFE FAMILIES, 1972 SAMPLE

	Working-Wife Families			Homemaker Families		
	II (Lower-Middle)	III (Middle)	IV (Upper-Middle)	II (Lower-Middle)	III (Middle)	IV (Upper-Middle)
Income	$9,076	$14,084	$22,337	$8,986	$13,518	$21,264
Taxes	$1,168	$1,920	$4,143	$1,054	$1,958	$3,709
Wife's earnings as a % of total income	29%	23%	26%	—	—	—
Financial assets	$1,271	$2,512	$5,852	$2,139	$3,557	$8,854
Net Δ (assets-liabilities)	$882	$231	$985	$890	$780	$2,925
Percentage owning homes	57%	82%	84%	61%	79%	90%
Average value of home	$20,254	$23,762	$29,275	$19,106	$24,436	$33,555
Proportion owning cars	97%	98%	99%	95%	99%	98%
1 car	43	24	21	43	36	25
2+ cars	54	74	78	52	63	73
Total disbursements as a % of after-tax income:	104%	91%	84%	98%	91%	85%
Nondurables	70	55	51	67	60	54
Durables	9	14	11	10	11	12
Services	8	7	6	7	6	6
Finance charges, insurance, and retirement	17	15	16	14	14	13

Expenditures on selected items as a
% of after-tax income:

Food, total	22%	17%	14%	20%	19%	14%
Food at home	18	13	10	17	15	11
Shelter, total	15	10	10	15	13	12
Clothing and drycleaning	8	6	7	7	6	7
Transportation	17	20	16	18	16	15
Recreation	4	6	7	5	6	7
Health expenses	6	5	4	6	5	4
Retirement and pensions	6	6	6	5	5	5

Note: These figures are representative of averages for husband-wife families of other sizes as well as for four-person families.

Source: Tabulations of Consumer Expenditure Survey, 1972 interview data. Only families with heads between the ages of 25 and 64 are included. Wife was classified as "employed" if she worked at least 14 weeks during the year or earned at least $900.

This approach permitted comparing the ways working-wife families spend their incomes with those of homemaker families who have similar resources and needs, as determined by their household composition. The results showed that for some categories of expenditures— house furnishings, furniture and appliances, and health care—the wife's work status made no significant difference.

For those expenditures that did prove to differ according to a wife's work status, the expenditures for a homemaker family and a working-wife family were calculated assuming that after-tax income, assets, and household composition for these families were the same as for the sample average. As Table 25 shows, the main expenditure differences between these two comparable homemaker and working-wife families are for transportation, Social Security, and clothing. These are precisely the categories in which additional expenses are incurred when a wife takes a job.

An Employed Wife's Work-Related Expenditures

When a wife works, neither the money she spends on work expenses nor the extra purchase of market goods and services that save housework time increases her family's consumption; the first represents a dead loss, and the second represents a change in methods of producing household services. Even though the two effects cannot be neatly separated, the excess expenditures by working-wife families over expenditures by homemaker families with the *same money income and family composition* are a conservative estimate of the total of the two effects, which will be designated work-related expenditures or expenses.[16] These expenditures, which do not include the decline in nonmarket work and leisure, are the minimum amount by which a wife's after-tax earnings should be adjusted downward before comparing her family's income to a homemaker family's income.

More than 70 percent of the increased expenditures of the working-wife family are for transportation and for retirement funds. The additional expenditures for retirement by the working wife are accounted

---

16. Under the assumption that the preference structure for different types of consumption does not vary systematically for working-wife and homemaker families with the same income and household composition, it can be shown that this expenditure comparison underestimates work-related expenditures. The estimate for the working-wife family's increased work-related and time-saving expenditures is biased downward by the homemaker family's higher expenditures in all categories made possible because its budget does not contain these work-related expenses.

Table 25

ESTIMATED EXPENDITURES FOR EMPLOYED WIVES, 1972

Average Annual Expenditures	Full-Time Homemaker Wife (1)	Wife Working Full Time (2)	(2)—(1) Difference
Transportation	$ 980	$1,261	$281
Social Security and pensions	116	323	207
Clothing	365	468	103
Food, total	1,555	1,602	47
Dry cleaning, clothing care	49	65	16
Insurance	82	97	15
Personal care	52	66	14
Domestic services and materials	18	22	4
Education	4	5	1
TOTAL	$3,221	$3,909	$688
Shelter	866	792	−72

Source: Regressions based on 1972–73 Consumer Expenditure Survey data.

for by her family's larger total contribution to Social Security.[17] Child care expenses, which are embedded in the categories of education (as nursery school or kindergarten) and in domestic services (as baby-sitting, child care centers, and domestic help), do not show up as important expenditures for the average working wife. The average amounts spent annually in these two categories of education and

17. Although both husband's and wife's earnings are taxed individually up to the Social Security ceiling, in most cases contributions made to the Social Security fund by a wife and her employer have little or no effect upon her and her family's benefits. This is also true of fringe benefits for the employed wife; many health plans cover the family rather than the individual, so the wife is already covered by the husband's plan.

The 1972 Social Security payroll tax on employees was 5.2 percent on a maximum of $9,000 earnings per worker. The Consumer Expenditure Survey recorded 88.5 percent of this tax under pensions and retirement and 11.5 percent under health expenses. Both homemaker and working-wife families pay Social Security taxes on the husband's first $9,000 earnings; the working-wife family also pays Social Security taxes on the wife's earnings. In the calculations made on the sample average, the additional $207 in retirement expenditures for the working wife represents the recorded payroll tax on $4,500 earnings, or slightly more than the average additional earnings ($4,200) of the working-wife family that are taxed.

domestic services/materials are so small that any difference between the two family types may be important in terms of the relative amounts spent, but the difference is not important in absolute terms for the family's budget.

Because we are comparing families with equal incomes, any increased expenditure in one category must be offset by a decreased expenditure in another category or by a decrease in savings. These results show that a working-wife family's increased expenditures are partially offset by decreased expenditures on shelter. Families with employed wives pay for their higher work-related expenses by spending a larger proportion of their incomes and by decreasing their shelter expenditures. The work-related expenditures averaged $688 for full-time working wives, or approximately 14 percent of these wives' earnings before income taxes. The income taxes on the wife's earnings in this example are estimated to be $950, so her work-related expenses and income taxes take 34 percent of her paycheck.[18] In other words, after paying for taxes and increased expenditures that accompany working, the wife who earns $4,800 actually increases her family's disposable income by only $3,160.

For the average middle-income or upper-middle-income household with a working wife, the household would drop to the next lower income class if the wife did not earn a paycheck. For example, if the working wife in an average middle-income family left the labor market, her family would become a lower-middle-income family. (Compare the middle-income working-wife family with the lower-middle-income homemaker family in Table 24.) Expenditures on food, clothing, transportation, recreation, and retirement would be 25 percent to 50 percent lower for the middle-income family if the wife were not employed; expenditures on shelter would be only slightly lower. For the upper-middle-income family with an employed wife, expenditures on clothing, transportation, recreation, and retirement would be 40 percent to 50 percent lower, and expenditures on food and shelter would be 15 percent to 20 percent lower if the wife were not employed. In general, expenditures on all items would be lower, although expenditures on nondurables (which include the necessities) would decline less than the other categories. In addition, the family would put less of its income into savings and other financial assets.

---

18. This example assumes after-tax income is $9,904 (sample mean) and the earnings of a full-time working wife are $4,800 (40 percent of the family's before-tax income of $12,000). The income taxes on the wife's earnings are estimated to be $950, or 20 percent, the implicit tax rate in the Consumer Expenditure Survey cross-tabulations.

The task of filtering out the differences in consumption and life-styles between families with employed wives and families with full-time homemakers is difficult because these two family types differ in fundamental ways other than the wife's work activities. In general, husbands in families with working wives earn less and are more likely to be less than fifty years old. Working-wife families also are smaller and have fewer children under age six. Although the average working-wife family has higher total income, it has less unearned and "other" income (i.e., income other than the wife's earnings) than the home-maker family has.[19]

Incremental Expenditures

The expenditures shown in Table 25 for these two family types having the same income compare a homemaker family with above-average income for such families and a working-wife family with below-average income for working-wife families. Alternatively, we can compare the two family types by holding their "other income" constant. This approach allows us to analyze how a wife's paycheck is spent, as opposed to how total family income is spent. Because other income is primarily the husband's earnings, "husband's earnings" will be used to designate the broader category of "other income."

In this comparison, the homemaker family has below-average husband's earnings for such families, and the working-wife family has above-average husband's earnings for working-wife families. The working-wife family's total income will exceed the homemaker family's income by the amount of the wife's earnings.

Expenditures were calculated for a working-wife family and a home-maker family with the same amount of husband's earnings and family composition, both of which were set equal to the sample average (see Table 26).[20] The results show that the wife's paycheck is spent on those items that represent the bulk of expenditures for any family— food (6 percent), shelter (5 percent), and transportation (13 percent),

---

19. See Robert Holbrook and Frank Stafford, "The Propensity to Consume Separate Types of Income: A Generalized Permanent Income Hypothesis," *Econometrica* 39 (January 1971): 1–21; and Strober, "Wives' Labor Force Behavior."

20. Although the wife's $5,000 earnings increased the family's income by 52 percent, recorded expenditures increased 35 percent. In addition to recorded expenditures, another 15 percent to 20 percent of the wife's earnings is absorbed by income taxes (based on the implicit tax rates in Table 24), and the remaining 25 percent is either saved or spent on unrecorded expenditures. The working-wife family in the current example spends 77 percent of its gross income on recorded expenditures, which is comparable to the 79 percent spent by the average working-wife family in income group III (Table 24).

along with clothing (5 percent), recreation (5 percent), and retirement (8 percent) (see Table 26, column 1).[21] Expenditures on food, shelter, and health increase at less than the average rate, and expenditures on domestic service, dry cleaning and clothing repair, clothing, transportation, personal care, insurance, and retiremént increase at more than twice the average rate (see Table 26, column 2).

How do these increased expenditures from a wife's paycheck compare with the way a homemaker family would spend a $5,000 increase in the husband's earnings? On average, a working-wife family spends a larger proportion of the wife's paycheck on dry cleaning and clothing repair, transportation, and Social Security than the homemaker family would spend with a comparable increase in the husband's earnings (Table 26, column 3). In contrast, expenditures on food, recreation, gifts and contributions, and especially shelter and personal care account for larger proportions of the additional expenditures that would be made by a homemaker family.

These results are compatible with the earlier estimation of work-related expenses.[22] In comparisons of both total and incremental expenditures made by the homemaker and working-wife families, the family with an employed wife had significantly greater expenditures on clothing, transportation, and retirement contributions and smaller money outlays on shelter. Although a wife's market job increases the income of her family and allows the outlays on food, shelter, and other goods to increase, a large proportion of the wife's paycheck is spent on income and payroll taxes and on work-related expenditures.

In short, a family whose income increases by $5,000 when the wife accepts a job is worse off than a homemaker family whose income in-

---

21. This comparison is calculated from the following regression, which was estimated using the 1972–73 Consumer Expenditure Survey:

$$\text{EXP}_i = \alpha_0 \prod_i X_i^{\alpha_1} \, E^{\sigma_2} \, Y^{\beta_1^{FT}} \, e^{\beta_2^{PT}}$$

where EXP_i represents expenditures on item i_1, X is a vector of explanatory variables representing assets, number of family members and their age groupings; E is the wife's gross earnings; Y is total family income *not* including wife's earnings; FT and PT are dummy variables signifying full-time and part-time work for the wife, respectively (defined as in Table 25).

22. The only exception is in personal care, a small category that includes services purchased at the beauty parlor or barber shop and the purchase and repair of hair dryers and electric shavers. In the first comparison (Table 25), a working-wife family spent more total income on personal care than a homemaker family did; Table 26 shows that a homemaker family spent a higher proportion of the $5,000 incremental income on personal care than the working-wife family did.

Table 26

ESTIMATES OF HOW A WORKING WIFE'S EARNINGS ARE SPENT

Recorded Expenditures	Expenditure Distribution of Wife's $5,000 Earnings[1] (percent)	Increase in Expenditures with Wife's Paycheck[2] (percent)	Proportion of Increased Expenditures: Working-Wife vs. Homemaker Families[3]
Total	58.0	35	—
Selected Items:			
Food, total	5.8	20	.87
Shelter	5.0	26	.54
Domestic service	.2	75	1.05
Dry cleaning and clothing repair	.7	77	1.84
Clothing	4.9	75	1.52
Transportation	12.9	75	1.70
Personal care	.2	78	.35
Recreation	5.3	70	.84
Health	2.1	32	1.00
Insurance	1.2	84	1.05
Social Security and retirement	7.8	442	4.10
Gifts and contributions	1.4	68	.74

1. Expenditures for a full-time working-wife family with $5,000 earnings and $9,524 other income were compared with the expenditures for a full-time homemaker family with $9,524 total income. Assets and household composition variables were set to the sample mean; $9,524 is the sample mean for income other than wife's earnings.
2. This column gives the percentage difference between expenditures made by the full-time working-wife family (with wife's earnings equal to $5,000 and total income equal to $14,524) compared with the full-time homemaker family (with total income equal to $9,524). The working-wife family's income is 52 percent (or $5,000) higher than the full-time homemaker family's income.
3. This column gives the proportion of the difference in recorded expenditures spent on each item by a working-wife family (from wife's $5,000 earnings) divided by the analogous proportion for a homemaker family whose income increases $5,000. The former family is assumed to have $5,000 wife's earnings and $9,524 other income, and the latter family to have $14,524 other income. Total recorded expenditures accounted for 58 percent of the incremental income from the wife's $5,000 earnings compared with only 30 percent of the increased $5,000 other income for the full-time homemaker family.

creases by $5,000 when the husband is "promoted." In the former case, the family loses its full-time homemaker and incurs work-related expenses, which may account for one-fifth of the wife's earnings.

When a wife takes a job outside the home, the following changes in housework activities may occur: (1) the family purchases market substitutes for some of the services normally provided within the home; (2) the wife decreases her housework time, and the husband and other family members increase their housework time; and (3) the provision of services at home diminishes in an absolute sense. Examination of expenditure patterns showed the first effect to be empirically unimportant. The importance of the second and third effects, therefore, determines what happens to the production of services at home when the wife is not a full-time homemaker.

THE WORK DONE IN THE HOME

In most American families headed by a husband and wife, the wife has the responsibility of supervising the household and generally does the bulk of the housework herself. In a time-budget study of household production in the late 1960s, Kathryn Walker found that wives who were full-time homemakers did 72 percent of the housework.[23] The Walker study also showed that the extent of sharing housework among family members was slight, whether the wife had an outside job or not. Even when wives were employed outside the home, they still did 61 percent of all the housework.

According to Walker, husbands did 14 percent of the housework when their wives were employed and 18 percent when their wives were employed. But the husband's greater share of housework does not represent more hours of housework; it reflects less total time spent on housework. The amount of time the husband devoted to housework varied primarily with his hours spent in paid labor; husbands employed less than forty hours were found to work fifteen hours per week at home, while those employed more than forty hours worked eight hours per week at home. The average husband spent about eleven hours on housework activities each week regardless of his wife's work status or their number of children. In fact, a husband with two or three children was found to contribute *less* time to housework on average when his wife was employed.[24]

---

23. Kathryn E. Walker and Margaret E. Woods, *Time Use: A Measure of Household Production of Family Goods and Services*, American Home Economics Association, 1976, Table 3.10. Wives who were employed less than fourteen hours per week were classified as homemakers or not employed (p. 13).

24. Ibid., p. 44, Tables 3.4, 3.10, 3.14, 3.15, 3.16.

The average weekly hours of housework contributed by the children did not vary with the mother's work status. Teenagers averaged eight hours per week, and six- through eleven-year-olds averaged four hours per week.[25]

A Comparison of the Housework Time of Working-Wife Families and Homemaker Families

According to Walker's data, husbands took part mainly in the non-physical care of children, marketing, yard and car care, and special house care (including maintaining the structure and making furnishings). Children participated primarily in after-meal cleanup, regular house care, marketing, and yard and car care. But the wife, employed or not, accounted for the majority of the time spent in all housework activities except yard, car, and special house care, with the additional exception that the employed wife accounted for less than the majority of the time spent in nonphysical care of family members, which is the only activity involving people other than the immediate family to any extent.[26]

Wives performed four major housework activities: (1) meal preparation and (2) cleanup, which together accounted for about 30 percent of her housework time; (3) care of family members, which accounted for 15 percent to 25 percent of her time and varied with her work status and the number of children; and (4) clothing care and regular house care, each of which accounted for about 15 percent of her time.[27] Wives with children averaged a minimum of thirty-six hours each week working in the home, whether or not they also had a paid job outside the home.

An employed wife spent less time on housework than a full-time homemaker did, in part because her family typically is smaller and her children older; hence the demand for services in the home is reduced. On average, the employed wife worked nineteen fewer hours per week (or 34 percent less time) in the home than the homemaker did; other family members (or others) made up only two hours per week of this difference. When the number and ages of her children are taken into account, the actual decline in the employed wife's time spent on housework was less than the average indicates. For example, a working wife with two children averaged seventeen fewer hours (or 30 percent less time) in housework each week than her homemaker counterpart did, but the difference was only twelve hours

25. Ibid., Table 3.6.
26. Ibid., Tables 3.10 and 3.12.
27. Ibid., Table 3.12.

(or 25 percent) if the youngest child was between two and eleven years old.[28]

The housework activity most affected by the wife's employment, Walker found, was the time spent caring for family members. The average working wife's time spent in physical care was 50 percent to 75 percent less and that in nonphysical care 25 percent to 50 percent less than the time spent by the average full-time homemaker with the same number of children. Other family members (or outsiders) did not make up much of the lesser amount of time the working mother spent in physical care because, as has been noted, working women's children typically are older and need less care.[29] In contrast, the shorter time working wives spent in the nonphysical care of family members was largely offset by the greater time input of other women who were not members of the immediate family.

The difference in the time working wives spent in other housework activities compared with homemakers' time was less dramatic. The average time spent in marketing and management activities was not affected by a wife's work status. The times spent on house care and clothing care were comparable, ranging from 15 percent to 35 percent and varying with the number of children. Other family members made up most of the lesser time the working wife spent on house care, but they made up only part of the shorter time she spent on clothing care. This asymmetry most likely reflects the differences in the ways these two services are purchased outside the home. Many clothing care services can be procured easily in the quantity desired at the local drycleaners and laundry. House care is not so easily purchased, because it involves hiring someone to come into the home to work under supervision for an agreed-upon time.

Walker classified the hours intended for the education and socialization of a child (as opposed to purely pleasurable activity) as "secondary time spent on nonphysical care of family members."[30] This component of a parent's housework constitutes an important part of the adult-child interaction in families with children. A close examination of the Walker study reveals that the major difference between an employed and a nonemployed wife's housework activities occurred in this important, but often unnoticed, category of secondary, nonphysical care (see Figure 15). Although an employed wife's total time in housework activities differs surprisingly little from that of a homemaker, much of her housework is done during a different time period,

---

28. Ibid., Table 3.5.

29. Ibid., Tables 5.4 and 5.5. In the Walker sample, only 31 percent of the employed wives had any children under six years old, compared with 60 percent of the homemakers who had children under age six.

30. Ibid., p. 106.

FIGURE 15

SECONDARY TIME FOR NONPHYSICAL CARE OF FAMILY MEMBERS IN HOMEMAKER AND WORKING-WIFE FAMILIES, 1976

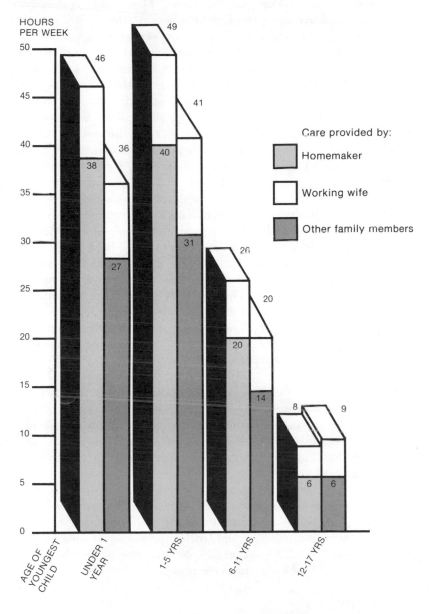

SOURCE: Calculated from Kathryn E. Walker and Margaret E. Woods, *Time Use: A Measure of Household Production of Family Goods and Services* American Home Economics Association, 1976, Table 5.8.

when her children are most likely doing homework, watching television, or sleeping.

Interestingly enough, the secondary time the husband of a working
wife spent with the children was little more than the time spent by
husbands whose wives were not employed. There was no difference
in the husband's average secondary interaction time if his youngest
child was younger than one year old or between the ages of six and
eleven. If his youngest child was between one and five, the husband's
average secondary, nonphysical time was 8.5 hours per week rather
than 7.7 hours. If his children were teenagers, the father spent 1.5
more hours each week (for a total of 3.5 hours) with them in indirect
interaction, and this greater amount more than offset the lesser time
his working wife spent with them.[31] This was not the case for the pre-
teenaged children—they simply received less secondary attention.
Children ages six to eleven received six fewer hours per week of their
mother's secondary time if she had a job, and children ages one to five
received nine fewer hours of their mother's secondary time.

Together, the expenditure patterns and the time budgets indicate
that families do not widely substitute market goods and services for
housework activities when the wife is employed. The average family
with a working wife spends slightly more money and less time on
clothing care and meal preparation than the average homemaker
family does. Expenditures for child care by the average working-wife
family are not sufficiently different to be distinguishable in the data.
Although the time spent in all housework activities except marketing
and management is less for employed wives, most of the difference is
in the parents' time (both primary and secondary) spent with their
children.

These observations lead to an important finding: The abstract
image of the working wife using her paycheck to buy market substitutes for her housework activities does not portray reality. Instead, a
wife's paycheck is used to purchase the same kinds of consumer goods
and services that the homemaker family buys, and the working wife
lengthens her work time in order to do the necessary housework.

The quality of the time spent in housework activities, especially
child rearing, has not been discussed here. The matter involves a
complex array of issues, including the psychological well-being of the
family members individually and collectively and is discussed in
Chapters 4 and 5 of this book. A simpler measure of well-being, the
total work time of husbands and wives, is explored here.

---

31. Ibid., Table 5.8.

The Total Weekly Work Time of Husbands and Wives

Although the Walker study is the only major collection of data on families' use of time in the United States in the late 1960s, the Survey Research Center at the University of Michigan collected time use data on individuals in 1965 and 1976. Some results from these studies, along with the data on hours at the job collected by the U.S. Bureau of Labor Statistics, are shown in Table 27.

When wives specialize in housework and their husbands specialize in market work, the Walker study shows a disparity in how many hours each works. The husband tends to work long hours at his job, averaging fifty-five hours per week (including commuting and volunteer work), and the wife works about the same number of hours at home. But the husband also contributes some time to housework, with the result that he works six hours, or 10 percent, more each week than his wife does.

The divergence in work hours is in the opposite direction in families in which the wife has a full-time market job. The full-time working wife, because she continues to do the equivalent of another job in running the house, averages seventy-one hours of work each week, or 30 percent more time than her husband's fifty-five hours. The long work week of the full-time homemaker's husband partially compensates for her not being employed, but still the family with both spouses employed full time devotes twenty-six more hours to paid work than the homemaker family does. In contrast, the husband and wife in the homemaker family reportedly spend twenty-three more hours on housework. A more equitable sharing of the workload apparently exists among families in which a wife works part time; but the wife still spends more than 70 percent of her work time in housework and her husband spends more than 80 percent of his work time in market work.

One similarity among family types does emerge from these numbers: The average total work time for all family types is the same (averaging 126 to 127 hours per week), even though the work effort is distributed differently between the husband and wife and even though the allocation of work time between paid work and housework varies substantially.

The results from the Survey Research Center (SRC) study at the University of Michigan are similar to those reported by Walker, although husbands and wives in the SRC survey cannot be compared since individuals (not families) were sampled. In general, the employed married women in the SRC sample displayed the same patterns of paid work and housework as the full-time working wives in the Walker

Table 27

AVERAGE TOTAL WEEKLY WORK TIME FOR
HUSBANDS AND WIVES, 1965–76

	Hours per Week		
	Labor Market[1]	Housework	Total Time
I. Walker Study, 1967–68[2]			
Homemaker families			
Wife	3	57	60
Husband	55	11	66
Part-time employed wife[3]			
Wife	18	47	65
Husband	51	11	62
Full-time employed wife[4]			
Wife	37	34	71
Husband	44	11	55
II. Survey Research Center (SRC) Study, 1965[5]			
Married women, employed	36	34	69
Married men, employed	48	13	61
Married women, not employed	1	54	55
SRC Study, 1976[5]			
Married women, employed	32	27	59
Married men, employed	44	14	58
III. Current Population Survey (CPS), 1965			
Married women, employed	35	—	—
Married men, employed	45	—	—
CPS, 1976			
Married women, employed	34	—	—
Married men, employed	43	—	—

1. Labor market time in the Walker study includes the time spent at the job and in volunteer activities, including travel time. Labor market time in the SRC studies includes the time spent at a job but not volunteer or commuting time. Labor market time in the CPS refers to the actual number of hours worked during the survey week.

2. In these homemaker families, which constituted 66 percent of the Walker sample, the wife did not engage in any paid labor; her 3 hours of labor market time represented volunteer work.

3. Part-time working wives were defined to include women who engaged in up to 30

sample, and the employed married men have the same patterns as the husbands of part-time working wives, who would be representative of the "average" husband in the Walker sample.

Unfortunately, little information on the use of time has been collected in the mid-1970s, so our knowledge about changes in the work done at home during the past decade of rapid increase in wives' labor force participation is somewhat speculative. One small sample collected by the Michigan Survey Research Center indicates that remarkable changes may have occurred in female work patterns between 1965 and 1976. The paid work time of employed married women was found to have dropped about 10 percent (from thirty-six to thirty-two hours) and their housework time to have dropped 20 percent (from thirty-four to twenty-seven hours). As a result, the total work week of the average employed wife reportedly decreased from sixty-nine to fifty-nine hours.

This outcome is at variance with the earlier Walker results, which found wives' housework time increased as their market time decreased. Employed married men also decreased their paid work hours between these two SRC surveys, but they did not increase their contribution to housework time by a corresponding amount, so their total work week fell slightly from sixty-one hours to fifty-eight hours.[32] The time pat-

---

32. These changes for the husband are consistent with the Walker data because more of the husbands in the 1976 SRC sample would have had employed wives (since the wives' participation rate had increased from 35 percent to 45 percent), and the average husband's paid work time would fall if he exhibited the same patterns as in the Walker sample. But the married men in the 1976 SRC sample spent three more hours each week on housework than husbands in the Walker sample did; although in absolute terms, this is a meager amount, it constitutes a 30 percent difference.

---

hours of paid labor per week. These women constituted 18 percent of the Walker sample.

4. Full-time working wives in the Walker study are wives who engaged in 30 or more hours per week of paid labor. They constituted 16 percent of the sample.

5. The SRC samples consisted of individuals rather than families, so husbands and wives cannot be compared. The 1965 sample contained 449 employed married men and 190 employed married women; the 1976 sample contained 147 employed married men and 93 employed married women.

Sources: Calculated from Walker and Woods, *Time Use,* Table 3.17; Survey Research Center (SRC) "Summary of United States Time Use Survey," University of Michigan, 1966, Table 1; Frank Stafford and Greg Duncan, "The Use of Time and Technology by Households in the United States," University of Michigan, 1977, Table 8; U.S. Department of Labor, Bureau of Labor Statistics, *Employment and Earnings,* January 1966, Table A-20, and January 1977, Table 31.

terns in the latest SRC survey demonstrate a trend toward an equaliza-
tion of the total work week for employed married men and women,
primarily as a result of the dramatic decline in the employed wife's
time spent on housework.

How representative for the country as a whole are the time patterns
of the SRC sample of ninety-three employed wives? As Table 26
shows, national data from the Current Population Survey (CPS) on
50,000 households differ in two major ways from the SRC data on
the hours of paid work. Compared with the SRC survey, the CPS
shows only a minor decline in a wife's average hours worked (1965 to
1976), and the labor market times reported in the SRC surveys are
higher than the work hours reported in the CPS (with the exception
of employed wives in 1976).[33] The CPS data indicate that the decline
in wives' (and husbands') hours on the job is overstated in the SRC
survey. Whether the decline in employed wives' work in the home is
also overstated cannot be ascertained until more data on housework
time are available.

If the decrease in work done in the home is corroborated, it will
signal important changes in how the household functions internally
and how it uses its work time. Changes in family composition could
account for only a minor part of any decline in housework, because
there was little difference in the age of the youngest child of employed
wives in 1965 and 1976, although the number of children probably
declined slightly.[34] Moreover, the increase in part-time work by em-

---

33. The labor market time in the SRC survey includes break time and other
nonpaid time spent at the work place, as reported by a diary kept by the respondent.
Labor market time in the CPS refers to the actual number of hours worked, as
reported by one individual in the household for all household members. If we
consider only *paid* work time in the SRC survey, it is uniformly lower than the
CPS work hours for both years. See Frank Stafford and Greg Duncan, "The Use of
Time and Technology by Households in the United States," University of
Michigan, 1977, pp. 19–20.

34. In 1965 and 1976, the distribution of employed wives by age of youngest child
was as follows: 46 percent had no children under eighteen years old, 33 to 34 percent
had children six to seventeen years only, and 20 to 21 percent had a child under
six years of age. (U.S. Department of Labor, Bureau of Labor Statistics, "Marital
and Family Characteristics of Workers in March 1965," *Special Labor Force Report
64*, Table F, and *U.S. Working Women: A Databook*, Table 19.) Although the
distribution of employed wives by number of children under eighteen years of age
is not published, the distribution of husband-wife families by number of children
shows that the proportion of husband-wife families with three or more children
declined while the proportion with two, one, or no children increased between
1965 and 1976. U.S. Department of Commerce, Bureau of the Census, *Statistical
Abstract, 1976*, nos. 40 and 58.

ployed wives (from 26 percent in 1965 to 29 percent in 1976) cannot be used to explain a decline in the employed wife's housework time.[35] On the contrary, an increase in part-time work would normally have been accompanied by an *increase* in employed wives' housework time. Forces other than changes in the composition of working-wife families, the decrease in paid work time of employed wives, or the housework done by husbands must be responsible for any drop in the hours of housework for employed wives during this period.

The 1976 SRC survey shows that men and women still divide their work time differently between paid and unpaid activities, although the total work weeks of the average employed married man and woman are almost equal. The work time for husbands and wives in the various family types most likely remains unequal, with the full-time homemaker working fewer hours than her husband and the wife who works full time putting in a longer total work week than her husband. The part-time employed wife and her husband most likely remain the couple with the most evenly distributed work loads. A central characteristic of home life remains the same—the average working wife still spends twice as much time in housework as the average working husband. Even though the 1976 SRC survey shows the division of labor becoming less specialized, housework still accounts for 46 percent of an employed wife's work time and only 24 percent of an employed husband's work time.

The time-budget studies from the late 1960s raised the question of how long a full-time working wife would be willing to work seventy-one hours each week while her husband works fifty-five hours. Although such an unequal distribution of work might be expected during the period when a wife's work role is changing, wives cannot be expected to work such long hours indefinitely. The 1970s survey indicates that an employed wife may decide that she is unable to do her two full-time jobs with equal dedication, and she may no longer run her home by the same standards as those of the full-time homemaker. Realization by a working wife and her husband that she can-

---

35. Part-time work means less than thirty-five paid hours per week. One-third of the increase in the proportion of employed wives on part time was attributable to economic (i.e., not voluntary) reasons. In addition to the increase in part-time work, the percentage of workers reporting more than forty hours of work during the survey week was 28 percent lower for married women and 16 percent lower for married men in 1976 compared with 1965. U.S. Department of Labor, Bureau of Labor Statistics, *Employment and Earnings*, January 1977, Table A-20, and January 1977, Table 31.

not run the home as if she were a full-time homemaker may eventually lead to additional contributions by her husband.

The rapid changes in women's work roles now occurring show every indication of continuing into the 1980s. Women's increased participation in the work force has become particularly noticeable because it has coincided with the labor force entry of young women born during the post-World War II baby boom.[36] If these women, who will be twenty-seven to forty-four years old in 1990, continue to display a stronger attachment to the labor market than do their female elders— as well as a heightened desire to integrate their market jobs more harmoniously with their personal and family lives—then they will continue to revolutionize the role of women and the ways that families live. Where these fundamental changes are taking us is unclear, since we are in the beginning of a transition period during which wives and their families are assimilating these transformed work and sex roles into their daily lives.

THE FUTURE OF WORK ROLES: SOME CONCLUSIONS

Many observers believe that employment of wives outside the home has increased the strain upon the family because less time is being devoted to fulfilling the personal needs of family members and to having the family operate as a unit. In addition, both spouses must deal with the stresses associated with their jobs in the absence of the support system traditionally provided by a full-time homemaker, who takes care of the "breadwinner's" physical needs and provides him with psychological sustenance. Although family life may deteriorate as wives become employed, turning back the clock may be impossible as well as undesirable. Because the occupation of homemaking demands one's full attention and energies only during the time that young children are in the home and because the family institution fails to guarantee security for members who do not have earnings, providing equal access to the labor market for all adults is a social imperative.

---

36. Since the early 1960s, the growth in the female labor force participation rate, which has been most pronounced for married women ages twenty to thirty-four, has occurred primarily through increases in the participation rates of each successive age group of women. U.S. Department of Commerce, Bureau of the Census, "Population Estimates and Projections," *Current Population Report*, series P-25, no. 704, 1977, Table 6; U.S. Department of Labor, Bureau of Labor Statistics, "Marital and Family Characteristics of Workers, March 1961," *Special Labor Force Report No. 20*, Table 20; and "Marital and Family Characteristics of the Labor Force in March 1976," *Special Labor Force Report No. 206*, Table B.

The family institution, necessary for raising children, must evolve to meet the new needs of its members. For example, in the nuclear family the husband must be willing to change his work role to incorporate more housework responsibilities. People may also experiment with forms of extended families, but the chance of success is unknown. Only one outcome is certain—women's desire to work outside the home will change men's work roles as well as women's. Until working wives can persuade their husbands to divide their energies more evenly between paid labor and work in the home, the two-earner family will show signs of strain caused by too much paid work and too little time devoted to homemaking.

Because there has been no offsetting move toward a shorter work week, the entrance of wives into the labor market has resulted in an overall shift in the family's work effort toward paid labor and away from household production. This trend could be reversed by a decrease in the standard work week for all workers, so that both husbands and wives would have time available to maintain their households and to attend to the needs of family members, especially children.

A shorter work week coupled with a more equitable husband-wife sharing of the housework would produce husband-wife workloads that are more similar both in hours and in types of work. If a shorter work week evolves only for women (and not for men), the outcome will be a new variety of sex-typed work roles. A female part-time worker who has important home responsibilities outside her market job cannot compete either in time or in devotion with a male full-time worker who has a wife providing a supportive home life. Instead of having a life's work of rearing children and running a home, a lifestyle common in the previous generation, women would be coupling their homemaking duties with part-time market jobs in which they do not compete directly with men. For many full-time homemakers, this work pattern may be considered an improvement over the current situation because it widens their opportunities and uses their talents better while avoiding the stresses and fatigue associated with being a full-time working wife. But this outcome is a far cry from the goal of sexual equality, and it would perpetuate the subordinate position of women in our society.

The entrance of wives into the labor market has increased the material well-being of their families, although in the initial stages this economic improvement has been at the expense of interaction of family members and the nonwork activities that provide a balanced life. Thus, the increase in a family's spendable income does not indicate a comparable increase in its well-being. Work roles are changing rapidly, and the options opening up evoke mixed reactions of exhilaration and fear. The transition of women's work from the home to the marketplace marks one more step in the process of advanced industrialization. Within this context, women's market work can be viewed strictly as a means of further increasing the material well-being of their families, or it can be viewed more broadly as a step toward achieving equality between the sexes in all work activities.

Chapter 7

INSTITUTIONAL RESPONSES: THE FEDERAL INCOME TAX SYSTEM

NANCY M. GORDON*

The basic question this chapter explores is the equitable treatment under the income tax system of people in different circumstances—married or single, participating in the labor market or not. As the previous chapters have indicated, during the past few decades women's and men's roles in American society have been changing rapidly and an increasing variety of family structures have been evolving.[1] These outcomes have resulted from the interaction of many factors. Life expectancies have increased, birthrates have fallen, divorce rates have

* The author would like to thank Walter Stromquist, formerly of the Office of Tax Analysis, U.S. Department of the Treasury, for his assistance with this chapter.

1. For example, between 1930 and 1975, the proportion of families headed by women increased from 4.2 percent to 9.5 percent. See Heather Ross and Isabel Sawhill, *Time of Transition: The Growth of Families Headed by Women* (Washington, D.C.: The Urban Institute, 1975).

risen, and women have strengthened their commitment to the labor force.

Consequently, the traditional view of the family is no longer valid. Most women do not marry and remain at home ·for the rest of their lives caring for their husbands and children. Rather, participation in the labor force commonly continues after marriage. A high proportion of women remain in the labor force while they rear young children. Many marriages end in divorce, thus increasing the number of children being reared by a single parent, usually the mother. And, despite women's increasing labor market experience, their wage rates remain at only 60 percent of those of men.[2]

All these factors prompt the question, how well are our social programs functioning? In answer, this chapter and the next will focus on two major institutions: first, the federal income tax system, and then the Social Security system.

To explore the treatment of different types of married couples and single persons under the federal personal income tax system, we need to identify the relative tax burdens of different types of people, the extent to which these different types are represented in the American population, and ways in which their representation will change in the future. We start with an elaboration of the demographic and social changes just outlined. Then we describe the development of the current tax system and the problems posed as a result of changing lifestyles, particularly the increasing commitment of married women to participation in the labor force and the increasing number of single workers. Following a comparison of the current tax system's effects in the years 1976 and 1990, we will identify some proposals for modifying the system, present some preliminary information with which we can examine the consequences of the proposals, and discuss issues requiring further consideration.

DEMOGRAPHIC AND SOCIAL CHANGES

In some respects, life-cycle patterns of women have not changed much since 1900. For example, the average age at which a woman first marries has ranged only from a high of 21.4 in the 1900s and 1930s to a low of 20.0 in the 1950s. The average age at which a married woman has her first child has ranged only from a high of 23.5 in the

---

2. Several factors contribute to the lower wages of women, including their disproportionate representation in low-paying occupations and continuing cases of lower pay for equal work.

1930s to a low of 21.4 in the 1950s. And the average age of a mother at the marriage of her youngest child has ranged only from a high of 55.4 in the 1900s to a low of 52.3 in the 1970s.[3]

Yet life expectancy has increased significantly: by almost ten years (from age 68.8 to 78.7) between 1930 and 1976 for white women who survive to age twenty. For black women alive at age twenty the increase has been even greater: eighteen years (from 57.2 to 74.9).[4] The increases for men who live to age twenty, however, have been considerably less: for whites, six years (from 66.0 to 71.6) and for blacks, eleven years (from 56.0 to 66.8). As a result, women can now expect to live many more years after all their children have married (and many children will have left home before marrying), and women can expect to be widowed for a longer period of time.[5]

A more dramatic change in the life cycle for women has occurred with respect to childbearing. In the 1930s and 1940s, a significant proportion of women continued to bear children during their thirties and forties, but now most women complete childbearing by their early thirties. If we compare live births per thousand women in 1930 and in 1976, we find little change for women between ages twenty and twenty-four (124.9 versus 112.1) or for women between ages twenty-five and twenty-nine (117.3 versus 108.8). For women between ages thirty and thirty-four, however, the number of live births dropped (from 87.7 to 54.5). This drop was even sharper for older women: between ages thirty-five and thirty-nine, from 56.1 to 19.0; between ages forty and forty-four, from 21.8 to 4.3; and between ages forty-five and forty-nine, from 2.4 to 0.2.[6]

This pattern is closely tied to the decline in the proportion of women who have large families. In 1965, among women ages fifteen to forty-four who had already borne at least three children, the fertility rate was 26.8 per thousand women; by 1976 the fertility rate among this group had fallen to 7.3 per thousand.[7] So, on average, women now have many more years of life during which all their children are in school

---

3. Paul C. Glick, "Updating the Life Cycle of the Family," *Journal of Marriage and the Family* 39 (February 1977): 3–15.

4. Races other than white or black are included with blacks.

5. U.S. Department of Commerce, Bureau of the Census, *Statistical Abstract of the United States, 1950*, nos. 89–90; *Statistical Abstract of the United States, 1978*, no. 100.

6. U.S. Department of Commerce, Bureau of the Census, *Statistical Abstract of the United States, 1950*, no. 70, and *1978*, no. 81. Figures refer to live births per thousand women in each age group.

7. U.S. Department of Health, Education, and Welfare, *Monthly Vital Statistics Report* (HRA) 77, 1120, vol. 25, December 30, 1976, Table 5.

or have left home. This factor has contributed to the increasing return of women to the labor force. At the same time, more and more women are remaining in the labor force when their children are young or leaving it for only a short time during that period.

The increasing labor force participation rates of women are also related to rising divorce rates. Divorced women are more likely to have to work to provide for themselves and their children, and women who are relatively independent economically may be more likely than others to terminate an unhappy marriage. For example, for every hundred marriages occurring in 1930, seventeen divorces occurred; in 1977, the ratio was forty-nine divorces per hundred marriages.[8] It took forty-five years, from 1920 to 1965, for the divorce rate to double, but it doubled again between 1965 and 1975.[9] Estimates of the proportion of marriages now being formed that will eventually end in divorce range from 30 percent to 40 percent.[10] Although many divorced women remarry, the proportion of families in which no adult male is present has increased from 4.2 percent in 1930 to 9.5 percent in 1975. Furthermore, most female heads of families in 1930 consisted of older women who most likely were widows; in 1975 female family heads were evenly distributed across all age groups over age twenty-five.[11]

As Chapter 1 indicated, women's participation in the labor force has been rising, and is likely to continue to do so. To recapitulate, in 1947, 32 percent of women ages sixteen and over were in the labor force, compared with 49 percent of women in that age group in March 1978. By 1990, this percentage is expected to increase to about 55 percent. In March 1948, only 11 percent of married women living with their husbands and having children younger than age six were in the labor force. In March 1978, 42 percent of such mothers were in the labor force, and by 1990, about 55 percent are expected to participate.

---

8. U.S. Department of Commerce, Bureau of the Census, *Statistical Abstract of the United States, 1978,* no. 78.

9. Ibid. Divorce rate refers to divorces per thousand population. As already noted in Chapter 4, the rate rose from 2.5 in the mid-1960s to 5.0 in the mid-1970s.

10. Population Reference Bureau, *Population Education Newsletter* 7 (January 1978): 1.

11. Population data from U.S. Department of Labor, Bureau of Labor Statistics, "New Labor Force Projections to 1990," *Special Labor Force Report No. 197,* Appendix; and from U.S. Department of Commerce, Bureau of the Census, *Historical Statistics of the United States, Colonial Times to 1957,* 1960, A22–A23. Household data from *Historical Statistics of the United States,* A230–A241, and *Statistical Abstract of the United States, 1978,* no. 66. Data for 1930 refer to women fourteen years of age and older, while data for 1975 refer to women eighteen years of age and older.

During this period of significant growth in women's labor force participation, the income tax system has been modified several times. Let us now look at the development of that system, focusing on the evolution of its treatment of single people and married couples.

THE CURRENT INCOME TAX SYSTEM

When the federal personal income tax was first introduced in 1913, individuals were taxed on their own incomes regardless of marital status or the incomes of their spouses. Hence, an individual paid the same income tax whether married or single. Married residents of community property states (i.e., those in which the income of a couple is legally deemed to belong equally to the two spouses) soon realized that they could reduce their total tax payments by asserting that each spouse was legally liable for the income tax due on *half* of the couple's income. The Supreme Court concurred with this interpretation (Poe vs. Seaborn) in 1930.

Because the federal income tax rate schedule is progressive, couples who can split their income and pay taxes on each half will enjoy a lower total payment than will the couple in which one spouse has to pay the tax on the total income.[12] Married couples who lived in "common law property" states (i.e., those in which the income of an individual was unaffected by marital status) objected strenuously to the difference in treatment of their incomes and the treatment that otherwise similar couples who lived in community property states received. Residents of common law property states lobbied for the right to compute their income taxes in the same way as those living in community property states, and between 1930 and 1948 several common law property states adopted community property laws. In 1948, Congress enacted a significant tax reduction by allowing married couples to file joint returns regardless of their state of residence, thereby giving all married couples the benefits of income splitting.

Single adults responsible for supporting dependents such as children or aged relatives soon argued that they, too, were entitled to receive the benefits of income splitting. In 1951, a new "head-of-household" rate schedule was established to give such individuals half the advantages of income splitting; that is, the head-of-household rate schedule was set exactly halfway between the single schedule and the

---

12. Recall that progressivity of the rate schedule means that the *percentage* of income paid in taxes increases as income goes up. For example, at the $20,000 level, income splitting would reduce the total tax owed from $3,667 (18 percent of income) to $2,442 (12 percent of income).

joint return schedule. In addition, in 1954 Congress extended entitle-
ment to file joint returns to certain widows and widowers for the first
two years after the deaths of their spouses.

Most recently, single individuals have successfully lobbied for a
change in their rate schedule. Prior to 1971, single persons were paying
as much as 40 percent more in taxes than married couples (and as
much as 20 percent more than heads of households) with the same
taxable income. But, as of that year, Congress responded to single
persons' arguments that their share of the tax burden was excessive
by lowering their rate schedule. Under the 1971 law, a single person
paid no more than 20 percent more tax than a married couple with
the same taxable income, and less than half the tax of a married
couple with twice the taxable income. Thus income splitting is no
longer a correct description of joint returns. Despite further modifications to the tax system, the rate schedule for single persons has
remained lower than the one for married couples; hence the so-called
"marriage penalty" remains.[13] Further modifications (such as the
adoption of zero brackets to replace the previous standard deduction
and the inclusion of the general tax credit) have, however, affected the
tax payment of a single person relative to that of a couple with the
same income. Single persons now usually pay at least 20 percent more
than couples with the same income pay.

The "tax on marriage" (the excess tax paid by a two-earner couple
over what the couple would pay if permitted to file as two single
individuals) for many two-earner couples is a major source of pressure
for further modification of the system. Table 28 shows the gains (in
terms of reduced taxes after marriage) for one-earner couples and the
losses (in terms of increased taxes after marriage) for two-earner
couples.[14] For example, when Andy (who earns $25,000 a year) marries
Barbara (who is not employed), Andy will pay $1,085 less in income
taxes. On the other hand, when Robert (who earns $12,500 a year)
marries Sheila (who makes the same salary), their income taxes will
increase by $465.

The current system is based on the premise that all married couples
with the same income should be treated alike. Hence, Barbara and
Andy will pay the same taxes as Sheila and Robert because both
couples have the same income, $25,000 a year. Taxes increase after

---

13. A married couple cannot avoid or even reduce the marriage penalty by using
the married-filing-separately schedule because it, too, is higher than the schedule for
single persons.

14. Figures in this chapter are based on the provisions of the 1978 law.

Table 28

THE MARRIAGE PENALTY

(Negative Numbers Indicate a Tax Reduction Upon Marriage;
Positive Numbers Indicate a Tax Increase Upon Marriage.)

Percentage Earned by the Lesser-Earning Spouse	0	10%	20%	30%	40%	50%
Total Family Income						
0	0	0	0	0	0	0
$ 3,000	0	0	0	0	0	0
5,000	−$278	−$199	−$118	−$43	0	0
7,000	−351	−232	−113	5	$118	$183
10,000	−460	−240	−49	141	194	204
15,000	−703	−353	33	176	256	277
20,000	−762	−240	137	274	423	463
25,000	−1,085	−324	114	330	429	465
30,000	−1,406	−399	98	430	567	565
40,000	−2,013	−599	244	731	1,034	1,188
50,000	−2,535	−714	444	1,188	1,743	1,910
100,000	−2,605	374	2,128	3,205	3,660	3,660

Note: Calculations are based on 1978 law, under the assumptions that all income is from wages eligible for the maximum tax and that deductible expenses are 16 percent of income.

Source: Office of Tax Analysis, Department of the Treasury.

marriage for one couple and decrease for the other because of the difference in the tax treatment of single persons and married couples.

To understand the changes in tax liabilities that occur upon marriage, we must compare the tax burdens of single individuals vis-à-vis married couples. Table 29 shows tax levels and the ratio of taxes paid by couples and by single persons with the same income. The relative difference in tax payments is greatest for modest income levels: at $7,000 per year, a single person pays more than twice the taxes that a couple with the same earnings must pay, largely because the couple has two exemptions while the single person has only one. This difference declines as income increases, but even at the $50,000

Table 29

THE SINGLES PENALTY

(A Comparison of the Tax Paid by a Single Individual and the Tax Paid by a Couple With the Same Income)

Income	Tax Paid by Singles	Tax Paid by Couples	Singles Tax Relative to Couples Tax
0	0	0	—
$ 3,000	0	0	—
5,000	$ 278	0	—
7,000	619	$ 268	2.31[1]
10,000	1,221	761	1.60
15,000	2,410	1,706	1.41
20,000	3,667	2,905	1.26
25,000	5,145	4,060	1.27
30,000	6,790	5,384	1.26
40,000	10,535	8,522	1.24
50,000	14,735	12,200	1.21
100,000	35,735	33,130	1.08

Note: Calculations are based on the same assumptions as those used for Table 28. 1. This difference is largely attributable to the fact that married couples may claim two exemptions, whereas single people may claim only one. At low income levels, the additional exemption has a large effect on the total tax due.

income level, the single individual pays 21 percent (or $2,535 per year) more than the couple pays. Since Andy was paying a "single's penalty," his marriage to Barbara provides the advantage of income splitting which exceeds the disadvantage of the higher rate schedule for couples; hence, their total taxes decline. In comparison, when Robert and Sheila marry, they gain nothing from income splitting (since their incomes are the same) but are forced to use the higher rate schedule for married couples; hence, their taxes increase.

How are these differences justified? Single individuals are assumed to have a greater "ability to pay" than are married couples with the same earnings—Andy is assessed less tax after marriage because he is supporting Barbara. This argument ignores the fact that Barbara is contributing to the couple's well-being in ways other than earning income and that no additional taxes are being paid on what we call her "imputed" income—her productivity in the home or her additional leisure. Depending on the value placed on her homemaking contribution, this couple's "income" exceeds to a greater or lesser extent that of a single person with the same earnings; hence the tax-paying ability of this couple should be compared with that of a single person who has a *larger* money income than the couple has.

The implication of this argument is that either the couple's tax should be higher or the single person's lower than it is. Because imputed income is difficult to measure, however, it is not feasible to increase the couple's tax by including imputed income in the tax system. Rather, the existence of imputed income suggests that single people may currently be assessed an excessive proportion of the tax burden in comparison with one-earner couples, and that the single persons' rate schedule should be lowered further.

Now consider the case of Sheila and Robert, both of whom are employed. Because the current system is based on the premise that all married couples should be treated alike, the proportion of the couple's income earned by each spouse does not affect tax payments. Hence, Sheila and Robert pay the same taxes as Barbara and Andy. But are these two couples really similar? Because Sheila and Robert both work full time, they actually resemble two single persons more closely than they resemble a one-earner couple. They lack the contributions provided by a full-time homemaking spouse, just as single people do. Although they may experience some "economies of scale" because of living together, single people often capture these same economies by sharing quarters. Justification for an increase in tax assessment for Robert and Sheila as a consequence of marriage is hard to find.

The underlying difficulty is that three goals of our tax system are in conflict: (1) progressivity, (2) treatment of the family as the tax-paying unit, and (3) marriage neutrality. Any two can be achieved simultaneously, but all three cannot. The current system has sacrificed the third goal. Proposals for reform question the desirability of the second. Because of the increasing variety of family structures in recent years, treating "families" in the same way now often results in treating *different* situations similarly rather than in achieving the intended goal of treating similar situations similarly.

Basically, the increasing participation of women, especially married women, in the labor force is changing the relative numbers of persons in various tax categories, with more and more couples experiencing a marriage penalty. The next section explains how the rising participation of married women in the labor force will affect the magnitudes of "marriage gains" and "marriage penalties" for couples in the future.

MARRIAGE TAX GAINS AND PENALTIES
IN 1976 AND 1990

The previous section described the gains of one-earner couples and the losses of many two-earner couples from filing jointly compared with filing as two single persons (which married couples are not now allowed to do). It also discussed the relative tax burdens of single persons and married couples with the same money incomes. But how many couples gain and how many lose from the joint filing system? What is the total magnitude of their gains and losses? How will these numbers change by 1990? Similarly, how many single taxpayers are there compared with married couples? Are they a growing or shrinking proportion of the tax-paying public? These questions and others are explored in this section.[15]

Certain assumptions must underlie any forecasts. The forecasts presented here assume that (1) marriage, divorce, and fertility rates will remain at their current levels; (2) mortality rates will continue to decline slightly; (3) the earnings gap between men and women will not narrow; (4) labor force participation rates for women will continue to increase until 1990; and (5) real wages will grow at 1.75 percent per year.[16] Should fertility be lower or divorce higher, or should women's wages rise relative to men's, we would expect the labor force participation of women to increase more quickly than is assumed. As a result, we would expect the growth of two-earner couples to exceed that indicated by these forecasts, thus increasing the number of married couples experiencing a marriage penalty and decreasing the number gaining from joint filing.

Let us start with the situation in 1976, considering first people who gain from joint filing. They include all one-earner couples and those two-earner couples in which the earnings of one spouse are so low relative to the other's that the advantage of income splitting outweighs

---

15. Although the data available are for 1976, the provisions of the 1978 law have been used throughout the analysis. Changes in the tax law adopted since 1976 have reduced the dollar size of the marriage penalty by increasing the relative tax burden of single people. If we had used 1976 law, we would have overstated the magnitude of the marriage penalty problem and understated the taxes paid by single individuals.

16. The forecasts were made by a microanalytic simulation model, DYNASIM. For a discussion of this model, see Guy H. Orcutt, Steven B. Caldwell, and Richard F. Wertheimer II, *Policy Exploration Through Microanalytic Simulation* (Washington, D.C.: The Urban Institute, 1976).

the disadvantage of the higher rate schedule for married couples.[17] In 1976, 28.3 million couples gained from joint filing. On average, they paid $633 less than they would have paid had they filed as two single persons. This total saving of $17.9 billion is equal to 18 percent of all taxes paid by married couples. Of the 28.3 million couples who gain from joint filing, 18.5 million (65 percent) consisted of one earner and a dependent spouse, while in 9.8 million cases (35 percent) both spouses were employed for at least part of the year. (See Table 30.)

In comparison, 8.5 million two-earner couples paid a "marriage penalty." That is, 23 percent of all tax-paying couples and 46 percent of all two-earner tax-paying couples paid more in taxes because they were married to each other than they would have paid had they been able to file as single persons. The amount of the penalty averaged $321. This total $2.7 billion penalty represented almost 3 percent of all taxes paid by married couples. Furthermore, despite the fact that both spouses in these couples were employed, they came from all segments of the income distribution. Ten percent of the couples had combined earnings less than $8,500, 25 percent had combined earnings less than $13,000, and 50 percent had combined earnings less than $20,000 per year. Only 10 percent had combined earnings of $35,000 a year or more.

How can this situation be expected to change by 1990?[18] The proportion of married couples in which only one spouse is employed will fall from 58 percent in 1976 to 51 percent in 1990. Furthermore, the percentage of two-earner couples who reap tax gains from marriage will fall from 54 percent to 35 percent. In all, 27.7 million or 63 percent of married couples will gain from joint filing, down from 77 percent in 1976. Of these gainers, 68 percent will be one-earner couples, and 32 percent will consist of two earners. Furthermore, the average amount of the marriage tax gain will fall substantially: from $633 in 1976 to $362 in 1990. The total gain in 1990 ($10 billion) will represent

17. In the empirical work, a one-earner couple is defined as any married couple in which one spouse earns 97.5 percent or more of the total earnings of the couple. Furthermore, all income is assumed to be from earnings. For calculations in which married couples are assumed to file tax returns as two single persons, deductions are split between spouses in proportion to earnings.

18. All monetary values for 1990 are expressed in 1976 dollars to facilitate comparisons between the two years. Tax calculations were based on income expressed in 1990 dollars using the 1978 rate schedules. Because this approach would increase total taxes as a percentage of total income, all tax amounts were then reduced proportionately to retain the same relationship between total tax and total income as occurred in 1976.

Table 30

MARRIAGE TAX GAINS AND PENALTIES: 1976 AND 1990

(Monetary Values Expressed in 1976 Dollars)

	1976	1990
Couples with Gains		
Average gain	$633	$362
Total number	28.3 million	27.7 million
Number with one earner	18.5 million	19.0 million
(percentage)	65%	68%
Number with two earners	9.8 million	8.8 million
(percentage)	35%	32%
Couples with Penalties[1]		
Average penalty	$321	$350
Total number	8.5 million	16.5 million
Two-Earner Couples		
Number with gain	9.8 million	8.8 million
(percentage)	54%	35%
Number with penalty	8.5 million	16.5 million
(percentage)	46%	65%

1. All couples with penalties consist of two earners.

only 7 percent of all taxes paid by married couples, compared with 18 percent in 1976.

In contrast, by 1990, 16.5 million married couples will pay a marriage penalty. These couples represent 37 percent of all married couples (up from 23 percent in 1976) and 65 percent of all two-earner couples (up from 46 percent). The average amount of the penalty is expected to remain about the same in real terms: $350 in 1990, compared with $321 in 1976. Because of the larger number of couples experiencing a marriage penalty, however, the total penalty should more than double, to $5.8 billion, 4 percent of all taxes paid by married couples. Again, these couples will be spread across the income distribution: 10 percent will have combined earnings of less than $11,000, 25 percent will earn less than $17,000, and 50 percent will earn less than $25,000. Only 17 percent will have combined earnings of $40,000 or more. (To compare this income distribution with that in 1976, recall that our assumption of real wage growth at 1.75 percent per year will have shifted the entire income distribution upward. For example, $15,000 in 1976 would correspond to $19,500 in 1990.)

Approximately 19.2 million single persons paid taxes totaling $23.4 million in 1976. Of these individuals, 32 percent had incomes less than $5,000 and paid an average tax of $178; 42 percent had incomes less than $10,000 and paid on average $828; and only 9 percent had incomes in excess of $15,000 and paid on average $5,247. These numbers contrast with those for married couples: 1 percent with incomes less than $5,000 and average taxes of $116; 18 percent with incomes less than $10,000 and average taxes of $453; and 54 percent with incomes greater than $15,000 and average taxes of $4,374.[19]

By 1990, the proportion of the population who are married should increase somewhat, from 60 percent to 63 percent. The proportion who have not yet married is expected to decline, from 26 percent to 21 percent. The percentage of persons who are separated, divorced, or widowed is expected to grow slightly, from 15 percent to 16 percent.

To summarize, by 1990 the number of married couples experiencing a marriage penalty will almost double and the amount paid in penalties will more than double. In contrast, the number of couples gaining from joint filing will fall slightly, and the average amount they gain will decline by almost half. Little change is expected in the number of single persons relative to the number of married couples. Hence, although the debate about the appropriate shares of the tax burden to be paid by married couples and single persons is likely to continue, neither group will change much in relative size. In contrast, the changing economic behavior of married women is shifting the distribution of married couples toward those with two earners, and we may expect to see increasing pressure for modification of the tax system to lower the relative tax burden of two-earner couples. Alternative tax policies that have been suggested to modify the tax treatment of two-earner couples are discussed in the next section.

POLICY RESPONSES

Three major policy responses to alter the relative tax burdens of one-earner couples, two-earner couples, and single people have been suggested: First, maintain joint taxation of married couples but allow some portion of the second earner's income to be tax-free. Second,

---

19. These numbers refer only to those individuals and couples whose incomes were sufficiently high that federal income taxes were paid. The large number of single taxpayers with incomes less than $5,000 includes many part-time workers such as students.

require all individuals to file their own tax returns based on their own incomes, regardless of marital status or the financial positions of spouses (mandatory individual filing). Third, allow married couples to choose between joint and individual filing, depending on which option is more advantageous in their circumstances (optional individual filing).

Most Western European countries vary tax payments owed by married couples according to the division of total earnings between the two spouses. In doing so, they take into account the loss, or partial loss, of the homemaking services of one spouse when both are employed. Many countries have chosen one of the first two options described, although in recent years there has been a move toward adopting mandatory individual filing. The remainder of this section compares the optional and mandatory individual filing systems with the filing system the United States currently uses.[20]

Mandatory Individual Filing

Returning to our data for 1976, adoption of mandatory individual filing with no change in the rate schedule for single persons would increase tax payments by current "gainers" by $17.9 billion and decrease tax payments by current "losers" by $2.7 billion for a net increase in total tax revenue of $15.2 billion. Because such an increase in total tax revenue is unintended, we assume that the tax schedule for the mandatory individual filing proposal is a proportionately reduced version of the current schedule for single filers. The proportionate reduction is chosen so as to maintain total tax revenue at the current system's 1976 level. So the mandatory individual filing proposal we examine consists of two parts: (1) eliminate all marriage tax gains and penalties described in Table 30 and (2) use the additional tax proceeds for a general tax cut of about 10 percent. When both parts of this proposal are considered, total tax payments by current gainers would increase by only $8.4 billion, which corresponds to an average increase of $296 per couple. Total tax payments by current losers would decline by $5.3 billion, which corresponds to an average decrease of $627 per couple. Single tax payers would find their taxes reduced by about 10 percent, the amount of the general tax cut.[21]

---

20. Future research will also examine the effects of excluding a portion of the second earner's income from taxation. The amounts suggested for such an exclusion are usually so small, however, that they are likely to leave many couples still experiencing a penalty.

21. Because of the lowered rate schedule, married couples filing separately would also have their tax payments reduced. Surviving spouses would no longer be given

For a specific example of the effects that mandatory individual filing would have, consider the two couples discussed earlier in the chapter. (This example and others to be discussed below are summarized in Table 31.) Recall that Andy earns $25,000 and his wife Barbara is a full-time homemaker, while Robert and Sheila are both employed full time, each earning $12,500. Both couples have family incomes of $25,000, and both currently pay $4,060 in federal income taxes. Under mandatory individual filing Robert's and Sheila's tax would decrease to $3,223. This decrease of $837 is considerably greater than the marriage penalty of $465 they currently experience and reflects both elimination of their current marriage penalty and their gain from the general tax cut. Conversely, Andy's and Barbara's taxes would increase to $4,613. Their increase of $553 is about half of their current gain of $1,085 from joint filing. (The general tax cut prevents their tax from increasing even further under this proposal.) The resulting difference of $1,390 in the two couples' taxes may be thought of as the tax paid on Barbara's "income," that is, on her contribution of homemaking services to the couple's welfare and any increased leisure she and her husband may have compared with Robert and Sheila.

If Robert and Sheila do not earn exactly the same amounts (although their total income remains $25,000), the effects of mandatory individual filing would be somewhat different. For example, if one spouse earns $17,500 and the other $7,500, their total taxes would decline by $716, or more than twice their current penalty of $330, because not only do they avoid the marriage penalty, but also they reap the benefits of the general tax cut that is part of adopting a system of mandatory individual filing. With earnings of $20,000 and $5,000 their taxes would decline by $522 as a result of the general tax cut, even though they are currently gaining from joint filing.

In contrast, a single person with earnings of $25,000 would find that the amount of income tax owed declines from the current $5,145 to $4,613 because of the general tax cut. As a result, this single person would be paying exactly the same amount as a one-earner couple with the same income, rather than 27 percent more as occurs under the current system. Under the mandatory individual filing system, married couples' tax liabilities would depend on the proportion of total income each spouse earned. If we compare our single person with

the advantage of income splitting (which they now enjoy for two years after their spouses' deaths) but they would gain from the general tax cut. Heads of households would no longer receive the partial benefits of income splitting for which they are now eligible, but they would benefit from the general tax cut.

Table 31

COMPARISON OF TAX LIABILITIES UNDER THREE SYSTEMS

	Earnings	Current System	Mandatory Individual Filing	Change from Current System	Optional Individual Filing	Change from Current System
Spouse 1 Sheila	$12,500	$4,060	$3,223	−$837	$3,,678	−$383
Spouse 2 Robert	12,500					
Spouse 1 Andy	25,000	4,060	4,613	+ 553	4,146	+ 86
Spouse 2 Barbara	0					
Single person 1[1]	12,500	3,595	3,223	− 372	3,678	+ 83
Single person 2	12,500					
Single person	12,500	1,797	1,611	− 186	1,839	+ 42
Single person	25,000	5,145	4,613	− 532	5,254	+ 109

Note: The tax liabilities are for 1976. For assumptions on which these numbers are based, see text.

1. The tax payments of these two single individuals have been combined to provide a basis for comparison with the two married couples examined below.

a couple such as Robert and Sheila, each of whom earns $12,500, we find that under mandatory individual filing the single person would pay $1,390—43 percent more than the couple's total taxes of $3,223. This is a natural result of the progressivity of the tax system. In fact, mandatory individual filing restores income splitting to the tax system for married couples whose income actually is split evenly.

We have seen that adoption of mandatory individual filing in 1976 would have redistributed $8.4 billion, or 6 percent of the total tax burden, by reducing taxes paid by both two-earner couples and single persons and by increasing taxes paid by couples who currently gain from joint filing. Single persons' taxes would fall relative to the taxes of one-earner couples and rise relative to those of two-earner couples. What would this redistribution entail if postponed until 1990? By then, adoption of mandatory individual filing with no change in the rate schedule would increase total tax revenue by $4.3 billion. If rates were adjusted proportionately so that total tax revenue remained the same as it would be under the current system, the general tax cut would amount to only about 2 percent. Those couples gaining from joint filing would find their total tax payments increasing by $7.8 billion, an average of $281 per couple. In contrast, those experiencing a marriage penalty would find their total tax payments decreasing by $6.9 billion, an average of $418 per couple. Single taxpayers, who are affected only by the general tax cut, would find their taxes reduced by 2 percent.

Optional Individual Filing

A second possible tax policy is optional individual filing, under which couples could choose to file jointly or as two single individuals, which-ever way was to their advantage. Adoption of this option in 1976 with no change in the rate schedules would have reduced total tax revenues by $2.7 billion, about 2 percent of total taxes. To avoid this unintended tax decrease, we examine an optional individual filing proposal that consists of two parts: (1) elimination of the tax penalties but not the tax gains shown in Table 30, and (2) a general tax increase of about 2 percent. In this way, total tax revenue under the optional individual filing proposal is maintained at the current system's 1976 level. When both parts of the proposal are considered, total tax payments of gainers from joint filing would increase by $1.6 billion, an average of $55 per couple. Single taxpayers also would pay about 2 percent more. Total tax payments by those currently experiencing a penalty would decline by $2.1 billion, an average of $251 per couple.

What effect would optional individual filing have on our two couples? Andy and homemaker Barbara would experience a slight tax increase: $86, which is 8 percent of their current gain from joint filing. At the same time, Robert and employed wife Sheila would find their taxes decreasing by $382, which is 82 percent of the $465 marriage penalty they are currently experiencing. If Sheila's and Robert's earnings were divided differently, for example, $17,500 and $7,500, they would find their taxes declining by $244, or 74 percent of their $330 current marriage penalty. With incomes of $20,000 and $5,000 their taxes would decline by only $24, which is 21 percent of their current $114 marriage penalty.

Single people would find their tax payments increasing by about 2 percent, the same increase as that experienced by one-earner couples. Hence the relative positions of single persons and one-earner couples would not change. A single person with earnings of $25,000 would continue to pay 27 percent more than a one-earner couple with the same income; with earnings of $15,000, the single person would continue to pay 41 percent more tax than the couple pays. The relative positions of single persons and two-earner couples who are currently experiencing a marriage penalty, however, would change. If optional individual filing were adopted, taxes owed by such two-earner couples would fall, while taxes owed by single people would increase slightly. For example, a single person with earnings of $25,000 would pay a tax of $5,254—43 percent more than a two-earner couple each member of which earned $12,500—again a basic implication of the progressivity of the tax system. But the single person earning $25,000 would pay exactly half the amount paid by a couple each member of which earned $25,000, instead of 42 percent as under the current system. (The last two columns of Table 31 summarize this example of the effects of optional individual filing.) If the single person earned $15,000, the tax owed would be $982 more than the taxes of a two-earner couple in which each member earned $7,500.

Adoption of optional individual filing would reduce taxes of two-earner couples, shifting some additional tax burden to both one-earner couples and single persons. The relative positions of single persons and one-earner couples would remain unchanged. What would happen if this option were not adopted until 1990? By then, a larger revenue loss, $5.8 billion, would be incurred. (Recall that this amount exactly equals the total amount of the marriage penalty under the current system, which is increasing as more married women are employed.) Maintaining total tax revenue would then result in a $2.8 billion increase in total tax payments by those who benefit from joint filing, an average of $102 per couple. Single taxpayers would find their taxes increasing by slightly more than 3 percent. Those experiencing a marriage penalty would find their total tax payments reduced by $4 billion, an average of $242 per couple.

FURTHER ISSUES AND CONCLUSIONS

What conclusions can be drawn from this analysis? As remarked earlier, value judgments must enter the determination of comparability between a filing unit consisting of one person and a filing unit consisting of a married couple. If one believes that single persons most closely resemble two-earner couples each partner of which earns the same as the single person, either mandatory or optional individual filing would result in equitable tax burdens for these two groups. But comparisons between single persons and one-earner couples are affected quite differently by the two proposals. Under optional individual filing, the relative burdens would remain the same as under the current system (see Table 31) which requires single people to pay considerably more than one-earner couples with the same incomes. Under mandatory individual filing, the tax burden of single persons would fall relative to that of one-earner couples. Instead of paying considerably more in taxes, single persons would pay exactly the same taxes as one-earner couples with the same earnings.

Another important question is whether the tax system should treat all married couples with the same income the same way. In this chapter we have argued that differences in the division of earnings between spouses should affect their tax payments. The current system makes no such differentiation. Yet, as Chapter 6 has shown, two-earner couples experience a lower standard of living than do one-earner couples with the same money income because of the two-earner couples' lack of time for activities in the home and for leisure. Both mandatory and optional individual filing create such a differentiation in tax payments. They differ in that mandatory individual filing would substantially increase the tax payments of many one-earner couples (and lower those of many two-earner couples), whereas optional individual filing would increase payments by one-earner couples only slightly, in return for a modest decrease in tax payments by two-earner couples currently experiencing a marriage penalty.

We conclude that the tax treatment of married couples should be modified and that the effects on married couples of optional individual filing are preferable to those of mandatory individual filing, both now and in 1990. The tax burden of single persons, however, appears excessive in comparison with that of one-earner couples because of the "imputed" income available to one-earner couples in the form of the homemaker's time. The optional individual filing proposal we examine does not address this second issue because it uses the 1978 rate schedules for both single and joint filers, thereby maintaining the current differences in tax treatment of single persons vis-à-vis one-earner couples. (Only those currently experiencing a marriage penalty would find their position changed relative to that of other groups under this specific proposal.) Hence we conclude that adjustment of the single rate schedule relative to the schedule for joint filers would improve the optional individual filing proposal.

It should be noted, though, that reduction in the schedule for single persons in response to the judgment that they are bearing a disproportionate share of the total tax burden would also decrease the tax burden of two-earner couples who filed as single persons relative to the burden of one-earner couples. Those who consider two-earner couples most similar to two single persons with the same earnings would support this modification as a way of reflecting the imputed income of the homemaker spouse in one-earner couples.

Other concerns about optional individual filing have also been raised. For example, options in the federal tax code have been resisted for two reasons: First, some taxpayers may incorrectly choose the option that is less advantageous for them. The author believes that this particular concern is exaggerated. Other countries have succeeded in educating their taxpayers in how to determine the best choice. Further, in the United States, three-quarters of all taxpayers do not itemize deductions. In such cases, it would be a simple matter for the Internal Revenue Service to confirm that the correct choice had been made when checking the arithmetical calculations.

A second concern is that introducing a choice into the tax system may complicate some couples' decision making in matters that have tax implications. For example, the after-tax effects of certain investment decisions may have to be calculated under both filing options—joint filing and filing as two single persons. Are these additional costs so large, or would they be imposed on so many people, as to exceed the total costs currently experienced by two-earner couples? The author believes not.

Another issue raised about individual filing concerns the treatment of married couples' unearned income. One possibility is that ownership of the asset generating the unearned income would determine the spouse to pay the tax.[22] This practice might encourage transfer of ownership from one spouse to the other to reduce the couple's total tax liability.[23] A second possibility is that the couple could allocate unearned income to the tax return of either spouse as preferred. This approach would continue to treat asset income (but not earnings) the same way the current system treats all income—as though it accrues equally to the two spouses. This approach would, however, avoid any incentive to transfer ownership and, what is more important, it would remove from the Internal Revenue Service any burden of determining ownership of assets within the family unit.

If adopted exactly as proposed, this option would tend to reduce tax payments of one-earner couples who had considerable unearned income relative to tax payments of one-earner couples who had the same total income but received all of it from earnings, since only the former couple could allocate income to the nonemployed spouse. This differentiation would affect relatively few people, because only 15 percent of all taxable income is not from wages and salaries. Further, slightly more complicated procedures that would affect only exceptionally high-income couples have been suggested to handle taxation of unearned income under individual filing in a way that would avoid this difficulty. Consequently, the author believes that solutions can be found to the concerns that have been raised regarding optional individual filing.

Society is now in a transition stage in which both one-earner and two-earner couples are about equally common. Joint filing now unfairly penalizes two-earner couples. Mandatory individual filing would result in immediate, and in some cases substantial, tax increases for one-earner couples whose decisions regarding the roles of husband and wife were made when joint filing was not questioned. Optional individual filing appears to be a desirable compromise between these two extremes.

---

22. Income from jointly held assets would be divided equally between husband and wife.

23. The substantial disincentive to transfer asset ownership imposed by the existence of transfer taxes suggests that this issue may be of less importance than it first appears.

Chapter 8

INSTITUTIONAL RESPONSES: THE SOCIAL SECURITY SYSTEM

NANCY M. GORDON

The changing social and demographic trends discussed earlier in this book are also of major importance for the Social Security system. The relative treatment of one-earner couples, two-earner couples, and single individuals must once again be addressed. In addition, the adequacy of old-age income protection for divorced homemakers is in question. Both of these issues arise because the Social Security system was designed to protect traditional families in which the husband is employed and the wife remains at home to care for dependent children. The exceptions to this tradition are increasing, however, with greater labor force participation by married women and the rising incidence of divorce. The provisions of the Social Security system are poorly suited to the growing proportion of the population that does not fit the traditional family pattern.

This chapter focuses on the retirement and aged-survivors portions of the Social Security system.[1] The first section examines the provisions of the current system and their undesirable consequences for certain groups. The next section describes the proposed policy alternatives and discusses their underlying rationales. Then comes analysis of the future costs of such options and their long-term effects on different groups of people. The chapter ends with the author's recommendations and a discussion of issues that need further consideration.

PROVISIONS AND EFFECTS OF THE CURRENT SYSTEM

From the inception of the Social Security system, benefits have been financed by payroll taxes paid equally by employers and employees.[2] In 1937, the combined employer and employee Social Security tax was 2 percent, paid on "covered" earnings up to a taxable maximum of $3,000; by 1979 the combined Social Security tax rate had increased to 12.26 percent, paid on covered earnings up to $22,900.[3] The combined tax rate is scheduled to increase to 13.30 percent by 1981 and to 15.30 percent for 1990 and beyond. Further increases in the maximum amount of covered earnings have also been scheduled—to $29,700 by 1981. In subsequent years, the maximum taxable earnings will increase according to the rate of growth of covered earnings in the economy.

Although taxes have increased substantially, even in real terms, benefits have increased even more. For example, in 1950 the average annual benefit awarded to male workers was $383 and the maximum benefit was only $542. Expressed in 1976 dollars, these amounts correspond to $906 and $1,283. By 1976 these amounts had risen to

---

1. Provisions affecting disabled workers and their dependents and young widows (and widowers) caring for children are not examined.

2. Self-employed persons are assessed at a higher rate than employed persons are, to reflect the lack of contribution by an employer. For example, in 1979, the self-employed rate was 8.10 percent, compared with the 6.13 percent each paid by employees and employers for a combined rate of 12.26 percent.

3. Social Security taxes are paid on "covered" earnings. Uncovered earnings are those earned by workers outside the system, for example, by employees of the federal government, of some state and local governments, and of some nonprofit institutions. These Social Security tax rates are for retirement, disability, health insurance, and survivors' benefits. Since 1965, a portion of the payroll taxes has been used to finance Medicare payments. In 1978, the total 12.1 percent payroll tax paid by employees and employers was allocated as follows: 8.7 percent for retirement and survivors' benefits, 1.2 percent for disability benefits, and 2.2 percent for health insurance benefits. This allocation, however, does not reflect exactly the relative annual expenditures on the three types of benefits.

$3,186 and $4,648.[4] Furthermore, the scheduled increases in the taxable maximum will mean that in the future the maximum benefit a high-income worker can receive will be much larger. Again, measuring benefits in 1976 dollars, it is estimated that the maximum benefit for a worker will be about $8,600 by the year 2000 and about $15,650 by 2020.

How are these Social Security benefits determined for individuals in different circumstances? When the Social Security system was designed in the mid-1930s, only individual workers were to receive retirement benefits. Within a few years, before any benefits were actually paid, the system was expanded to include dependents' benefits. That system is essentially intact today. When workers retire, their benefits are based on their indexed, covered earnings, averaged over their working years.[5] Once awarded, benefits are automatically increased as the overall cost of living rises. The formula used to calculate benefits is progressive; that is, benefits replace a higher proportion of earnings for people with low earnings than for those with high earnings. In 1979, Social Security monthly benefits will replace 90 percent of the first $180 of average indexed monthly earnings (AIME), 32 percent of the next $905 of AIME, and 15 percent of any remaining amount of AIME. It should be noted that the progressivity of the benefit formula is a particularly valuable feature for women. Because women both earn less and are out of the labor force completely or

---

4. As a result of the provision of benefits to workers' dependents (described later), in 1976, an aged couple consisting of a worker and a dependent spouse received, on average, $4,779 and a maximum of $6,972.

5. Starting in 1979, past earnings will be indexed before averaging according to the average amount of wage growth in the economy. The benefit formula is adjusted each year in the same way to reflect growth in covered wages. Earnings will be averaged over the highest twenty years for 1979, but the number of years over which earnings are averaged will increase by one year each year up to thirty-five years for 1994 and thereafter. Years in which there were no covered earnings are included in the averaging process when necessary. The resulting amount of average indexed monthly earnings (AIME) forms the basis for benefit calculations. Further, at least forty quarters of coverage (quarters in which covered earnings were at least fifty dollars) are necessary to receive a retirement benefit in 1979. Full benefits are paid to individuals who retire at age sixty-five or older. For workers receiving benefits between ages sixty-two and sixty-four, benefits are actuarially reduced. Moreover, all beneficiaries are subject to benefit reductions if their annual earnings exceed the earnings limit. For persons sixty-five to seventy-one years old, the limit is now $4,000, but it is scheduled to increase to $6,000 in the near future. Benefits are reduced by fifty cents for each dollar of earnings in excess of the allowed amount.

work part time for a greater portion of their lives than men, their average indexed monthly earnings are lower. Were the benefit formula proportional (as is the case in many European countries), women's benefits would be far lower than they are.

In addition to the workers' benefits described above, aged spouses of retired workers are entitled to dependents' benefits equal to 50 percent of their spouses' benefits. Aged spouses who are also entitled to benefits as workers in their own right receive the larger of the two possibilities. When workers die, their aged spouses are eligible for survivors' benefits equal to the amount of the deceased workers' benefits, or to their own benefits as workers, whichever amount is higher. The same spouse benefits are provided to workers' divorced wives who do not remarry, provided the marriage lasted at least ten years before dissolution.[6] Like widowed spouses, divorced wives also receive either their own benefits as workers or their benefits as divorced wives, whichever amount is higher; they do not receive both. Benefits paid to current spouses are not reduced because of benefits paid to divorced wives.[7]

As an example, consider Betty and George, a couple who have followed traditional sex roles throughout their lives.[8] Although Betty worked in covered employment for a short time before her marriage to George, she did not accumulate the forty quarters of coverage necessary to receive Social Security benefits as a worker. George has worked in covered employment most of his life and will have average

---

6. Prior to January 1979, the marriage had to have lasted at least twenty years for the divorced wife to be eligible for these benefits.

7. The provisions affecting divorced persons currently apply only to women and are being litigated. Even if these provisions were not related to gender, however, few men would gain from them because few men have benefits in their own right that are less than half the benefits of their divorced wives. Those who do usually worked primarily for employers not covered by the Social Security system, such as local, state, and federal governments. The system still differentiates on the basis of gender in some other specific provisions, too, but relatively few individuals are affected and the provisions are likely to be changed soon. Generally, these provisions provide benefits to women under conditions more liberal than those that apply to men. For a discussion of these provisions, see *The Report of the HEW Task Force on the Treatment of Women Under Social Security*, U.S. Department of Health, Education, and Welfare, Washington, D.C., February 1978, Appendix A, pp. 75–76. See also *Social Security and the Changing Roles of Men and Women*, U.S. Department of Health, Education, and Welfare, Washington, D.C., February 1979.

8. The examples are based on the 1979 benefit formula. The amounts are basic annual benefits for individuals reaching age sixty-two in 1979, without actuarial reductions for early retirement. "Average earnings" refers to average annual wage-indexed earnings that are used to calculate benefits.

Table 32

REPRESENTATIVE ANNUAL BENEFITS UNDER THE
CURRENT SYSTEM

	Retirement	Survivor
One-earner couple[1] (Betty and George)	$7,640	$5,093
Divorced wife (Betty)	2,547	5,093
Two-earner couple[2] (Helen and Tom)	7,882	5,093
Divorced wife (Helen)	2,789	5,093
Two-earner couple[3] (Cathy and John)	6,346	3,173
Divorced wife (Cathy)	3,173	3,173
Single person[4]	3,173	NA
Single person[5]	5,093	NA

1. The one-earner couple includes one spouse with average indexed annual earnings equal to $12,000 and one with no earnings.
2. This two-earner couple consists of one person with average indexed annual earnings of $12,000 and one person with average annual indexed earnings of $4,800.
3. This two-earner couple consists of two individuals, each of whom has average indexed annual earnings of $6,000.
4. This single person has average indexed annual earnings of $6,000.
5. This single person has average indexed annual earnings of $12,000.

earnings of $12,000 when he retires. Consequently, his benefits will be $5,093 per year.[9] As a dependent Betty will receive benefits of $2,547 per year, half of George's benefits. In all, they will receive total Social Security benefits of $7,640 annually. Even if Betty and George had recently been married, their benefits would be the same, provided Betty had not earned benefits on her own as a worker in excess of her benefits as a spouse. If George had been previously married to someone other than Betty for more than ten years, his ex-wife would also be entitled to benefits as a dependent of $2,547 annually, unless her benefits as a worker exceeded this amount or she had remarried. Upon George's death, Betty and his ex-wife would each receive $5,093 annually as his survivors. (The benefits used in this and subsequent examples are summarized in Table 32.)

---

9. His monthly benefits (based on his average indexed monthly earnings of $1,000) are calculated as follows: $(.90)(\$180) + (.32)(\$820) = \$424.40$, resulting in annual benefits of $5,093.

Why is this system now being criticized? First, there has been a dramatic increase in the number of two-earner couples relative to the number of one-earner couples. Because the design of the original system was based on the assumption that women were economically dependent upon their husbands, these two-earner couples receive smaller benefits relative to the Social Security taxes they pay than do one-earner couples. Spouses with irregular participation in the labor force often have little increase in benefits as a result of their Social Security tax payments. Some find that the benefits to which they are entitled as retired workers are actually less than the benefits to which they are entitled as dependent spouses. For these people, prior Social Security tax payments make no difference in retirement benefits compared with what they would have received had they remained at home and paid no Social Security taxes whatsoever.

This lack of equal treatment for families with the same total lifetime income and the same number of members at retirement is now being questioned. Even if one believes that families are the correct units to consider, and even if the benefits received at retirement are the same for two families that differ only in terms of labor force participation of the wives, the problem remains. The family with two earners is likely to have paid considerably more Social Security taxes than the family with only one earner. Furthermore, the survivor of the two-earner couple will probably receive *lower* benefits than the survivor of the one-earner couple will receive.

A second reason the system is now being criticized is that benefits received by divorced homemakers who do not remarry tend to be low, especially while their ex-husbands are alive. In addition, as long as marriages last ten years, no distinction is made between homemakers whose marriages lasted most of their lives and those who divorced at a younger age. Homemakers divorced late in life are able to work in paid employment for only a limited number of years. Because the system bases pensions on earnings averaged over an extended period, these women have difficulty generating adequate Social Security pensions in their own right as workers. Furthermore, the small benefits to which a divorced homemaker may be entitled as a retired worker cannot be combined with her benefits as a divorced wife; she receives only the higher of the two amounts.[10]

To illustrate some of these concerns, compare full-time homemaker Betty and her husband George with another couple of the same age,

---

10. It should be noted, however, that after the death of her ex-husband, the benefits to which she is entitled as a divorced wife double.

Helen and Tom. Helen worked for a short time before marriage, as did Betty, but after Helen's children were grown, she returned to the labor force. Because of Helen's lower wages and years out of the labor force, her average earnings are only $4,800; whereas Tom's average earnings are $12,000, the same as George's. Helen's benefits as a worker will equal $2,789 annually; Tom's benefits will be the same as George's, $5,093 annually.[11] Consequently, Helen and Tom will receive a total of $7,882 in Social Security benefits, compared with the $7,640 received by Betty and George. The excess of $7,882 over $7,640, only $242 a year, is the gain that Helen perceives she is receiving in exchange for all the Social Security taxes she has paid while working.

Of course, Helen's children would receive survivors' benefits in the event of her death and, starting five years after she returned to work, Helen would receive Social Security benefits in the event of her total disability. Yet the combined value of these benefits plus the small increase in retirement benefits over what her retirement benefit would be as Tom's wife seem little compensation for the additional Social Security taxes that Helen and Tom have paid compared with those paid by Betty and George. Furthermore, should Betty and Helen be widowed, each would receive exactly the same Social Security benefits, because each would receive survivors' benefits based on her husband's average earnings of $12,000.

For illustration of the problem regarding divorced homemakers, suppose Helen and Tom divorced after their children had left home. Tom remarried, but Helen did not and she returned to work. On reaching age sixty-five she would receive $2,789 annually in Social Security benefits as a worker. These benefits are slightly more than those she would receive as a divorced wife but they are only 37 percent of the $7,640 received by Tom and his second wife, who receives benefits as a dependent spouse since she was employed too few years to receive benefits herself as a worker. Should Tom die before Helen, her benefits as a surviving divorced wife would increase substantially, from $2,789 to $5,093—the same amount Tom's second wife would receive.

Another comparison, this time with Cathy and John, illustrates further problems with the current benefit structure. Both Cathy and John worked most of their lives in covered employment, but each

---

11. Helen's monthly benefits are calculated as follows: (.90)($180) + (.32)($220) = $232.40; consequently, her annual benefits are $2,789. Because this amount exceeds the $2,547 to which she is entitled as a dependent, she receives her benefits as a worker.

earned only half of George's salary. Because each has average earnings of $6,000 per year, each will receive annual retirement benefits of $3,173, for a total of $6,346. Because Cathy's and John's combined salaries have equaled George's salary alone, both "couples" have paid the same amount of Social Security taxes over the years. Yet Cathy's and John's total benefits of $6,346 will be $1,294 (20 percent) less than the benefits received by Betty and George ($7,640). Should Cathy and Betty be widowed, the divergence of benefits would be even more extreme. Cathy would receive only $3,173 (her own benefits, since her benefits as John's survivor are not higher), but Betty would receive survivors' benefits of $5,093. As we argued in Chapter 7, it is difficult to justify this difference of $1,920 (61 percent), especially inasmuch as Betty and George have had the advantage of a full-time homemaker throughout their lives and hence have been better off than Cathy and John, who have both been employed full time.

Finally, consider a single person who has never married and who has earned the same amount as Cathy and John each earned. The single earner has paid half the Social Security taxes that Cathy and John together paid and will receive half their benefits: $3,173. This earner also paid half the taxes George and Betty paid but will receive only 42 percent of that couple's combined benefits. Had the single person's earnings equaled George's, the earner would have paid the same Social Security taxes but would have received only two-thirds the benefits, $5,093 compared with $7,640. The single person also would have paid the same taxes as Cathy and John together paid, but would have received only 80 percent of their benefits, $5,093 compared with $6,346. These comparisons illustrate the effects of two factors: provisions of dependents' benefits to spouses and the progressivity of the benefit formula. The former provides relatively greater benefits to one-earner couples, and the latter provides relatively greater benefits to those with lower earnings.

Almost everyone agrees the current Social Security system needs improving. It seems unfair to vest all Social Security pensions claims in an employee when the spouse, although not in the labor force, has contributed to the family's economic position by work at home and often has enabled the employed worker to earn more than would have been possible without the spouse's help. It also seems inequitable for two-earner couples to pay substantially more taxes for roughly the same protection. Moreover, the protection for divorced women is often inadequate.

What is being sought in this chapter is a Social Security system that would—

- impose no large penalties on one-earner couples relative to the current system;
- improve the relative treatment of those couples in which both partners work in paid employment for substantial periods of their lives as well as the relative treatment of single individuals; and
- increase protection for divorced homemakers.

Opinions differ about how best to balance these sometimes inconsistent goals. The next section discusses several different views.

POLICY RESPONSES

The underlying difficulties with the Social Security system are not the gender-specific provisions (which are likely to be revised soon), but rather the interdependencies between the system's benefit structure and the differences in the labor market behavior of men and women. The lower benefits that women typically receive stem from the fact that their labor force participation patterns and earnings differ from those of men. Women, on average, not only drop out of the labor force in order to rear children, but they also earn less when they are employed. Because the system averages earnings over a long period of time, irregular participation and low earnings mean low benefits. (Recall that were it not for the progressivity of the benefit formula, women's benefits would be even lower.)

One response to differences in the behavior of men and women has been to add dependents' and survivors' benefits. This alternative was more appropriate in the past (although, even then, many people did not fit into the traditional family model) than it is today for several reasons. The employment of wives has increased dramatically. Moreover, the rise of feminist consciousness had led many people to argue that women should not be viewed primarily as the dependents of men, but rather as individuals in their own right, with their own independent claims to retirement income. Furthermore, as divorce rates have risen and multiple marriages have become more common, vesting pension rights with the individual is seen as one obvious solution to shifting family relationships.

Some feminists argue that Social Security protection should be improved through changes in sex roles; men and women should share more equally work in the home and work in the marketplace, thereby accumulating their own claims to future Social Security benefits. This view would lead to adopting a system of benefits for workers only, with no provisions for the dependents or the survivors of workers. Such a comprehensive approach would address the relative treatment of one-earner couples vis-à-vis two-earner couples and single individuals, but also would reduce benefits for people who still chose to be full-time homemakers.

Other people, however, are more concerned about maintaining and strengthening the traditional family structure. Although they agree that protection for divorced women should come through individually vested claims to retirement pensions, they contend that such claims should be financed in part through societal contributions for Social Security benefits for homemakers. They argue that it is important not to force women into the labor market if they prefer to remain at home with their children, and that the gains to society of mothers' remaining at home more than repay the costs of providing them free claims to Social Security benefits. This option, however, continues subsidization of one-earner couples at the expense of both two-earner couples and single people, including single parents who are employed.

A compromise proposal would split equally between spouses the claims to Social Security benefits accumulated during marriage. This approach would result in individually vested claims to benefits for homemakers and would take into account all of a couple's covered earnings in computing benefits, even if one spouse was employed only sporadically.[12] The following sections examine these comprehensive approaches: individually based benefits, homemaker credits, and earnings sharing.

Individually Based Benefits

Under a system of individual benefits, all dependents' and survivors' benefits would be eliminated. At the same time, government policies would be adopted to encourage women to seek paid employment and men to increase their share of responsibility for child rearing and

---

12. Several specific solutions to particular problems have been proposed. Unfortunately, such proposals often unintentionally create additional difficulties. For example, one proposal increases workers' benefits by 12.5 percent and reduces dependents' benefits from 50 percent to 33.3 percent of the workers' benefits. Under this proposal, benefits received by one-earner couples would be essentially unaffected, while benefits received by two-earner couples and single people would increase. Thus this proposal would reduce differences in retirement benefits between one-earner couples and both two-earner couples and single individuals; but the proposal actually would exacerbate differences in the treatment for survivors of one-earner couples vis-à-vis survivors of two-earner couples and would worsen protection for divorced homemakers. Such proposals have been analyzed thoroughly by the Department of Health, Education, and Welfare Task Force on the Treatment of Women Under Social Security and are not discussed further here. The reader is referred to the *Report of the HEW Task Force on the Treatment of Women Under Social Security.*

other home-related activities. Then each adult would receive retirement or disability benefits based only upon his or her own earnings record, accumulated while that person was engaged in covered employment.[13]

Proponents of such a system do not suggest that it be put into effect quickly. Rather, they advocate gradual implementation during a transition period of perhaps twenty to thirty years. Such a transition period would provide time for individual women and men to adapt their behavior in response to the new provisions. In addition, it would prevent any significant changes in benefit levels from those expected by individuals who will retire in the near future.

One difficulty with the current Social Security system is that benefits paid to dependent spouses duplicate rather than supplement benefits earned through paid employment. Another problem is that although society often encourages individuals, especially women, to remain at home caring for their families for a significant portion of their lives, adequate retirement income is provided only if the marriage remains intact. Despite the fact that husband and wife decide jointly that one of them will be a homemaker, in the event of divorce the costs of that decision are imposed primarily upon the homemaker. An individually based system responds to the first of these concerns by eliminating benefits for dependents, thereby equalizing treatment of one-earner couples, two-earner couples, and single persons, but it would provide little or no protection for divorced individuals who had decided to devote full time to homemaking activities.

The rationale underlying this approach is similar to the prevailing philosophy in Sweden: that men and women should have similar roles, sharing equally the responsibility for providing income for the family through market work and the responsibility for providing services in the home, including the rearing of children. A major distinction between this approach and the Swedish system is that the latter consists of two separate tiers, often referred to as a "double decker" system. Every resident of a certain age is eligible to receive the first tier of benefits, a fixed amount per year. In addition, workers who have paid social insurance taxes on covered earnings receive benefits proportional to the indexed value of their covered earnings. The two-tier system separates the social goal of ensuring a minimum amount of income to older residents from that of replacing the earnings of retired workers. If such a system were adopted in the

---

13. Most proposals such as this one would retain benefits for surviving children and for surviving spouses who were caring for surviving children younger than a specified age (such as seven years old), subject to an earnings test.

United States, the progressivity currently embodied in the benefit formula would be replaced by the first tier of benefits and income replacement for those with covered earnings would occur in a proportional way.[14]

By providing comparable treatment for workers regardless of whether they are members of one-earner couples or two-earner couples, or are single, such a system avoids many problems of unequal treatment of individuals. In addition it would provide minimal retirement income protection for full-time homemakers, who would automatically receive the first tier of benefits. Finally, it would take into account all the Social Security taxes paid by either spouse, regardless of how little one might have worked in covered employment.

How would these two versions of individually based benefits affect single people relative to married couples? As is the case in the income tax system, single persons currently bear a disproportionate share of the total burden of providing Social Security benefits. They pay Social Security taxes on the same amount of earnings at the same rate as do married workers. Yet one-earner couples (and two-earner couples in which one spouse earns substantially more than the other) receive both greater absolute benefits than those of single persons and greater benefits relative to the taxes they have paid. These differences result from the benefits the present system provides for dependents and survivors of workers.

The differences in treatment between single persons and most married couples would be eliminated if a one-tier, individually based system were adopted. If a two-tier system were adopted (with earnings-related benefits proportional to one's own earnings), differences in benefits still might result from the provision of the first-tier benefits to all people meeting the age requirement.[15] Although eligibility would not be related to marital status, the probability of being a full-

---

14. Adoption of this system in the United States would also resolve difficulties resulting from the fact that some employment, especially federal government employment, is outside the Social Security system. Now well-to-do individuals who have worked most of their lives in noncovered employment can achieve relatively high Social Security benefits through relatively small tax payments made over ten years of their working life (for example, in part-time jobs) because of the progressivity of the benefit formula which was designed to help persons with low incomes.

15. Note that the two-tier system could incorporate several alternative ways of providing the second tier of earnings-related benefits. For example, one could provide survivors' benefits based on the earnings-related benefits of both spouses, or one could share earnings records between spouses upon divorce. In other words, under a two-tier system the second tier of benefits does not have to be proportional to earnings on which Social Security taxes have been paid by the individual.

time homemaker is likely to be related to marital status. Another difference between single persons and married couples would occur in a two-tier system if survivors' benefits were based on the total earnings-related benefits received by a couple rather than on the amount of an individual's own benefits.

Both variations of individually based benefits would provide benefits to individuals based on their own behavior rather than on that of people to whom they are related, thereby meeting the second goal listed above—namely, improving the relative treatment of two-earner couples and single individuals. Only the two-tier system, however, could meet the first and third goals of not imposing large penalties on one-earner couples and of increasing protection for divorced home-makers. Whether these goals were actually achieved would depend largely upon the size of the first-tier benefits.

Even the two-tier system, however, may have an important negative feature. Unless the first-tier benefits were quite large, this system would provide a strong disincentive against any individual's choosing to remain out of the labor force for an extended period of time. That is, it would operate in the same way as mandatory individual filing, one of the proposals for modifying the federal income tax system examined in the preceding chapter. In fact, many groups who favor individually based benefits seek precisely this goal. Others, including the author, argue that it would be preferable not to penalize individuals who choose to allocate their time to homemaking for a portion of their lives. Within the tax system, optional individual filing would provide such a choice, because it would continue a large portion of the tax reduction currently received by one-earner couples (through filing joint returns) while at the same time eliminating the penalty imposed upon two-earner couples (who would be free to file as two single individuals). What is being sought here is a Social Security system that would also be neutral regarding individuals' labor force participation decisions, as well as meeting the three goals we identified earlier. The next section examines another proposal.

Homemaker Credits

The general approach of homemaker-credits proposals is to provide entries in Social Security earnings records for individuals who are not employed so that they can receive Social Security benefits as workers do now. Many different suggestions have been made about ways to determine eligibility and about the amount of the credits. For example, all homemakers might be eligible, or only those caring for young children, or there might be a maximum number of years for which credits could be received.

Perhaps the most important distinction among proposals is whether Social Security taxes would be assessed for such credits. If Social Security taxes were to be paid for homemaker credits received, most of the problem in the treatment of one-earner vis-à-vis two-earner couples would be resolved. The issue of the employer contribution for credits received by homemakers might be partially resolved by assessing taxes for homemakers at the self-employment tax rate (which exceeds that paid by an employee but is less than the combined employee-employer rate). Opponents of this proposal argue that paying such Social Security taxes would be difficult if not impossible for one-earner couples at relatively low income levels, and it is these lower-income homemakers who most need additional protection.

Yet if credits were provided to homemakers without taxes' being assessed, some of the problems of the current system would be perpetuated—namely, more benefits would be provided for one-earner couples than for two-earner couples with the same income and the same Social Security tax payments. For example, the full-time home-maker spouse of a worker earning $20,000 would receive free home-maker credits; but a two-earner couple consisting of two full-time workers together earning $20,000 would not be eligible for free credits. Hence, they would pay the same Social Security taxes as the one-earner couple but receive considerably less protection.

In response to this concern, other supporters of the free homemaker-credits approach suggest the following modification: that the spouse with the lower earnings in the two-earner couple (or an eligible single person) be excused from paying Social Security taxes on earnings up to the amount of the homemaker credits.[16] This response would treat eligible one-earner couples equally with two-earner couples and single persons, but it would cost considerably more than other homemaker-credits proposals—and people not eligible for the credits would be subsidizing those who were to an even greater extent.

The amount of homemaker credits to be provided would depend on whether corresponding taxes were assessed. If taxes were paid for them, individuals might be obligated to purchase a minimum specified amount of credits with additional amounts (up to the taxable maximum for a single person) available at their discretion. If the credits

---

16. If the earnings were less than the credits, this proposal would supplement the earnings record of an eligible person up to the level of the credits and no Social Security taxes would be assessed.

were free, the largest amount likely to be provided is the full-time minimum wage, about $6,000 for the year 1979.[17]

Finally, how should benefits for survivors be determined under a homemaker-credits approach? The rationale that homemaker credits eliminate the need for derived benefits suggests that no additional survivors' benefits should be provided. Failure to provide survivors' benefits, however, would probably result in quite low benefits for survivors who had been full-time homemakers. A way to avoid this problem would be to award survivors their own benefits or two-thirds of the couple's benefits when both were alive, whichever amount was higher. This arrangement would enable the survivor to maintain the same standard of living as the couple had enjoyed, but again it would increase the total cost of the proposal.

Proponents of homemaker credits argue the necessity to recognize the economic value of homemaking and to provide protection against the loss of this imputed income due to age or disability of the homemaker. Concern for the rearing of children in their homes also contributes to arguments supporting homemaker credits. Supporters believe that it is better for children to be cared for by their parents than for them to grow up in day care centers or in family day care. They fear that in many cases only low quality care is available for children whose mothers work outside the home. Furthermore, they argue that in addition to family benefits, society may gain from parental care for children. If so, public subsidy of parental care for preschoolers might be justified. Certainly the public school system represents a similar special subsidy for child rearing.

Opponents of homemaker-credits plans agree that homemakers contribute economically to their families, but they reach a different conclusion from this observation. They suggest that the provisions of homemaker credits without corresponding taxes is likely to be expensive, and that neither couples in which both members work nor employed single persons should have to pay additional taxes to subsidize persons who remain at home. They argue further that although retirement protection should be available for men or women who remain at home with their children, this protection should be paid for by the couple making that decision. After all, the goods and services produced by a homemaker and the increased leisure consumed by the one-earner couple are not taxed as income; as a result, one-

---

17. If credits in excess of this amount were provided, workers earning the minimum wage would pay Social Security taxes and receive less retirement income protection than others would receive without paying at all.

earner families actually have a higher standard of living than two-earner families with the same total money income. Thus, society should not subsidize the Social Security benefits of one-earner couples at the expense of two-earner couples and single persons who have the same money income. Rather, subsidies should be limited to those provided for poorer individuals through the progressivity of the benefit formula.

Even if taxes were assessed for homemaker credits, the question remains of the adequacy of protection that would be provided to full-time homemakers who eventually divorced. If one believes that marriage is a partnership and that both spouses participated in the decision that one of them would stay home, then after divorce each should have the same claim to benefits based on the period of marriage. Under the present system they do not, and homemaker credits probably would do little to amend this situation. Providing homemaker credits at the same level as the full-time minimum wage would leave a divorced homemaker with relatively low benefits, perhaps not much higher than those under the current system. Divorced homemakers who enter the paid labor market, however, would have the advantage of combining protection received through the credits in their role as homemakers with protection earned later as workers.

How would homemaker credits affect treatment of single people vis-à-vis married couples? If taxes were paid for homemaker credits, differences in treatment of these groups would be small. If the home-maker credits were provided free, the effects on these groups would depend largely on eligibility requirements. If eligibility depended only on a person's being out of the paid labor force or caring for young children, there would be no difference in treatment of single or married persons. If eligibility were tied to marriage to a spouse working in covered employment, then single persons would not be eligible for the credits. Moreover, assuming that the adoption of homemaker-credits plans was tied to elimination of survivors' benefits, this major advantage of married workers over single workers would be ended.

How well would these homemaker-credits plans meet the three goals we have identified? In order to move toward meeting the goal of equal treatment of two-earner couples and single individuals, either taxes would have to be assessed for the credits, or earnings of eligible individuals would have to be excluded from Social Security taxable earnings up to the amount of the credits. These approaches would treat all individuals eligible for the credits in the same way; the remaining subsidy would be from those not eligible for the credits to those who were eligible, for example, from those without young children to those with them.

Whether the goals of not imposing large costs on one-earner couples and of improving protection for divorced homemakers would be met by the homemaker-credits approach would depend on the amount of the credits.[18] Furthermore, as noted earlier, only the option in which earners eligible for the credits also receive them would be neutral with regard to labor force participation decisions.

The next section addresses the third comprehensive approach to modifying the Social Security system, earnings sharing.

Earnings Sharing

Under earnings-sharing proposals, Social Security earnings records would be shared equally between spouses each year the couple is married. A couple would receive retirement benefits as individuals, based on their own shared records. Benefits for survivors of married couples could be determined in several ways: they could be based on the survivors' own shared records, or survivors could receive a proportion (perhaps one-half or two-thirds) of the total benefits that the couples had been receiving when both spouses were alive, or survivors could receive whichever of these two amounts was higher. Alternatively, spouses of deceased workers could inherit the workers' earnings records and combine them with their own up to the maximum amount of earnings covered by Social Security each year. The underlying rationale for these proposals is that marriage is a partnership. One can view Social Security earnings records as another monetary asset accumulated during marriage, because they are claims to future retirement income. Hence, shared records closely resemble community property.

Those who favor earnings sharing argue that it would establish individual claims to retirement benefits and therefore would protect homemakers whose marriages end in divorce. The penalties under the existing system that are incurred primarily by women who divorce after many years as homemakers would be shared by both spouses who make the decision that one of them not be employed. Women, then, would be penalized less under an earnings-sharing option (and their ex-husbands more) than under the current system in which all pension rights are vested in the earner. Earnings sharing might cost more than the present system, however, because of the progressivity of the benefit

---

18. Later our empirical analysis will examine the effectiveness with which homemaker credits equal to full-time minimum wage earnings would meet these two goals.

formula. The cost of earnings sharing depends largely on the provisions regarding survivors' benefits. If no survivors' benefits were provided, total costs might decline compared with costs under the current system. On the other hand, if survivors' benefits were provided at two-thirds of the total family benefits (rather than individuals' continuing to receive only benefits based on their own shared records), the cost might exceed that of the current system.

Opponents point out that an earnings-sharing system would tend to reduce benefits for couples in which only one member had ever worked, because dependents' benefits would be eliminated. However, benefits even for this rare couple in which one spouse never worked would be considerably higher than the worker's benefits under the current system because of the progressivity of the benefit formula.[19] Because the percentage of women who will never participate in paid employment is already only 10 percent[20] and is expected to decline further in the future, earnings sharing appears likely to meet the first goal we identified, that is, it would not impose large costs on one-earner couples.

Another major advantage of earnings sharing is that it would equalize the benefits for one- and two-earner couples with the same total covered earnings because they would then have identical earnings records. That is, all couples with the same total covered earnings would be treated in the same way regardless of the division of earnings between the spouses. Hence, earnings sharing meets part of the second goal by equalizing the treatment of two-earner couples relative to one-earner couples with the same covered earnings. Earnings sharing would, however, retain some difference in the treatment of one-earner and two-earner couples with the same total earnings in cases in which total earnings exceeded the taxable maximum.[21]

---

19. Under the current system, one-earner couples receive benefits based on the total earnings of the workers plus dependents' benefits of 50 percent. Under earnings sharing, one-half of each worker's earnings would be used to compute benefits for the husband and the other half to compute benefits for the wife. Because the benefit formula replaces a higher proportion of earnings at lower earnings levels, each of these benefits under an earnings-sharing system would exceed half of the worker's benefits under the current system. In general, under earnings sharing, each one-earner couple would receive approximately 130 percent of the worker's benefits under the current system compared with the 150 percent they now receive. If the basically homemaker spouse had ever paid any Social Security taxes, the couple would receive even higher benefits.

20. U.S. Department of Labor, Bureau of Labor Statistics, unpublished statistics.

21. This difference in treatment also exists under the current system. It occurs in both systems because such a two-earner couple pays Social Security taxes on a higher

What about the remainder of the second goal, which concerns the treatment of single people? Earnings sharing would perpetuate some of the disparity in benefits received by a married couple and those received by a single person with the same income. However, this disparity results from the progressivity of the benefit formula, rather than from the provision of dependents' benefits. A single person would receive less than a married couple with the same earnings because each spouse would be credited with only half the couple's earnings, and benefits would replace a higher proportion of each half, resulting in higher total benefits for the couple than for the single earner. Furthermore, if survivors' benefits were set higher than 50 percent of the couples' benefits—for example, at two-thirds—it would be possible for some survivors of couples in which both had been high earners to receive benefits larger than the maximum paid to single workers who had always earned the maximum amount taxed by Social Security. To avoid this possibility, survivors' benefits might be subject to a ceiling equal to the maximum possible benefits for single persons.[22]

---

amount of earnings than does the one-earner couple. Consider, for example, a one-earner couple earning $35,000 in 1979 versus a two-earner couple in which one member earns $20,000 and the other $15,000. Despite the fact that both couples have the same total money income, the one-earner couple would pay Social Security taxes on only $22,900, while the two-earner couple would pay Social Security taxes on the entire $35,000. In return for their greater tax payment, however, the two-earner couple receives larger earnings records and would have larger retirement benefits.

This difference in treatment could be removed if the taxable maximum for a couple were set at twice the maximum for two individuals. One-earner couples would then be required to pay any deficit in their Social Security taxes when filing their income tax return for the year. Although this proposal is unlikely to be popular, in practice, raising the taxable maximum for everyone may have much the same effect. The taxable maximum has been increasing over time and will continue to increase, to $29,700 by 1981. Hence, a declining number of one-earner couples will have incomes exceeding the taxable maximum. In addition, unless the economic position of women changes greatly, fewer two-earner couples will have total earnings in excess of the taxable maximum. However, should the economic position of women improve so that a higher percentage of two-earner couples have combined earnings in excess of the taxable maximum, additional pressure would probably be generated for changing this aspect of the Social Security system.

22. This response would, however, reinstate some disparity in treatment of married couples. Benefits for survivors of two couples could be the same (the maximum paid to a single worker) even though Social Security tax payments during the working years had been quite different. Basically, when maximum survivors' benefits are limited in this way, the survivor of a two-earner couple in which each had high earnings would get low benefits (in relation to the couple's total tax payments) compared with the survivor of a couple who had lower covered earnings. Suppose the maximum benefits paid to a single worker (and hence the maximum

Finally, how effective is earnings sharing in meeting the goal of improving the protection of divorced homemakers? Earnings sharing would mean that both spouses shared equally in the financial loss occurring in the event of divorce, with the outcome for each spouse directly related to the length of marriage. A short marriage would have little effect on the benefits provided to each spouse. A longer marriage would tend to reduce the benefits of the higher earner and to increase the benefits of the lower earner or the homemaker spouse. Because claims to retirement benefits based on shared earnings during years of marriage could be combined with a divorced homemaker's own earnings in subsequent years, protection for a woman in these circumstances is likely to increase compared with the protection under the current system when the ex-husband remains alive.[23] The comparison of benefits after his death, if it precedes hers, depends on the amount of her own earnings. This is because, under the current system, divorced widows usually receive their ex-husbands' entire benefits; in contrast, under earnings sharing the homemakers' own earnings would contribute to higher benefits. We can conclude, however, that earnings sharing would smooth the time pattern of benefits for divorced homemakers. Rather than receiving low benefits while their ex-husbands are alive and then double those amounts upon their ex-husbands' deaths, divorced women would, under earnings sharing, have the same level of benefits in all years.[24]

Despite the few remaining differences in the treatment of one-earner couples, two-earner couples, and single individuals, earnings-sharing proposals have an appeal similar to that of optional individual filing for the federal income tax system. Earnings sharing occupies an intermediate position between providing homemaker credits and providing benefits only on an individual basis. Homemaker credits would continue to subsidize primarily one-earner couples at the expense of two-earner couples and single individuals; but benefits based solely on one's own employment would strongly penalize in-

---

survivors' benefits) were $8,000. This sum would be paid to the survivor of a one-earner couple who had been receiving $6,000 plus $6,000 (since two-thirds of $12,000 is $8,000) as well as to the survivor of a two-earner couple each member of which had been receiving $8,000. Yet the latter couple would have paid considerably more Social Security taxes during their lifetimes.

23. Recall that this comparison is valid only for divorced female homemakers, because the current system provides such benefits only for women.

24. Of course, as is true of all Social Security benefits, they would increase each year as the cost of living increases.

dividuals who preferred to allocate a substantial proportion of their time to home activities.

Earnings sharing also would enable divorced homemakers to combine the protection they receive in their roles as homemakers with that they receive subsequently in their roles as workers, just as homemaker-credits proposals would. But earnings sharing would provide higher earnings records, and hence higher benefits, for many divorced homemakers than would homemaker-credit plans. In 1979, for example, home-makers whose spouses earned more than $12,000 (twice the full-time minimum wage) would receive greater protection under earnings sharing than under a homemaker-credits proposal in which the credits equaled the full-time minimum wage. Correspondingly, however, earnings sharing would reduce the benefits received by divorced men who do not remarry. Such a reduction would not occur under homemaker-credits proposals in which the worker's record is unaffected.

This section has discussed several proposals for modifying the Social Security system, their underlying rationales, and the effects they would have on different groups of people. In order to evaluate the desirability of these proposals, however, we need more specific information. We need to know both the sizes of the different groups that would be affected and the extent of changes in benefits that would occur under the alternative systems. The next section provides some of these answers.

EFFECTS OF SPECIFIC POLICY OPTIONS

This section discusses the results of our analysis of four specific policy options: (1) the current system; (2) individually based benefits; (3) homemaker credits; and (4) earnings sharing. The provisions of the current system have already been described.[25] The other policy options

---

25. The provisions of the Social Security system, as amended in 1977, formed the basis for our calculation of benefits. In particular, benefits are provided to divorced wives who did not remarry provided the marriage had lasted ten years or more. Also, we have used the 1979 benefit formula as shown below to calculate an individual's primary insurance amount, which is the amount of benefits paid if retirement does not occur before age sixty-five:

Averaged Indexed Monthly Earnings (AIME)	*Primary Insurance Amount*
Less than $180	90 percent of AIME
$180 to $1,085	$162 plus 32 percent of (AIME minus $180)
$1,086 or more	$452 plus 15 percent of (AIME minus $1,085)

would retain the wage-indexed earnings and benefit formula of the current system but would replace the dependents' and survivors' benefits of the current system with one of the following sets of provisions.

- In the case of individually based benefits, all persons would receive the benefits that are payable on their own records as workers. There would be no dependents' or survivors' benefits provided for adults.

- Under the homemaker-credits proposal, each adult over age twenty-five would have an earnings record at least as large as the full-time minimum wage that year. This record could be provided for homemakers with or without corresponding taxes' being assessed.[26] In the former case, Social Security taxes for recipients would be assessed at the self-employment rate.

- The earnings-sharing proposal allocates the earnings records of spouses equally to each during each year of marriage. Upon retirement, each spouse would receive benefits based on his or her own individual record. Upon the death of one spouse, the survivor would receive either his or her own benefits or two-thirds of the couple's total benefits when both were alive, whichever amount was higher.[27]

The analysis is based on data created by a microsimulation model, DYNASIM.[28] This microsimulation model simulates the behavior of

---

26. Because we considered Congress unlikely to adopt a free homemaker credits plan, we did not analyze such a proposal. In any event, the focus in this chapter is on benefit levels rather than on the comparison between benefit levels and tax payments. Those who advocate providing homemaker credits without assessing corresponding taxes can examine the benefit levels that would result from such a plan under the assumption that the source and method of payment for the credits would be changed.

27. If no survivors' benefits were provided, the surviving spouse would continue to receive his or her own benefits (which would be based on the shared earnings record). This amount would seldom be sufficient to maintain the survivor at the same standard of living the couple had enjoyed, but providing the survivor with two-thirds of the couple's benefits would do so. Allowing the survivor to continue receiving his or her own benefits, if higher than the two-thirds option, protects survivors who had recently married persons with exceptionally low benefits. This provision was not incorporated in the homemaker-credits proposal for two reasons: (1) it would not have been consistent with supporters' views that the provision of credits would eliminate the need for benefits derived from spouses' claims; and (2) such a change would have increased considerably the cost of the homemaker-credits proposal.

28. For a description of the DYNASIM model, see Guy H. Orcutt, Steven B. Caldwell, and Richard Wertheimer II, *Policy Exploration Through Microanalytic Simulation* (Washington, D.C.: The Urban Institute, 1976). For a description of the revised DYNASIM model as it affects this analysis, see Richard Wertheimer II

Table 33

COMPARISON OF TOTAL BENEFITS OF
THREE PROPOSED OPTIONS AS PERCENTAGES OF THE
CURRENT SYSTEM'S BENEFITS

	(percent)
Current system	100
Individually based system	88
Homemaker credits	102
Earnings sharing	101

Note: Because we are considering only the age group that will reach age sixty-five in the years 1998 to 2000, the total cost of their benefits does not indicate the total cost of the Social Security system. Hence, we have reported amounts only in relative terms.

a random sample of the American population over future years. One age group was extracted—persons who were ages twenty-five to twenty-seven in 1960, who would reach age sixty-five between 1998 and 2000.[29] Benefits each individual in this group would receive at age sixty-five (with no actuarial reduction for early retirement) were then computed under the assumption that the provisions of each of the four options had been in place throughout the individual's lifetime. As a result it is possible to examine the long-term effects of each option that would occur if it were fully implemented.[30]

The next sections discuss the relative costs under the four options of providing benefits to the specific age group described above, the effects of the four options on men and women of different marital statuses, and then the detailed implications of the homemaker-credits plan and the earnings-sharing proposal.

First, consider the total amounts of benefits that would be paid to members of the group when they reached age sixty-five. These amounts are shown in relative terms for the four policy options in Table 33. The individually based system is significantly less expensive (12 percent

and Sheila R. Zedlewski, "The Aging of America: A Portrait of the Elderly in 1990," The Urban Institute Working Paper 1224–01, December 1978.

29. For a description of the particular data used for this analysis, see Gary Hendricks, Russell Holden, and Jon Johnson, "A File of Simulated Family and Earnings Histories Through the Year 2000: Contents and Documentation," The Urban Institute Working Paper 985–3, revised April 1977.

30. As noted earlier, however, any new system should be phased in slowly to allow people to adapt to the new provisions.

less) than the current system. Both the homemaker-credits and the earnings-sharing proposals are slightly more expensive (2 percent and 1 percent, respectively) than the current system.

Recall from Chapter 7 that, for purpose of comparison, tax liabilities under each option were increased or decreased proportionately so as to maintain total tax revenue at a constant amount. We have not scaled the Social Security benefits under the three policy options to maintain total costs of the systems at the same level as the current system because we lack adequate information to do so—only one specific age group is examined. Moreover, for many years after adoption, the total cost of each option would be strongly influenced by the choice of transition mechanism from the current system. Consequently, in the case of the individually based system under which benefits decline for many people without a corresponding increase for others, a decline in the total expenditure for all Social Security benefits would result. These resources could be reallocated among all beneficiaries, for example, by changing the benefit formula.

With this caveat in mind, consider now the average benefits under the four policy options.[31] Table 34 displays average benefits expressed in 1976 dollars for women and men in different marital status categories, plus the combined benefits received by husbands and wives. Under the current system, we see that married women receive slightly more than half the benefits married men receive. The average married couple who will reach age sixty-five between the years 1998 and 2000 will receive benefits of $11,210.[32] Divorced women receive somewhat more than married women, but considerably less than widows. Divorced men receive slightly less than married or widowed men.

Under the individually based system, married women would receive on average about $700 less each year than they do under the current system. In general, men would receive almost exactly the same benefits as under the present system. Hence, average couples' benefits would drop, from $11,210 to $10,500. Divorced women would receive considerably less than they do under the current system, $3,990 compared with $4,870. Widows would receive markedly lower benefits, $3,435 compared with $6,040 under the current system.[33]

---

31. We assume that all individuals wait to collect benefits until age sixty-five. Individuals who die prior to retirement are omitted from the analysis.

32. Spouses in a marriage are often of different ages. Hence, we have examined the benefits the couple would receive after both members have reached age sixty-five.

33. Benefits received by widowers would be affected only in those few cases in which the men were dependents or survivors of their wives. In our sample, we see no change from the current system.

Table 34

COMPARISON OF AVERAGE BENEFITS UNDER FOUR POLICY OPTIONS

Plan	Marital Status and Sex[a]						
	Married		Couple	Divorced		Widowed	
	Women	Men		Women	Men	Women	Men
Current system	$3,960	$7,250	$11,210	$4,870	$7,020	$6,040	$7,160
Individually based	3,250	7,250	10,500	3,990	7,020	3,435	7,160
Homemaker credits	4,560[b]	7,270[b]	11,830	4,980	7,040	4,760	7,180
Earnings sharing	5,420	5,800	11,220	5,100	6,260	6,630	7,120

a. Persons who had never married would receive the same retirement benefits ($5,320 for women, $7,000 for men) under the current system, the individually based system, and the earnings-sharing system. Benefits would be slightly higher ($5,660 for women, $7,030 for men) under the homemaker-credits plan.

b. Estimated.

Now consider the homemaker-credits proposal. By requiring each person to have an earnings record at least the size of the full-time minimum wage, benefits for married women would increase by about $600 annually. Benefits for married men would increase minimally, for a total increase in average couples' benefits from $11,210 to $11,830. Under this homemaker-credits proposal, divorced women would receive about $100 more annually on average. Benefits for divorced and widowed men would be the same as under the current system. The one startling difference applies to widows; they would receive significantly lower benefits than they do now, only $4,760 compared with the current $6,040. This drop is the result of replacing survivors' benefits with the widows' own benefits based on a combination of homemaker credits and their own work histories.

Finally, relative to the current system, the earnings-sharing proposal would increase benefits for married women, decrease benefits for married men, and maintain the total average benefits for married couples at a level almost identical to that under the current system. The average benefits for divorced women would increase from $4,870 to $5,100, while the average benefits for divorced men would fall from $7,020 to $6,260. The provisions of survivors' benefits equal to two-thirds the couples' benefits or the individuals' own benefits, whichever amount was higher, would increase the average widows' benefits from $6,040 to $6,630, while benefits for widowers would remain about the same as under the current system.

What can we conclude from this initial information about the four policy options? First, an individually based system seems totally inappropriate to the way our society is now organized in the United States. Although benefits for married couples would decline only slightly, benefits for divorced women and widows would decline substantially. Even though all benefits could be increased without exceeding the cost of benefits under the current system, increasing benefits proportionately would still result in amounts for divorced women and widows significantly lower than they now are. (At the same time, benefits for married couples and divorced and widowed men would increase in comparison with current benefits.) Consequently this system would provide strong incentives for all individuals to devote most of their lives to paid employment in order to avoid the large penalties that would result from remaining at home for any significant period. We conclude that, given the current position of American women, providing benefits based solely on the individual's own working history is too extreme a policy change.

Would the provision of homemaker credits improve upon the present Social Security system? Advocates of homemaker credits have maintained that benefit levels for divorced women would increase substantially, and that if homemakers had their own earnings records to rely upon, they would no longer need survivors' benefits. As Table 34 indicates, however, in practice neither of these suppositions appears likely to result. Although benefits for married women would increase about $600 annually, benefits for divorced women would change very little.

Although the treatment of one-earner and two-earner couples could be more balanced under a homemaker-credits plan than under the current system, this improvement would occur only if the credits were provided to eligible individuals regardless of whether they had participated in the labor force or if corresponding taxes were assessed. Otherwise the system might well exacerbate current problems in the differential treatment of one-earner versus two-earner couples.

Finally, as noted above, under the homemakers-credit proposal benefits paid to widows would decline substantially. In effect, the proposal would reallocate benefits paid to married couples: a retired couple would receive higher benefits while both were alive, but widows would receive less than under the current system. Table 35 shows the increase in couples' benefits that would result from the homemaker-credits proposal for couples in which the wife had been employed for varying numbers of years.[34] In all cases, benefits would be greater than under the current system, but the longer a wife works, the less impact homemaker credits would have on the couple's benefits. However, if one refers back to Table 34, it is apparent that this advantage does not compensate for eliminating survivors' benefits—widows' benefits are considerably smaller than under the current system.

Why does this undesirable reallocation occur? The homemaker-credits proposal would require that each person have an earnings record at least the size of the full-time minimum wage. Although the minimum wage is not much lower than the average wage women now receive, an average married woman works about half time, not full time. The homemaker-credits proposal, then, would increase the earnings records not only of full-time homemakers, but also of the many women who are in the labor force part time. Consequently, because of their homemaker credits many women would receive higher

---

34. Any year in which a wife worked at least 520 hours (quarter time) is considered to be a year of employment.

Table 35

COMPARISON OF AVERAGE BENEFITS FOR MARRIED COUPLES UNDER CURRENT SYSTEM AND UNDER HOMEMAKER-CREDITS PROPOSAL, BY YEARS WIFE EMPLOYED

Years Wife Employed	Current System	Homemaker Credits	Change
41+	12,810	12,970	+$750
0–10	$10,160	$10,910	+ 890
11–20	10,490	11,380	+ 680
21–30	10,920	11,600	+ 300
31–40	11,900	12,200	+ 160

benefits while their husbands were alive than the benefits they now receive because of their own earnings or as dependents of their husbands.

The situation for widows' benefits is reversed. Those who propose homemaker credits argue that once homemakers are provided with their own earnings records, they will no longer need survivors' benefits. What has not necessarily been realized is that substituting homemaker credits for survivors' benefits would substantially lower benefits for most widows because men on average earn considerably more than the full-time minimum wage and, under the current system, most widows receive their husbands' benefits.

To summarize, under the homemaker-credits proposal, the position of divorced women would not be significantly improved and widows would find their benefits lower. If the credits were provided by assessing corresponding taxes, the treatment of one-earner and two-earner couples would be more balanced than under the current system. If not, the system might well exacerbate the already inequitable treatment of two-earner couples vis-à-vis one-earner couples. We conclude that this policy option responds to the difficulties of the current system by creating new ones.

What would be the implications of adopting an earnings-sharing proposal? As noted earlier, married men would find their benefits significantly reduced. Benefits to married women would increase substantially, with the result that, on average, married couples would receive almost exactly the same total benefits as those they receive under the current system. But would there be significant transfers between different types of married couples?

Table 36 shows benefits for couples under the current system and under the earnings-sharing proposal according to the number of years the wife was employed. Here we see that benefits for couples in which the wife was employed less than ten years would be lower on average, by about $500 annually under the earnings-sharing system than under the current one. Benefits for couples in which the wife was employed between eleven and twenty years would be higher by more than $500 annually. Benefits for couples in which the wife was employed twenty-one years or more would be only slightly higher, by between $60 and $150 annually.

These results follow from a combination of effects. Eliminating dependents' benefits reduces the benefits paid to one-earner couples, although this effect is offset to some extent because of the progressivity of the benefit formula. Under the current system, the Social Security tax payments of wives who worked between ten and thirty years probably has little effect on benefits. Yet such payments would count toward benefits under earnings sharing. Wives who worked for a relatively long period of time are likely to have average earnings that are closer to their husbands' earnings; hence, sharing earnings records would have little impact on the average earnings of each spouse and consequently little effect on their total benefits.

Because earnings sharing would treat couples with the same total covered earnings identically, regardless of the division of those earnings between spouses, this proposal responds directly to the issue of similar treatment of one- and two-earner couples. But what would it imply for benefits for divorced individuals? Table 37 shows benefits that divorced women and men would receive according to the number of years the individual had spent in paid employment. Divorced

Table 36

COMPARISON OF AVERAGE BENEFITS FOR
MARRIED COUPLES UNDER CURRENT SYSTEM AND UNDER
EARNINGS-SHARING PROPOSAL, BY YEARS WIFE EMPLOYED

Years Wife Employed	Current System	Earnings Sharing	Change
0–10	$10,160	$ 9,650	−$510
11–20	10,490	10,500	+ 560
21–30	10,920	11,070	+ 150
31–40	11,900	11,990	+ 90
41+	12,810	12,870	+ 60

Table 37

COMPARISON OF AVERAGE BENEFITS FOR
DIVORCED PERSONS UNDER CURRENT SYSTEM AND
UNDER EARNINGS-SHARING PROPOSAL,
BY YEARS EMPLOYED

Years Employed	Divorced Women			Divorced Men		
	Current System	Earnings Sharing	Change	Current System	Earnings Sharing	Change
0–10	$3,350	$3,810	+$460	—	—	—
11–20	3,930	4,430	+ 500	—	—	—
21–30	4,720	4,990	+ 270	—	—	—
31–40	5,540	5,620	+ 80	$6,680	$5,840	−$840
41+	5,820	5,880	+ 60	7,110	6,370	− 740

women would find that their benefits would increase no matter how many years they had been employed, with the largest increases (about $500) occurring for those employed twenty years or less. Modest increases ($270) would also occur for those employed between twenty-one and thirty years, and relatively small increases would occur for those employed longer.

These benefit increases for divorced women are less than the decreases experienced by divorced men who remain divorced by the time they retire. Although the number of divorced men who remarry is far greater than the number of divorced women who remarry (resulting in fewer retired divorced men than women), such men would find their annual benefits approximately $800 less than their benefits under the current system. Men who divorced but remarried prior to retirement are included in the married couples' tables, and their benefits would be almost identical with those under the current system.

Another way to address the question of the effect of earnings sharing on divorced men is to examine the extent of their benefit reduction under an earnings-sharing system compared with the current system.[35] For the year 2000, we find that under earnings sharing only

35. These results are based on a different DYNASIM simulation from the one used for the analysis described above and include divorced men of all ages who would be receiving Social Security benefits in the year 2000. A transition mechanism to phase in earnings sharing between 1979 and 1999 was included in this simulation.

3 percent of divorced men would receive benefits substantially lower than those they would receive under the current system (between 50 percent and 75 percent of current benefits). Fifteen percent would receive benefits of 75 percent to 90 percent of those they would receive under the current system. Twelve percent would receive benefits of 90 percent to 95 percent of those under the current system. Seventy percent would receive benefits between 95 percent and 105 percent of their value under the current system. Thus most divorced men would receive benefits approximately the same as their benefits under the current system, some would experience a modest reduction, and a few would experience severe reductions in benefits.

What would earnings sharing imply for widows and widowers? Table 38 shows a pattern in benefits for widows similar to that observed for married couples. Widows who had been in the paid labor market for ten years or less would experience a small decline in their benefit levels, $100 annually. All other widows could expect an increase in benefits, ranging from $400 annually for those in the labor force between eleven and twenty years to $1,100 annually for those in the labor force for thirty-one years or more. Benefits for widowers would remain essentially the same as benefits under the current system, declining by between $10 and $60 a year, depending on the number of years the husband was employed.

Table 38

COMPARISON OF AVERAGE BENEFITS FOR
WIDOWS AND WIDOWERS UNDER CURRENT SYSTEM AND
EARNINGS-SHARING PROPOSAL, BY YEARS EMPLOYED

Years Employed	*Widows*			*Widowers*		
	Current System	Earnings Sharing	Change	Current System	Earnings Sharing	Change
0–10	$6,030	$5,930	−$ 100	—	—	—
11–20	5,900	6,310	+ 410	—	—	—
21–30	6,060	6,670	+ 610	—	—	—
31–40	6,070	7,100	+1,030	$7,040	$7,030	−$10
41+	6,320	7,430	+1,110	7,200	7,140	− 60

Hence, older divorced men who received benefits early in the transition period would be less affected by the adoption of earnings sharing than would those who retired in later years.

RECOMMENDATION

We recommend that the earnings-sharing approach be incorporated into the Social Security system because this approach meets all three goals identified earlier in this chapter. First, earnings sharing would impose no large penalties on one-earner couples relative to the current system. Even those few couples in which the wife never participated in the labor force would experience only a moderate reduction in benefits. Second, married couples with the same covered earnings would be treated identically, regardless of the division of earnings between the spouses. Third, protection for divorced homemakers would be improved, because the implications of divorce for retirement income would be the same for both husband and wife, rather than retaining the same benefits for the husband and providing low benefits for the wife as occurs under the current system. Furthermore, all three goals probably could be met with little increase in the total cost of the system.

In designing a legislative proposal to implement the earnings-sharing approach, several decisions have to be made. For example, would disability and young survivors' benefits continue to be based on one's own earnings record, with the shared record used for retirement and aged survivors' benefits only, or would all benefits be based on the shared record? The former option would mean that homemakers would not receive disability protection, but that they would have greater protection in the event of death or disability of their spouses—the earners in these one-earner couples. The latter option would provide protection when homemakers are disabled or die, but at the expense of considerably reduced benefits to the couple should the employed spouse be disabled or die.

Also, when would earnings records be shared, annually or in the event of retirement, divorce, or death of an aged worker? The administrative burden of adopting earnings sharing probably would be least if records were shared only upon retirement, divorce, or death of an older worker. However, the definition of "retirement" should be when both spouses have applied for benefits. Otherwise, when one spouse applies for benefits, but the other does not, benefits might be unacceptably low. This situation is most likely to occur in the case of a one-earner couple in which the worker is several years older than the homemaker. The benefit reduction that would result from sharing earnings records upon the retirement of the worker would impose undue hardship on the couple until the homemaker was old enough to receive benefits.

Should earnings sharing be adopted, a transition scheme to move gradually, perhaps over twenty or thirty years, from the current to the new system would be advisable. Such a scheme would avoid disrupting the financial plans of people who will retire in the near future. Further, such a transition would minimize the effect on couples in which the wife never worked. This follows because current forecasts indicate that in the future it will be extremely rare to find a couple in which the wife has never worked. Further, any such couples could modify their behavior slightly in light of the new system, thereby maintaining their benefits at the same level as under the current system. Although some supporters of earnings sharing may be frustrated at the suggestion of such a gradual phase-in, in the long run we will have achieved the advantages that earnings sharing presents and we will have avoided imposing costs on those whose decisions about family and employment roles were made in past years.

Perhaps the most important reason that the author favors earnings sharing is that it is the most neutral policy regarding labor force participation decisions of married women. Both the current system and homemaker credits encourage women to remain in the home and to devote the bulk of their lifetimes to family responsibilities. Yet both systems impose large costs on some homemakers--the current system imposes them on women whose marriages dissolve, and the homemaker-credits proposal imposes them on widowed homemakers. Conversely, the individually based proposal would provide strong incentives for all individuals to participate in paid employment most of their lives.

We are currently in a time of transition when many women are choosing whether to be full-time homemakers, to pursue careers, or to combine both roles. In addition, many women have made decisions in the past that cannot be reversed. Consequently the author believes that we should adopt social institutions that encourage individuals to base their labor force participation decisions on factors within their personal lives, such as their and their spouses' preferences and value judgments. With regard to the Social Security system, only earnings sharing meets this criterion of neutrality.

SELECTED BIBLIOGRAPHY

Abramowitz, Susan and Stuart Rosenfeld, eds. *Declining Enrollments: The Challenge of the Coming Decade.* Washington, D.C.: National Institute of Education, 1975.

Abt Associates. "National Day Care Study: Preliminary Findings and Their Implications." Cambridge, Mass., 1978.

Angrist, Shirley S.; Judith R. Lave; and Richard Mickelson. "How Working Mothers Manage: Socioeconomic Differences in Work, Child Care, and Household Tasks." *Social Science Quarterly* 56 (1976): 631–37.

Bane, Mary Jo. *Here to Stay: American Families in the Twentieth Century.* New York: Basic Books, Inc., 1976.

Baruch, G. K. "Maternal Influences Upon College Women's Attitudes Toward Women and Work." *Developmental Psychology* 6 (1972): 32–37.

Becker, Gary S. *Human Capital: A Theoretical and Empirical Analysis.* New York: Columbia University Press, 1964.

Becker, Gary S.; Elizabeth M. Landes; and Robert T. Michael. "Economics of Marital Instability." National Bureau of Economic Research Working Paper No. 153, Stanford, Calif., October 1976.

Bergmann, Barbara R. "Reducing the Pervasiveness of Discrimination." In Eli Ginzberg, ed. *Jobs for Americans.* By the American Assembly. Englewood Cliffs, N.J.: Prentice-Hall, Inc., 1976.

————. "Sex Discrimination in Wages: Comment." In Orley Ashenfelter and Albert Rees, eds. *Discrimination in Labor Markets.* Princeton: Princeton University Press, 1973.

Birnbaum, J. A. "Life Patterns, Personality Style and Self Esteem in Gifted Family Oriented and Career Committed Women." Unpublished Ph.D. dissertation, University of Michigan, 1971.

Blake, Judith. "Demographic Science and Redirection of Population Policy." *Journal of Chronic Diseases* 18 (1965): 1181–1200.

Blinder, Alan S. "Wage Discrimination: Reduced Form and Structural Estimates." *Journal of Human Resources* 8, Fall 1973.

Blood, Robert O., Jr. "The Husband-Wife Relationship," in F. Ivan Nye and Lois Wladis Hoffman, eds. *The Employed Mother in America.* Chicago: Rand McNally, 1963.

Blood, Robert O., Jr., and Donald M. Wolfe. *Husbands and Wives: The Dynamics of Married Living.* New York: Free Press, 1960.

Bowlby, J. A. "Some Pathological Processes Engendered by Early Mother-Child Separation." In M. Senn, *Infancy and Childhood.* New York: Josiah Macy, Jr., Foundation, 1953.

Brito, Patricia K. and Carol L. Jusenius. "Occupational Expectations for Age 35." In U.S. Department of Labor. *Years for Decision.* Vol. 4. R&D Monograph No. 24, 1978.

Broverman, Inge; S. R. Vogel; D. M. Broverman; F. E. Clarkson; and P. S. Rosenkrantz. "Sex Role Stereotypes: A Current Appraisal." *Journal of Social Issues* 28 (1972): 59–78.

Brown, Gary D. "How Type of Employment Affects Earnings Differences by Sex." *Monthly Labor Review* 99 (July 1976): 25–30.

Buric, Olivera and Andjelka Zecevic. "Family Authority, Marital Satisfaction and the Special Network in Yugoslavia." *Journal of Marriage and the Family* 29 (May 1967): 325–36.

Burke, Ronald J. and Tamara Weir. "Relationship of Wives' Employment Status to Husband, Wife and Pair Satisfaction and Performance." *Journal of Marriage and the Family* 38 (May 1976): 278–87.

Business and Professional Women's Foundation. *Hours of Work When Workers Can Choose.* Washington, D.C., 1975.

Cain, Glen. *Married Women in the Labor Force: An Economic Analysis.* Chicago: University of Chicago Press, 1966.

Carnegie Corporation. "Average Day Care: Harmful or Beneficial?" *Carnegie Quarterly* 25 (Summer 1977): 5–6.

Cherlin, Andrew. "The Effect of Children on Marital Dissolution." *Demography* 14 (August 1977): 273–84.

Chiswick, Barry; J. Fackler; June O'Neill; and Solomon Polachek. "The Effect of Occupation on Race and Sex Differences in Hourly Earnings." *Proceedings of the American Statistical Association,* 1974, pp. 219–28.

Clarke-Stewart, Allison. *Child Care in the Family: A Review of Research and Some Propositions for Policy.* New York: Academic Press, 1977.

Cromwell, R., and D. C. Olson, eds. *Power in Families.* New York: John Wiley (Halstead), 1975.

Cronkite, Ruth. "Determinants and Changes in Normative Preferences of Spouses." Research Memorandum, Center for the Study of Welfare Policy, Stanford Research Institute, Menlo Park, Calif., 1977.

Cutright, Phillips. "Components of Change in the Number of Female Household Heads Aged 15–44: United States 1940–1970." *Journal of Marriage and the Family* 36 (November 1974): 714–21.

Dickinson, Katherine. "Child Care." In Greg J. Duncan and James Morgan, eds. *Five Thousand Families.* Vol. 3. Ann Arbor: Institute for Social Research, University of Michigan, 1975.

Dippo, Cathryn; John Coleman; and Curtis Jacobs. "Evaluation of the 1972–73 Consumer Expenditure Survey." Bureau of Labor Statistics. Paper presented at the annual meeting of the American Statistical Association, Chicago, August 1977.

Doeringer, Peter B. and Michael J. Piore. *Internal Labor Markets and Manpower Analysis.* Lexington, Mass.: D. C. Heath and Company, 1971.

Douvan, E. "Employment and the Adolescent." In F. Ivan Nye and Lois Wladis Hoffman, eds *The Employed Mother in America.* Chicago: Rand McNally, 1963.

Doyle, Anna-Beth. "Infant Development in Day Care." *Developmental Psychology* 2 (September 1975): 655–56.

Duncan, Greg J. "Unmarried Heads of Households and Marriage." In Greg J. Duncan and James Morgan, eds. *Five Thousand Families.* Vol. 4, Ann Arbor: Institute for Social Research, University of Michigan, 1976.

Eastwood, Mary. "Legal Protection Against Sex Discrimination." In Ann H. Stromberg and Shirley Harkess, eds. *Women Working.* Palo Alto, Calif.: Mayfield Publishing Company, 1978.

Etaugh, Claire. "Effects of Maternal Employment on Children: A Review of Recent Research." *Merrill Palmer Quarterly* 20 (1974): 71–98.

Feld, S. "Feelings of Adjustment," in Ivan Nye and Lois Wladis Hoffman, eds. *The Employed Mother in America.* Chicago: Rand McNally, 1963.

Feldman, H. and M. Feldman. "The Relationship Between the Family and Occupational Functioning in a Sample of Rural Women." Department of Human Development and Family Studies, Cornell University, 1973.

Ferree, Myra Marx. "Working Class Jobs: Housework and Paid Work as Sources of Satisfaction." *Social Problems,* April 1976, pp. 431–41.

Freedman, Ronald; Pascal K. Whelpton; and Arthur A. Campbell. *Family Planning, Sterility, and Population Growth.* New York: McGraw Hill, 1959.

Freeman, Jo. "The Legal Basis of the Sexual Caste System." *Valparaiso Law Review* 5 (1971): 213–30.

—————. *The Politics of Women's Liberation.* New York: Longman, 1975.

Fullerton, Howard N., Jr., and James J. Byrne. *Length of Working Life for Men and Women, 1970.* U.S. Department of Labor, Bureau of Labor Statistics, Special Labor Force Report No. 187. Washington, D.C.: U.S. Government Printing Office, 1977.

Gianopulos, Artie and Howard E. Mitchell. "Marital Disagreement in Working Wife Marriages as a Function of Husband's Attitude Toward Wife's Employment." *Journal of Marriage and the Family* 19 (November 1957): 373–78.

Glenn, Norval D. "The Contribution of Marriage to the Psychological Well-Being of Males and Females." *Journal of Marriage and the Family* 37 (August 1975): 594–601.

Glick, Paul C. "Updating the Life Cycle of the Family." *Journal of Marriage and the Family* 39 (February 1977): 3–15.

Glick, Paul C. and Arthur J. Norton. "Marrying, Divorcing, and Living Together in the U.S. Today." *Population Bulletin* 32 (1977): 3–39.

Goldberg, Phillip A. "Are Women Prejudiced Against Women?" *Transaction* 5 (May 1968): 28–30.

Gordon, Nancy M. and Thomas E. Morton. "The Staff Salary Structure of a Large University." *Journal of Human Resources* 11 (Summer 1976): 374–82.

Gover, David A. "Socioeconomic Differential in the Relationship Between Marital Adjustment and Wife's Employment Status." *Marriage and Family Living* 25 (November 1963): 452–56.

Grossman, Allyson Sherman. "Almost Half of All Children Have Mothers in the Labor Force." *Monthly Labor Review* 100 (June 1977): 41–44.

————. "Children of Working Mothers." *Monthly Labor Review* 101 (January 1978): 30–33.

————. *The Labor Force Patterns of Divorced and Separated Women.* U.S. Department of Labor, Bureau of Labor Statistics, Special Labor Force Report No. 198. Washington, D.C.: U.S. Government Printing Office, 1977.

Gustafsson, Siv. *Cost-Benefit Analysis of Early Childhood Care and Education.* Stockholm: The Industrial Institute for Economic and Social Research, 1978.

Hall, Arden and Samuel Weiner. "The Supply of Day Care Services in Denver and Seattle." Center for the Study of Welfare Policy. Research Memorandum 33, Stanford Research Institute, Menlo Park, Calif., June 1977.

Hannan, Michael T. and Nancy Brandon Tuma. "Income and Marital Events: Evidence from an Income-Maintenance Experiment." *American Journal of Sociology* 82 (May 1977): 1186–1211.

Hayge, Howard. *Marital and Family Characteristics of the Labor Force.* U.S. Department of Labor, Bureau of Labor Statistics, Special Labor Force Report No. 183. Washington, D.C.: U.S. Government Printing Office, 1976.

Hedges, Janice Neipert. "Flexible Schedules: Problems and Issues." *Monthly Labor Review* 100 (February 1977): 62–64.

Heer, David M. "The Measurement and Bases of Family Power: An Overview." *Marriage and Family Living* 25 (1963): 133–39.

Hendricks, Gary; Russell Holden; and Jon Johnson. "A File of Simulated Family and Earnings Histories Through the Year 2000: Contents and Documentation." The Urban Institute Working Paper 985-3 , revised April 1977.

Hofferth, Sandra L.; Katharine Fisher; and Donna Heins. "Occupational Segregation in Construction: A Case Study in Washington, D.C." The Urban Institute, Washington, D.C., 1977. Mimeographed.

Hofferth, Sandra L. and Kristin A. Moore. "Age at First Childbirth: Labor Force Participation and Earnings." The Urban Institute Working Paper 1146-4. Washington, D.C., 1978.

Hoffman, Lois Wladis. "Effects of the Employment of Mothers on Parental Power Relations and the Division of Household Tasks." *Marriage and Family Living* 22 (February 1960): 27–35.

————. "Effects of Maternal Employment on the Child: A Review of the Research." *Developmental Psychology* 10 (1974): 204–28.

Hoffman, Lois Wladis and F. Ivan Nye, eds. *Working Mothers.* San Francisco: Jossey-Bass, 1974.

Hoffman, Saul and John Holmes. "Husbands, Wives, and Divorce." In Duncan and Morgan, eds. *Five Thousand Families.* Vol. 4, pp. 23–76.

Holbrook, Robert and Frank Stafford. "The Propensity to Consume Separate Types of Income: A Generalized Permanent Income Hypothesis." *Econometrica* 39 (January 1971): 1–21.

Howrigan, Gail. "Effects of Working Mothers on Children." Center for the Study of Public Policy, Cambridge, Mass., August 1973.

Johnson, Beverly L. "Women Who Head Families, 1970–77: Their Numbers Rose, Income Lagged." *Monthly Labor Review* 101 (February 1978): 32–37.

Jones, Carol Adaire; Nancy M. Gordon; and Isabel V. Sawhill. "Child Support Payments in the United States." The Urban Institute Working Paper 992–03, Washington, D.C., October 1976.

Kamerman, Sheila and Alfred J. Kahn. "European Family Policy Currents: The Question of Families with Very Young Children." Columbia University School of Social Work, preliminary draft, 1976.

King, Karl; Thomas J. Abernathy; and Ann H. Chapman. "Black Adolescents' Views of Maternal Employment as a Threat to the Marital Relationship." *Journal of Marriage and the Family* 38 (November 1976): 733–37.

Komarovsky, Mirra. *Dilemmas of Masculinity.* New York: W. W. Norton and Co., 1976.

Lamale, Helen H. *Methodology of the Survey of Consumer Expenditures in 1950.* Philadelphia: University of Pennsylvania, 1959.

Len, Carol and Robert W. Bednarzik. "A Profile of Women on Part-Time Schedules." *Monthly Labor Review* 101, October 1978.

Levitan Sar A. and Robert Taggart III. *Employment and Earnings Adequacy: A New Social Indicator.* Baltimore: Johns Hopkins University Press, 1974.

Locke, Harvey J. and Muriel Mackeprang. "Marital Adjustment and the Employed Wife." *American Journal of Sociology* 54 (May 1949): 536–38.

Low, Seth and Pearl Spindler. *Child Care Arrangements of Working Mothers in the United States.* Washington, D.C.: U.S. Government Printing Office, 1968.

McCarthy, Maureen. "Federal and State Activities: Report of a Survey of Alternative Work Schedules in State Governments." In a Resource Packet for the National Conference on Alternative Work Schedules, Chicago, March 1977.

McIntire, Walter; Gilbert D. Nass; and Donna L. Battistone. "Female Misperceptions of Male Parenting and Expectancies." *Youth and Society* 5 (1974): 104–12.

Maklan, David Mark. "How Blue-Collar Workers on 4-Day Workweeks Use Their Time." *Monthly Labor Review* 100 (August 1977): 18–26.

Mason, Karen Oppenheim; John L. Czajka; and Sara Arber. "Changes in U.S. Women's Sex-Role Attitudes 1964–1974." *American Sociological Review* 4 (August 1976): 573–96.

Mason, Karen Oppenheim and L. L. Bumpass. "U.S. Women's Sex Role Ideology, 1970." *American Journal of Sociology* 80 (1975): 1212–19.

Matessich, Paul. "Childlessness and Its Correlates in Historical Perspective: A Research Note." *The Journal of Family History*, 1978.

Meissner, Martin; Elizabeth W. Humphreys; Scott M. Meis; and William J. Scheu. "No Exit for Wives: Sexual Division of Labour and the Cumulation of Household Demands." *Canadian Review of Sociology and Anthropology* 12 (1975): 424–39.

Michael, Robert T. "Factors Affecting Divorce: A Study of the Terman Sample." National Bureau of Economic Research Working Paper No. 147. Stanford, Calif., 1976.

Michel, A. "Comparative Data Concerning the Interaction in French and American Families." *Journal of Marriage and the Family* 29 (May 1967): 337–44.

Miller, Shirley Matile. "Effects of Maternal Employment on Sex Role Perception, Interests, and Self Esteem in Kindergarten Girls." *Developmental Psychology* 11 (May 1975): 405–06.

Mincer, Jacob. "Investment in Human Capital." *Journal of Political Economy* 66, August 1958.

———. "Labor Force Participation of Married Women: A Study of Labor Supply." In *Aspects of Labor Economics.* Princeton: Princeton University Press, 1962.

————. "Market Price Opportunity, Costs, and Income Effects." In C. F. Christ, ed. *Measurement in Economics: Studies in Mathematical Economics and Econometrics in Memory of Yehuda Grunfeld*. Palo Alto: Stanford University Press, 1963, pp. 67–82.

Mincer, Jacob and Solomon W. Polachek. "Family Investments in Human Capital: Earnings of Women." *Journal of Political Economy* 82 (March/April 1974): S76–S108.

Moore, Kristin A. and Linda J. Waite. "Early Childbearing and Educational Attainment." *Family Planning Perspectives* 9 (1977): 220–25.

Moore, Kristin A.; Linda J. Waite; Sandra L. Hofferth; and Steven B. Caldwell. "The Consequences of Age at First Childbirth: Marriage, Separation, and Divorce." The Urban Institute Working Paper No. 1146–3, Washington, D.C., 1978.

Mott, Frank L. and Sylvia F. Moore. "The Socioeconomic Determinants and Shortrun Consequences of Marital Disruption." Paper presented at the annual meeting of the Population Association of America, St. Louis, April 20–22, 1977.

Mott, Frank L. and David Shapiro. "Work and Motherhood: The Dynamics of Labor Force Participation Surrounding the First Birth." In *Years for Decision*. Vol. 4. Columbus: Ohio State University, 1977, pp. 65–111.

Mullis, I. V.; S. J. Oldefendt; and D. L. Phillips. *What Students Know and Can Do: Profiles of Three Age Groups*. Denver: National Assessment of Educational Progress, 1977.

Murray, Ann D. "Maternal Employment Reconsidered: Effects on Infants." *American Journal of Orthopsychiatry* 45 (October 1975): 773–79.

National Commission for Manpower Policy. *An Interim Report to the Congress*. Vol. I. Washington, D.C., March 1978.

National Council for Alternative Work Patterns. "Summary of Alternative Work Schedule and Related Legislation Pending Before the 95th Congress." In a Resource Packet for the National Conference on Alternative Work Schedules, Chicago, March 1977.

Neimi, Beth. "Geographic Immobility and Unemployment." In Cynthia B. Lloyd, ed. *Sex, Discrimination, and the Division of Labor*. New York: Columbia University Press, 1975.

Newman, Winn. "Combatting Occupational Segregation: Policy Issues." In Martha Blaxall and Barbara Reagan, eds. *Women and the Workplace*. Chicago: University of Chicago Press, 1976, pp. 265–72.

Nickols, Sharon. "Work and Housework: Family Roles in Productive Activity." Paper presented at the annual meeting of the National Council on Family Relations, October 19–23, 1976, New York.

Nolan, F. L. "Rural Employment and Husbands and Wives." in F. Ivan Nye and Lois Wladis Hoffman, eds. *The Employed Mother in America*. Chicago: Rand McNally, 1963.

Nye, F. Ivan. "Husband-Wife Relationship," in Lois Wladis Hoffman and F. Ivan Nye, eds. *Working Mothers*. San Francisco: Jossey-Bass, 1974.

————. "Marital Interaction." In Nye and Hoffman, eds. *The Employed Mother in America*. Chicago: Rand McNally, 1963.

————. "Personal Satisfactions." In Nye and Hoffman, eds. *The Employed Mother in America*. Chicago: Rand McNally, 1963.

Olson, David H. and Carolyn Rabunsky. "Validity of Four Measures of Family Power." *Journal of Marriage and the Family* 34 (May 1972): 224–34.

Oppenheimer, Valerie Kincade. "Divorce, Remarriage, and Wives' Labor Force Participation." Paper presented at the annual meeting of the American Sociological Association, September 1977.

————. *The Female Labor Force in the United States: Demographic and Economic Factors Governing Its Growth and Changing Composition*. Berkeley: University of California, 1970.

Orcutt, Guy H.; Steven B. Caldwell; and Richard F. Wertheimer II. *Policy Exploration Through Microanalytic Simulation*. Washington, D.C.: The Urban Institute, 1976.

Orden, Susan R. and Norman M. Bradburn. "Working Wives and Marriage Happiness." *American Journal of Sociology* 74 (January 1969): 392–407.

Organization for Economic Cooperation and Development. *The Treatment of Family Units in OECD Member Countries Under Tax and Transfer Systems*. Paris, 1977, pp. 15–17.

Owen, John D. "Flexitime: Some Management and Labor Problems of the New Flexible Hour Scheduling Practices." *Industrial and Labor Relations Review* 30 (January 1977): 152–61.

Parrish, John B. "Employment of Women Chemists in Industrial Laboratories." *Science*, April 30, 1965.

Pearl, Robert B. "The 1972–73 Consumer Expenditure Survey: A Preliminary Evaluation," University of Illinois. Paper presented at the annual meeting of the American Statistical Association, Chicago, August 1977.

Pinchbeck, Ivy. *Women Workers and the Industrial Revolution*. London: G. Routledge, 1930.

Polachek, Solomon W. and Francis W. Horvath. "A Life Cycle Approach to Migration: Analysis of the Perspicacious Peregrinator." In Ronald G. Ehrenberg, ed. *Research in Labor Economics*. Vol. 1. Greenwich, Conn.: Jai Press, 1977.

Powell, K. S. "Family Variables." In F. Ivan Nye and L. W. Hoffman, eds. *The Employed Mother in America*. Chicago: Rand McNally, 1963.

Presser, Harriet B. "Female Employment and the Division of Labor Within the Home: A Longitudinal Perspective." Paper presented at the annual meetings of the Population Association of America, St. Louis, Mo., April 20–23, 1977.

Preston, Samuel H. and Alan Thomas Richards. "The Influence of Women's Work Opportunities on Marriage Rates." *Demography* 12 (May 1975): 209–22.

Rappoport, Rhona; Robert Rappoport; and Michael Fogarty. *Sex, Career, and Marriage*. Beverly Hills, Calif.: Sage, 1971.

Ridley, Carl A. "Exploring the Impact of Work Satisfaction and Involvement on Marital Interaction when both Partners are Employed." *Journal of Marriage and the Family* 35 (May 1973): 229–37.

Ross, Heather and Isabel V. Sawhill. *Time of Transition: The Growth of Families Headed by Women*. Washington, D.C.: The Urban Institute, 1975.

Saario, Terry Tinson. "Title IX: Now What?" In Allan C. Ornstein and Steven I. Miller. *Policy Issues in Education*. Lexington, Mass.: Lexington Books, D. C. Heath and Company, 1976.

Safilios-Rothschild, Constantina. "A Comparison of Family Power Structure and Marital Satisfaction in Urban Greek and French Families." *Journal of Marriage and the Family* 29 (May 1967): 345–52.

————. "The Influence of the Wife's Degree of Work Commitment Upon Some Aspects of Family Organization and Dynamics." *Journal of Marriage and the Family* 32 (November 1970): 681–91.

————. "The Study of Family Power Structure: A Review, 1960–1969." *Journal of Marriage and the Family* 32 (November 1970): 539–52.

Sandell, Steven H. and David Shapiro. "The Theory of Human Capital and the Earnings of Women: A Re-examination of the Evidence." *Journal of Human Resources* 13 (Winter 1978): 103–117.

Sawhill, Isabel V. "The Economics of Discrimination Against Women: Some New Findings." *Journal of Human Resources* 8 (Fall 1973): 383–96.

Sawhill, Isabel V.; Gerald E. Peabody; Carol A. Jones; and Steven B. Caldwell. "Income Transfers and Family Structure." The Urban Institute Working Paper 979–03, Washington, D.C., 1975.

Schwartz, J. Conrad. "Social and Emotional Effects of Day Care: A Review of Recent Research." Paper presented to the Society for Research in Child Development Study Group on the Family, University of Michigan, Ann Arbor, October 1975.

Shortlidge, Richard L., Jr., and Patricia Brito. "How Women Arrange for the Care of Their Children While They Work: A Study of Child Care Arrangements, Costs, and Preferences in 1971." Center for Human Resource Research. Columbus: Ohio State University, January 1977.

Silverman, W. and R. Hill. "Task Allocation in Marriage in the United States and Belgium." *Journal of Marriage and the Family* 29 (May 1967): 353–59.

Smith, Ralph E. *The Impact of Macroeconomic Conditions on Employment Opportunities for Women.* U.S. Congress, Joint Economic Committee. Series on Achieving the Goals of the Employment Act of 1946. Washington, D.C.: U.S. Government Printing Office, 1977.

————. *Women in the Labor Force in 1990.* Washington, D.C.: The Urban Institute, 1979.

Spitz, R. A. "Hospitalism: An Inquiry into the Genesis of Psychiatric Conditions in Early Childhood." *Psychoanalytic Studies of the Child* 1 (1945): 53–74.

Stafford, Frank and Duncan, Greg. "The Use of Time and Technology by Households in the United States." University of Michigan, 1977.

Staines, Graham L.; Joseph H. Pleck; Linda J. Shepard; and Pamela O'Connor. "Wives' Employment Status and Marital Adjustment: Yet Another Look." University of Michigan, Institute for Social Research, 1978.

Stein, Aletha Houston. "The Effects of Maternal Employment and Educational Attainment on the Sex Typed Attributes of College Females." *Social Behavior and Personality* 1 (1973): 111–14.

Steiner, Gilbert V. *The Children's Cause*. Washington, D.C.: Brookings Institution, 1976.

Stone, Philip J. "Child Care in Twelve Countries." In Alexander Szalai, ed. *The Use of Time*. The Hague: Mouton, 1972.

Strober, Myra H. "Wives' Labor Force Behavior and Family Consumption Pattern." *American Economic Review*, February 1977, pp. 410–17.

Strober, Myra H. and Charles B. Weinberg. "Working Wives and Major Family Expenditures." *Journal of Consumer Research*, December 1977, pp. 141–47.

Szinovacz, Maximiliane E. "Role Allocation, Family Structure and Female Employment." *Journal of Marriage and the Family* 39 (November 1977): 781–91.

Tuma, Nancy Brandon; Lyle P. Groeneveld; and Michael T. Hannan. "First Dissolutions and Marriages: Impacts in 24 Months of the Seattle and Denver Income Maintenance Experiments." Research memorandum. Center for the Study of Welfare Policy, Stanford Research Institute, 1976.

Underwood, Lorraine A. *Women in Federal Employment Programs*. Washington, D.C.: The Urban Institute, 1979.

U.S. Civil Service Commission. *Equal Employment Opportunity Statistics*. Washington, D.C.: U.S. Government Printing Office, 1978.

————. Manpower Statistics Division. *Study of Employment of Women in the Federal Government 1975*. Washington, D.C.: U.S. Government Printing Office, 1975.

U.S. Department of Commerce. Bureau of the Census. "Characteristics of American Children and Youth: 1976." *Current Population Reports,* series P-23, no. 66, 1978.

————. "Daytime Care of Children: October 1974 and February 1975." *Current Population Reports*, series P-20, no. 298, 1976.

————. "Family Composition," *1970 Census of Population, Subject Reports*, no. PC(2)-4A, 1972.

————. "Fertility of American Women: June 1976." *Current Population Reports*, series P-20, no. 308, 1977.

————. "Marital Status and Family Status, March 1968." *Current Population Reports*, series P-20, no. 187, 1969.

————. "Marital Status and Living Arrangements: March 1976." *Current Population Reports*, series P-20, no. 306, 1977.

————. "Marital Status and Living Arrangements: March 1977." *Current Population Reports*, series P-20, no. 323, 1978.

————. "Money Income and Poverty Status of Families and Persons in the United States: 1977." Advance report. *Current Population Reports*, series P-60, no. 116, 1978.

————. "Money Income in 1976 of Families and Persons in the United States." *Current Population Reports*, series P-60, no. 114, 1978.

————. "Number, Timing and Duration of Marriages and Divorces in the United States: June 1975." *Current Population Reports*, series P-20, no. 297, 1976.

————. "Nursery School and Kindergarten Enrollment of Children and Labor Force Status of Their Mothers: October 1967 to October 1976." *Current Population Reports*, series P-20, no. 318, 1978.

————. "Projections of the Population of the United States: 1976 to 2050." *Current Population Reports*, series P-25, no. 601, 1975. •

————. "Projections of the Population of the United States: 1977 to 2050. *Current Population Reports*, series P-25, no. 704, 1977.

————. "A Statistical Portrait of Women." *Current Population Reports*, series P-20, no. 58, 1976.

U.S. Department of Health, Education, and Welfare. *The Appropriateness of the Federal Interagency Day Care Requirements: Report of Findings and Recommendations*. Washington, D.C.: U.S. Government Printing Office, 1978.

————. "Current Estimates from the Health Interview Survey," *Vital and Health Statistics*. Washington, D.C.: U.S. Government Printing Office, 1967.

————. *The Persistence of Preschool Effects: A Long Term Follow-Up of Fourteen Infant and Preschool Experiments*. Washington, D.C.: U.S. Government Printing Office, 1977.

————. "Pregnant Workers in the United States." Public Health Service: National Center for Health Statistics, no. 11, September 1977.

————. *The Report of the HEW Task Force on the Treatment of Women Under Social Security*. Washington, D.C., February 1978.

————. *Social Security and the Changing Roles of Men and Women*. Washington, D.C., February 1979.

U.S. Department of Labor. Bureau of Labor Statistics. *Employment and Earnings*, January 1966, 1977, 1978, and 1979.

————. *New Labor Force Projections to 1990*. Special Labor Force Report No. 197, Appendix. Washington, D.C.: U.S. Government Printing Office, 1976.

————. *Work Experience of the Population in 1976.* Special Labor Force Report No. 201. Washington, D.C.: U.S. Government Printing Office, 1977.

U.S. Department of Labor. Employment and Training Administration. *Women and Work.* Manpower Research Monograph No. 46. Washington, D.C.: U.S. Government Printing Office, 1977.

————. *Employment and Training Report of the President, 1977.* Washington, D.C.: U.S. Government Printing Office, 1977.

————. *Employment and Training Report of the President, 1978.* Washington, D.C.: U.S. Government Printing Office, 1978.

U.S. Department of Labor, Employment Standards Administration, Women's Bureau. *1975 Handbook on Women Workers.* Washington, D.C.: U.S. Government Printing Office, 1976.

U.S. Department of Labor, Women's Bureau. *Facts About Women's Absenteeism and Labor Turnover.* Washington, D.C.: U.S. Government Printing Office, 1969.

————. *U.S. Working Women: A Databook.* Washington, D.C.: U.S. Government Printing Office, 1977.

U.S. General Accounting Office. *Part-time Employment in Federal Agencies.* Washington, D.C.: U.S. Government Printing Office, 1976.

Vanek, Joann. "Time Spent in Housework." *Scientific American* 231 (November 1974): 116–20.

Vickery, Clair; Barbara R. Bergmann; and Katherine Swartz. "Unemployment Rate Targets and Anti-Inflation Policy as More Women Enter the Workforce." *American Economic Review* 68 (May 1978): 90–98.

Voss, Paul. "Social Determinants of Age at First Marriage in the United States." Unpublished dissertation. University of Michigan, 1975.

Waite, Linda J. "Projecting Female Labor Force Participation From Sex-Role Attitudes." *Social Science Research*, forthcoming.

Waite, Linda J. and Ross M. Stolzenberg. "Intended Childbearing and Labor Force Participation of Young Women: Insights from Nonrecursive Models." *American Sociological Review* 41 (April 1976): 235–52.

Waldron, I. "Why Do Women Live Longer Than Men?" *Social Science and Medicine* 10 (August 1976): 349–62.

Walker, Kathryn E. "Household Work Time: Its Implication for Family Decisions." *Journal of Home Economics* 65 (October 1973): 7–11.

Walker, Kathryn E. and Margaret E. Woods. *Time Use: A Measure of Household Production of Family Goods and Services.* American Home Economics Association, 1976.

Wallace, Phyllis A. "Employment Discrimination: Some Policy Implications." In Orley Ashenfelter and Albert Rees, eds. *Discrimination in Labor Markets.* Princeton: Princeton University Press, 1973.

Wallace, Phyllis A., ed. *Equal Employment Opportunity and the AT&T Case.* Cambridge, Mass.: The MIT Press, 1976.

Wallston, Barbara. "The Effects of Maternal Employment on Children." *Child Psychology* 14 (1973): 81–95.

Weller, Robert H. "The Employment of Wives, Dominance, and Fertility." *Journal of Marriage and the Family* 30 (August 1968): 437–42.

———. "Wives' Employment and Cumulative Family Size in the United States, 1970 and 1960." *Demography* 14 (February 1977): 43–65.

Wertheimer, Richard II and Sheila R. Zedlewski. "The Aging of America: A Portrait of the Elderly in 1990." The Urban Institute Working Paper 1224–01, December 1978.

Westat Research Inc. "Day Care Survey 1970: Summary Report and Basic Analysis." Westinghouse Learning Corporation, 1971.

Yarrow, M. R.; P. Scott; L. DeLeeuw; and C. Heinig. "Child-rearing in Families of Working and Nonworking Mothers." *Sociometry* 25 (1962): 122–40.

INDEX

273